Out of the Shadows

Also by E. Fuller Torrey

Ethical Issues in Medicine (ed.)

International Collaboration in Mental Health (ed.)

The Death of Psychiatry

Why Did You Do That?

Schizophrenia and Civilization

Witchdoctors and Psychiatrists

Surviving Schizophrenia: A Manual for Families, Consumers and Providers

The Roots of Treason: Ezra Pound and the Secret of St. Elizabeth's

Nowhere to Go: The Tragic Odyssey of the Homeless Mentally Ill

Care of the Seriously Mentally Ill: A Rating of State Programs (with Karen Erdman, Sidney M. Wolfe, and Laurie M. Flynn)

Criminalizing the Seriously Mentally Ill: The Abuse of Jails as Mental Hospitals (with Joan Stieber, Jonathan Ezekiel, Sidney M. Wolfe, Joshua Sharfstein, John H. Noble, and Laurie M. Flynn)

Frontier Justice: The Rise and Fall of the Loomis Gang

Freudian Fraud: The Malignant Effect of Freud's Theory on American Thought and Culture

Schizophrenia and Manic-Depressive Disorder: The Biological Roots of Mental Illness as Revealed by the Landmark Study of Identical Twins (with Ann E. Bowler, Edward H. Taylor, and Irving I. Gottesman)

OUT OF THE SHADOWS

CONFRONTING AMERICA'S MENTAL ILLNESS CRISIS

E. FULLER TORREY, M.D.

John Wiley & Sons, Inc.

New York • Chichester • Weinheim • Brisbane • Singapore • Toronto

Library of Congress Cataloging-in-Publication Data:

Torrey, E. Fuller (Edwin Fuller), 1937–
    Out of the shadows : confronting America's mental illness crisis /
by E. Fuller Torrey.
        p.   cm.
    Includes index.
    ISBN 0-471-16161-6 (cloth : alk. paper). — ISBN 0-471-24532-1 (pbk. : alk. paper)
    1. Mental health policy—United States.   2. Mentally ill—Care—
United States.   3. Mentally ill—Deinstitutionalization—United
States.   4. Mental health laws—United States.   5. Mentally ill—
Social conditions—United States.   I. Title.
RA790.6.T673   1996
362.2'0973—dc20   96-7716

Printed in the United States of America

10 9 8 7 6 5 4 3 2 1

For my faithful friends
Elsie Boyle and Edith Hansen

Between the idea
And the reality
Between the motion
And the act
Falls the Shadow.

T. S. Eliot
The Hollow Men

Preface

I have written this book for anyone who has wondered why there are so many severely mentally ill men and women living on the streets of our cities and towns. And why there are so many severely mentally ill people in jails and prisons. And why there are so many episodes of violence by sufferers of mental illnesses, especially since we know that when such people are treated they are not more violent than the general population. This book has been written because I wondered, too.

The American health care system in general, and the psychiatric care system in particular, are undergoing massive changes. The era of Freud and the era of deinstitutionalization are ending. The era of neurobiology has begun and promises to revolutionize our understanding of the brain and its diseases. For those of use who are interested in mental illness, it is an exciting, perplexing, chaotic time, a time of crisis that demands confrontation.

I believe we know how to solve our mental illness problems, but for a variety of reasons we do not do so. This book is about those reasons. It is drawn from what I have learned from people with severe mental illnesses, from their families, and from a handful of impressively competent and caring professionals. I learned it during eight years working on the wards of a public psychiatric hospital, fourteen years running a clinic for mentally ill persons who are homeless, and visits to public shelters in eighteen states and jails in fourteen states.

Most important, I bring to this book what I have learned from my sister, who has had the misfortune to have suffered from schizophrenia for forty years. The care she has received has varied from very good to grossly negligent. She too has suffered because of the failure of the mental illness treatment system. And she too has lived much of her life in the shadows.

Some of my recommendations may not be politically correct, but I believe they are factually correct.

E. Fuller Torrey

Acknowledgments

I am indebted to many people for help with this book. Robert Taylor and Sidney Wolfe allowed me to pick their brains and criticized an early draft of the manuscript. D. J. Jaffe and Harry Schnibble not only were helpful readers but also provided many useful clippings. Faith Dickerson, C. J. Dombrowski, Marilyn Moon, and Sally Satel offered additional suggestions, and the book is better because of their help.

Many people responded politely and patiently to my calls and requests for information: I want especially to thank Debbie Allness, Carol Bush, Camille Callahan, Winifred Carson, Kenneth Dudek, Richard Elliott, James Finley, Joyce and Harold Friedman, William Goldman, David Hanig, Michael Hogan, Alan Kaufman, Susan Kuper, Alana Landey, Carolyn Lewis, Chris Matkovich, Bentson McFarland, Mark Olfson, Edie Raffel, William Shaw, Peggy Straw, Mary Sullivan, Mary Ann Test, and Steven Veit.

I also wish to thank Larry Allen, Iowa Department of Human Services, for permission to use his diagram of funding sources for mental health services and Debra Srebnik, University of Washington, for permission to quote from their evaluation surveys.

Patrice DeHaven, Laverne Corum, and Dera Thompson helped with library work and the location of obscure references. Kyle Christiansen assisted with the figures and graphs.

Judy Miller typed and edited the manuscript in her usual cheerful and meticulous manner. Jo Ann Miller encouraged the idea and gave it a home at John Wiley & Sons.

My largest debt is to Barbara, my wife, best reader, and best friend.

Contents

1   PEOPLE IN THE SHADOWS: The Many Faces of
Mental Illness   1

2   NOWHERE TO GO: Homelessness and Mental Illness   13

3   JAILS AND PRISONS   25

4   WALKING TIME BOMBS: Violence and the Mentally Ill   43

5   PSYCHIATRIC GHETTOS: Communities and Families   61

6   LOOKING BACKWARD: Where We Have Been   81

7   NEW INITIATIVES IN FUNDING   91

8   FROM LEGAL FOLLY TO COMMON SENSE: The Right
to Get Well   141

9   FROM THE WOODY ALLEN SYNDROME TO
BRAIN DISEASE   167

10   LOOKING FORWARD: Where We Should Be Going   193

Appendix: THE MAGNITUDE OF DEINSTITUTIONALIZATION   205

References   209

Index   237

Chapter 1

PEOPLE IN THE SHADOWS: THE MANY FACES OF MENTAL ILLNESS

Well, we have to take our share of the illnesses of our time, and it seems after all only right that having lived for years in relatively good health—we should sooner or later receive our part. As for me, you must know that I shouldn't precisely have chosen madness if there had been any choice, but once such a thing has taken hold of you, you can't very well get out of it. [1]

—VINCENT VAN GOGH, from an 1889 letter written while he was involuntarily confined in a psychiatric hospital

In the shadows of mental illness there are many faces. One is that of Thomas McGuire (not his real name), a 45-year-old human resource specialist who for 15 years had been employed by a large manufacturing firm. A college graduate, he had served with the Air Force in Vietnam, had been married for 22 years, and had a teenage son and daughter. He lived in a large city in the eastern United States and used a prestigious university teaching hospital for emergency medical care.

On March 19, 1985, Mr. McGuire went to the emergency room complaining of chest pain and shortness of breath. An electrocardiogram confirmed he was having a heart attack. He was admitted to the hospital and treated for his heart problem. During the admission process, doctors carefully explored precipitating risk factors such as hypertension, cholesterol level, smoking, and work stress. Upon discharge, Mr. McGuire was enrolled in a follow-up program to decrease his cholesterol level and thereby reduce the chances of his having another heart attack.

1

Ten years later, on November 14, 1995, Mr. McGuire went to the same emergency room. He had called 911 and described suicidal symptoms. According to the notes of the physicians who saw him, Mr. McGuire had lost almost 50 pounds in the previous six months; was sleeping very little; had spent thousands of dollars foolishly, including mailing a postcard with $70 in stamps on it; had written numerous letters to his congressman offering to reorganize the government and "ship icebergs to Africa and reforest the Sahara"; and claimed to be a prophet who was "ushering in the millennium." Mr. McGuire's wife told the emergency room doctors that he had been hospitalized for one previous manic episode 20 years before, and had a history of periodic episodes of hypomania (minor attacks of mania) for which he had not been treated. The resident psychiatrist diagnosed Mr. McGuire as having acute manic-depressive illness (bipolar disorder) and recommended his admission to the hospital. Mr. McGuire refused voluntary admission, so his wife and son offered to testify to support an involuntary admission. The senior psychiatrist, however, refused to admit Mr. McGuire involuntarily, writing in his hospital chart: "There are no issues of danger to self [or] others. . . . Though patient is mentally impaired he does not at present present enough evidence to warrant detention." Mr. McGuire was released from the emergency room without being given any medication. A few hours later he hung himself with a rope he found in the basement of his home. His wife found him, and paramedics brought him to the emergency room from which he had just been released. He was pronounced dead there.

The contrast between the treatment Mr. McGuire was given for his heart attack and the treatment he received for his manic-depressive illness vividly illustrates what is wrong with our psychiatric health care system. Both conditions are well-established medical emergencies, one involving dysfunction of the heart, the other of the brain. Both conditions demand immediate hospitalization and the rapid administration of medication. Once stabilized, both conditions should be followed up with a plan for decreasing risk factors that might trigger recurrence and for providing education about early warning signs.

The reasons Mr. McGuire received excellent care for his heart attack but disgraceful treatment for his manic-depressive illness can be surmised from the notes of his psychiatrists and from what is known about psychiatric services in the state where he lived. It is a state that has closed over 80 percent of its public psychiatric beds in an effort to shift costs from the state government to the federal government (as will be discussed in Chapter 7). Increasing numbers of psychiatric emergencies have been referred to that university hospital and to other general hospitals in the community, many of which are already overcrowded and unprepared to treat such severely ill patients. It is a state in which civil rights lawyers and other advocates have waged a highly publicized fight to limit the grounds for involuntary psychiatric hospitalization to danger-to-self-or-others, and to have this interpreted as narrowly as possible in the courts (as will be discussed in Chapter 8). It is also a state with a long history of promoting "mental health" issues. And some members of the staff at the university hospital at which Mr. McGuire sought treatment still adhere to a psychoanalytic, rather than a medical understanding of mental illness. It is possible that the senior psychiatrist who released Mr. McGuire without treating him did not consider manic-depressive illness to be a medical emergency but rather to be a product of intrapersonal and interpersonal conflict that should be treated with long-term psychotherapy.

Mr. McGuire's negligent treatment is not an aberration. Similar examples occur throughout the United States virtually every day. Mr. McGuire did not seek help in a rural area with no trained psychiatrists, nor in a city such as Miami, Houston, or Los Angeles, which are known to have very poor public psychiatric services, nor in a public psychiatric hospital such as Hawaii State Hospital, which has been designated as the worst public psychiatric hospital in the United States.[2] Mr. McGuire sought treatment in a prestigious university hospital in a city reputed to be a regional medical Mecca.

The mental illness crisis, then, consists of hundreds of thousands of men and women like Mr. McGuire who represent a large percentage of the estimated 2.2 million Americans with untreated severe mental illnesses. On any given day, approximately 150,000 of them are homeless, living on the streets or in public shelters. Another 159,000 are incarcerated in jails and prisons, mostly for crimes committed because they were not being treated. Some of them become violent and may terrorize their families, towns, or urban neighborhoods. A very large number have died prematurely as a result of accidents and suicide. Tragically, most of these instances of homelessness, incarcerations, episodes of violence, and premature deaths are unnecessary. We know what to do, but for economic, legal, and ideological reasons we fail to do it.

Who Are the Severely Mentally Ill and What Is Wrong with Them?

"Mental illness" is a nonspecific term that covers a broad array of brain disorders, human behaviors, and personality types. The term commonly designates one end of an amorphous mental health–mental illness spectrum. This book is concerned only with *severe mental illnesses*, defined in 1993 by the National Advisory Mental Health Council, an arm of the National Institute of Mental Health, as including "disorders with psychotic symptoms such as schizophrenia, schizoaffective disorder, manic-depressive disorder, autism, as well as severe forms of other disorders such as major depression, panic disorder, and obsessive-compulsive disorder."[3] The Council determined that over a one-year period, 2.8 percent of the adult population in the United States is affected by such severe mental illness. Additional studies estimated that 3.2 percent of children and adolescents ages 9 through 17 have a severe mental illness in any given six-month period. Based on the total 1995 U.S. population of 262 million, this means that during that year approximately 5.6 million people ages 9 or older had a severe mental illness. According to the National Advisory Mental Health Council, the cost of their care was $27 billion for direct treatment costs and $74 billion if indirect costs such as maintenance and lost productivity are included. These numbers do not include people with a primary diagnosis of alcohol or drug addiction, although many severely mentally ill people also abuse alcohol or drugs.

Research over the past decade has clarified what is wrong with those diagnosed with severe mental illnesses. They have neurobiological disorders of their brains that affect their thinking and moods and that can be measured by changes in both brain structure and function. Figure 1.1 illustrates these changes as shown on MRI (magnetic resonance imaging) scans of two pairs of identical twins. In one pair, one twin has schizophrenia and his identical cotwin is well, and in the other pair, one twin

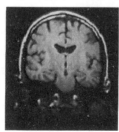 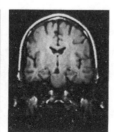 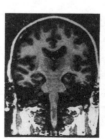 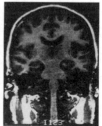

| Twin with schizophrenia | Well twin | Twin with manic-depressive disorder | Well twin |

FIGURE 1.1   MRI scans of two pairs of identical twins showing enlarged cerebral ventricles in affected twins.

has manic-depressive illness and her cotwin is well. In both cases, the affected twin has larger cerebral ventricles, the fluid-carrying spaces in the brain, suggesting that the affected twins have had some loss of brain tissue associated with their illnesses. Not everyone with schizophrenia and manic-depressive illness has enlarged cerebral ventricles, but many do.

Research on schizophrenia, schizoaffective disorder, manic-depressive disorder, autism, and severe forms of major depression, panic disorder, and obsessive-compulsive disorder has also revealed a variety of functional disease-related changes in the brains of affected individuals. These include changes in the neurochemistry, metabolism, electrical activity, neurological function, and neuropsychological function of the brain. Some of these changes may be caused by the medication being taken for the illness, but the majority are not medication-related and can be found in those who have never taken medication.

It has now been established that severe mental illnesses, as defined by the National Advisory Mental Health Council, are neurobiological disorders of the brain. These illnesses are thus in the same category as other brain disorders such as Parkinson's disease, Alzheimer's disease, and multiple sclerosis. Like severe mental illnesses, each of these disorders is associated with measurable abnormalities in brain structure and function. And, as with severe mental illnesses, it is not yet known what factors—genes, developmental effects, viruses, toxins, or metabolic defects—contribute to the biological chain of events causing these disorders.

Can They Be Treated and Are They Being Treated?

A persistent myth about severe mental illness is that it cannot be treated. In fact, according to the 1993 report of the National Advisory Mental Health Council, "The efficacy of many treatments for severe mental disorders is comparable to that in other branches of medicine, including surgery."[4] For schizophrenia and schizoaffective disorder (a mixture of schizophrenia and manic-depressive disorder) research has shown that standard antipsychotic medication will "reduce psychotic symptoms in 60 percent of patients and in 70–85 percent of those experiencing symptoms for the first time."[5] Newer antipsychotics such as clozapine are effective in an additional one-third of people who do not respond to the standard antipsychotics. For manic-depressive illness, approximately 75 percent of sufferers respond to lithium, carbemazepine, or a combination of ancillary medications. For severe depression, at least 80 percent respond to tricyclic (Elavil, Norpramin), selective serotonin reuptake inhibitor (SSRI) (Prozac, Zoloft, and others) or monoamine oxidase inhibitor, (MAOI) (e.g., Nardil, Parnate) antidepressants; some of the nonresponders can be successfully treated using electroconvulsive therapy (ECT). For severe panic disorder, between 70 and 90 percent of sufferers respond to an antidepressant or a benzodiazepine class of medication. And for severe obsessive-compulsive disorder, approximately 60 percent react at least moderately well to one or more antidepressants. Of all the severe mental illnesses, only autism has no effective medication at this time.

It should be emphasized that medications are not the only treatment for those with severe mental illnesses. Many also require rehabilitation and supportive counseling. Excellent model programs have been developed to provide these, including the Program in Assertive Community Treatment (PACT), which originated in Madison, Wisconsin; clubhouse programs patterned after New York City's Fountain House; and employment programs such as Fairweather Lodges, transitional employment programs, and job skills training. I will discuss these in Chapter 7, but for now the important point to remember is that we have effective treatments for the majority of people with severe mental illnesses. The medications do not cure the illnesses, but rather control the symptoms just as insulin does in diabetes. *The mental illness crisis, then, has not occurred because we do not have effective treatments. Rather, it exists because we do not use these treatments for a substantial number of those afflicted.* As we will see, the reasons for this failure say more about our national politics and ideology than about our scientific progress.

Of the 5.6 million individuals who had a severe mental illness in 1995, how many were receiving treatment? According to the National Advisory Mental Health Council, approximately 60 percent of severely mentally ill adults receive treatment in any given year.[6] For schizophrenia, the treatment rate appears to be even lower; for example, a 1981 study of people with schizophrenia living in Baltimore reported that only 50 percent were receiving treatment.[7] If we use an estimated overall treatment rate of 60 percent, then 40 percent are not receiving treatment. Based on the total of 5.6 million, that means that approximately 2.2 million severely mentally ill people are not being treated. These are the men, women, and children at the heart and core of the mental illness crisis.

Who are these people? Mr. McGuire was one of them. Among the thousands of others in the shadows are the following individuals whom I have known:

◇ A woman with schizophrenia who lived with her parents, and later with her unmarried brother, for 45 years until her recent death. She had originally become ill at age 16 and was hospitalized for six months, but that took place before antipsychotic medications were available. Over the years, her family periodically encouraged her to see a psychiatrist, but she refused. Her family provided for all her needs, and she lived an isolated, hermitlike existence, spending most of the time in her own room.

◇ A man now in his late 30s, who has suffered from periodic episodes of severe depression for almost 20 years. He also abuses alcohol and occasionally drugs, and it is these problems that he and his family focus on. His depression has never been treated.

◇ A woman in her 40s with manic-depressive illness who dropped out of school in the eighth grade because of severe "emotional difficulties." She lives in a rural area, and the nearest mental health center is a two-hour drive away. Her family is not well educated and does not understand why she "thinks funny" and sometimes stays in her room for weeks at a time. In one episode, when she became manic, her elderly parents locked her in the attic for several days so she would not run away.

◇ A 56-year-old man with paranoid schizophrenia, a graduate of an Ivy League university, who has spent the past 20 years wandering the country, often sleeping in public shelters or in the woods. He believes the FBI implanted microchips in his brain and that these broadcast voices in his head. His family has tried on several occasions to get him involuntarily committed to a hospital for treatment, but in court the man is calm, articulate, and able to convince the judge that he has the right to live his alternate lifestyle.

◇ A 28-year-old man with schizoaffective disorder (a mixture of schizophrenia and manic-depressive disorder) who lives beneath a bridge in a large eastern city. He spent five years in a South Carolina prison for manslaughter, and he periodically threatens people on the street who refuse his demands for money, most of which he uses to buy marijuana and alcohol. Since he left prison, he has received no treatment.

People like these can be found in every city, town, and rural area in the United States.

In addition to the 2.2 million people who receive no treatment, there is another group who are often forgotten: those who, like Mr. McGuire, have died as a direct or indirect result of not being treated. Suicide is the most common cause of their death: The lifetime suicide rate among those with schizophrenia is 10 to 13 percent and among those with manic-depressive illness 15 to 17 percent, as opposed to about 1 percent among the general population. In addition to suicide, many people with severe mental illnesses die prematurely because of accidents and untreated physical illnesses. We don't know how many of them would be alive today if they had received adequate treatment, but almost certainly hundreds of thousands have paid with their lives for an illness that need not have been fatal.

Deinstitutionalization: A Psychiatric *"Titanic"*

Deinstitutionalization is the name given to the policy of moving severely mentally ill people out of large state institutions and then closing part or all of those institutions; it has been a major contributing factor to the mental illness crisis. (The term also describes a similar process for mentally retarded people, but the focus of this book is exclusively on severe mental illnesses.)

Deinstitutionalization began in 1955 with the widespread introduction of chlorpromazine, commonly known as Thorazine, the first effective antipsychotic medication, and received a major impetus 10 years later with the enactment of federal Medicaid and Medicare. Deinstitutionalization has two parts: the moving of the severely mentally ill out of the state institutions, and the closing of part or all of those institutions. The former affects people who are already mentally ill. The latter affects those who become ill after the policy has gone into effect and for the indefinite future because hospital beds have been permanently eliminated.

The magnitude of deinstitutionalization of the severely mentally ill qualifies it as one of the largest social experiments in American history. In 1955, there were 558,239 severely mentally ill patients in the nation's public psychiatric hospitals. In 1994, this number had been reduced by 486,620 patients, to 71,619, as seen in Figure 1.2. It is important to note, however, that the census of 558,239 patients in public psychiatric hospitals in 1955 was in relationship to the nation's total population at the time, which was 164 million.

By 1994, the nation's population had increased to 260 million. If there had been the same proportion of patients per population in public mental hospitals in 1994 as there had been in 1955, the patients would have totaled 885,010. The true magnitude of deinstitutionalization, then, is the difference between 885,010 and 71,619. In effect, approximately

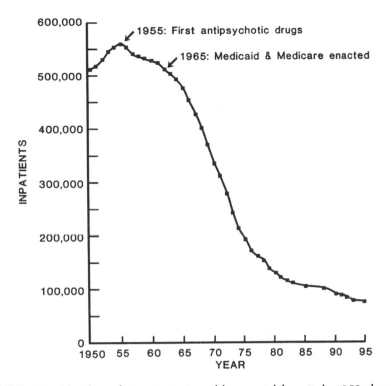

FIGURE 1.2   Number of inpatients in public mental hospitals 1950 through 1995.

92 percent of the people who would have been living in public psychiatric hospitals in 1955 were not living there in 1994. Even allowing for the approximately 40,000 patients who occupied psychiatric beds in general hospitals or the approximately 10,000 patients who occupied psychiatric beds in community mental health centers (CMHCs) on any given day in 1994, that still means that approximately 763,391 severely mentally ill people (over three-quarters of a million) are living in the community today who would have been hospitalized 40 years ago. That number is more than the population of Baltimore or San Francisco.

Deinstitutionalization varied from state to state. In assessing these differences in census for public mental hospitals, it is not sufficient merely to subtract the 1994 number of patients from the 1955 number, because state populations shifted in the various states during those 40 years. In Iowa, West Virginia, and the District of Columbia, the total populations actually decreased during that period, whereas in California, Florida, and Arizona, the population increased dramatically; and in

Nevada, it increased more than sevenfold, from 0.2 million to 1.5 million. The table in the Appendix takes these population changes into account and provides an effective deinstitutionalization rate for each state based on the number of patients hospitalized in 1994 subtracted from the number of patients that would have been expected to be hospitalized in 1994 based on that state's population. It assumes that the ratio of hospitalized patients to population would have remained constant over the 40 years.

Rhode Island, Massachusetts, New Hampshire, Vermont, West Virginia, Arkansas, Wisconsin, and California all have effective deinstitutionalization rates of over 95 percent. Rhode Island's rate is over 98 percent, meaning that for every 100 state residents in public mental hospitals in 1955, fewer than 2 patients are there today. On the other end of the curve, Nevada, Delaware, and the District of Columbia have effective deinstitutionalization rates below 80 percent.

Most of those who were deinstitutionalized from the nation's public psychiatric hospitals were severely mentally ill. Between 50 and 60 percent of them were diagnosed with schizophrenia. Another 10 to 15 percent were diagnosed with manic-depressive illness and severe depression. An additional 10 to 15 percent were diagnosed with organic brain diseases—epilepsy, strokes, Alzheimer's disease, and brain damage secondary to trauma. The remaining individuals residing in public psychiatric hospitals had conditions such as mental retardation with psychosis, autism and other psychiatric disorders of childhood, and alcoholism and drug addiction with concurrent brain damage. The fact that most deinstitutionalized people suffer from various forms of brain dysfunction was not as well understood when the policy of deinstitutionalization got under way.

Thus deinstitutionalization has helped create the mental illness crisis by discharging people from public psychiatric hospitals without ensuring that they received the medication and rehabilitation services necessary for them to live successfully in the community. Deinstitutionalization further exacerbated the situation because, once the public psychiatric beds had been closed, they were not available for people who later became mentally ill, and this situation continues up to the present. Consequently, approximately 2.2 million severely mentally ill people do not receive any psychiatric treatment.

Deinstitutionalization was based on the principle that severe mental illness should be treated in the least restrictive setting. As further defined by President Jimmy Carter's Commission on Mental Health, this ideology rested on "the objective of maintaining the greatest degree of freedom, self-determination, autonomy, dignity, and integrity of body, mind, and spirit for the individual while he or she participates in treatment or receives services."[8] This is a laudable goal and for many, perhaps for the majority of those who are deinstitutionalized, it has been at least partially realized.

For a substantial minority, however, deinstitutionalization has been a psychiatric *Titanic*. Their lives are virtually devoid of "dignity" or "integrity of body, mind, and spirit." "Self-determination" often means merely that the person has a choice of soup kitchens. The "least restrictive setting" frequently turns out to be a cardboard box, a jail cell, or a terror-filled existence plagued by both real and imaginary enemies. Even one Thomas McGuire is too many; hundreds of thousands are a disgrace.

Chapter 2

NOWHERE TO GO:
HOMELESSNESS AND MENTAL ILLNESS

*No vision haunts America's conscience more than the sight of the street people. . . .
The irrationality and anguish that grip so many of these individuals leap out
during any encounter, whether in Washington or Albuquerque.*[1]

—SENATOR PETE V. DOMENICI

The mental illness crisis also wears the face of Phyllis Iannotta. When she was murdered, on April 23, 1981, there was already abundant evidence that many severely mentally ill persons were falling through the cracks of deinstitutionalization and were not receiving treatment.

For those who were paying attention, there had been harbingers of an impending crisis since the early 1970s. Large numbers of mentally ill people began forming psychiatric ghettos in cities such as Long Beach, New York, near Pilgrim State Hospital; San Jose, California, near Agnews State Hospital; and Tacoma, Washington, near Western State Hospital. As large often run-down boarding homes filled with discharged psychiatric patients from the nearby hospitals, the intended policy of deinstitutionalization increasingly looked rather like transinstitutionalization—the exchange of one impersonal institution for another. At the same time, the availability of single-room occupancy hotels and other low-rent housing was declining precipitously in urban areas as redevelopment and gentrification shifted into high gear. Where were the thousands of former patients supposed to live, one might have asked.

While this urban psychiatric ghettoization and decline in low-rent housing was taking place, it was also becoming apparent that many of the discharged patients were not receiving ongoing psychiatric treatment. Theoretically, they were to have received medication and rehabilitation services from the federally funded community mental health centers, but in most cases this did not happen. As early as 1972, a study commissioned by the National Institute of Mental Health reported, "Relationships between community mental health centers and public mental hospitals serving the same catchment area exist only at a relatively minimal level between the majority of the two types of organizations."[2] By 1979, the Inspector General of the U.S. Department of Health, Education and Welfare was more blunt, saying, *"The relationship between the CMHCs [community mental health centers] and public psychiatric hospital is difficult at best, adversarial at worst* [emphasis in original]."[3]

By the early 1980s, then, some unintended consequences of deinstitutionalization were becoming manifest. More and more very sick people were living on the streets and in public shelters. Many of them were being arrested for misdemeanors associated with not receiving treatment and were ending up in city and county jails. Episodes of violence by untreated mentally ill persons were being reported in newspapers and newscasts. The mentally ill were also contributing to a deterioration of the quality of life in American cities, and their families were confronting the personal tragedies and deplorable consequences of the largest failed social experiment in twentieth-century America.

The Murder of a Shopping Bag Lady

At birth, Phyllis Iannotta did not seem destined to be a shopping bag lady.[4] She was born in Italy on May 8, 1914, to parents who emigrated to New York City shortly after her birth. Her father supported the family by selling items from a pushcart, and during the Depression, Phyllis quit school and went to work in a factory to help her family. She worked for 22 years supporting her parents and was "a real friend and wonderful company" according to her best friend. She was remembered as "very outgoing and very direct; if she liked you she'd tell you straight out." She worked hard, saved her money, and helped her family move from the poor neighborhood of Red Hook to Sunset Park, then Bensonhurst, and finally middle-class Bay Ridge. She was pursuing the American dream.

Then, in her early 40s, something went wrong. Phyllis Iannotta's brain began playing tricks on her. Initially, she believed her neighbors were trying to hurt her, then she started hearing voices, and finally she developed delusions that she was having conversations with the President. She was hospitalized in Staten Island's South Beach Psychiatric Center, diagnosed as having schizophrenia, and started on chlorpromazine. The medication markedly alleviated her symptoms, but like approximately half of all schizophrenic sufferers, she had little insight about her illness and so did not understand that she needed to continue taking the medicine once she left the hospital. She was supposed to obtain the chlorpromazine at a psychiatric outpatient clinic but, according to a social worker there, "after a while she just stopped coming." Her parents had died and she was on her own.

With no medication and no support, Phyllis Iannotta's life quickly went downhill, the slide greased by the symptoms of her schizophrenia. She lost her assets and contact with her friends, and within three years she had become homeless. She sometimes lived in the Dwelling Place, a shelter for women run by nuns, and it was clear to everyone who met her there that she was severely psychiatrically ill. After her death, one of the nuns was asked why they hadn't had her hospitalized. According to the author of a book about Iannotta, "The nun laughed without a trace of humor. 'Well, she wasn't about to commit herself to a hospital,' she said. 'And the state wouldn't commit her unless she was homicidal or suicidal. That's the law. Phyllis wasn't holding a gun to anybody's head, so she couldn't get the help she needed. Simple as that. That's a fact of life around here.'"[5]

When not living in the shelter, Phyllis Iannotta lived on a bench in the Port Authority Bus Terminal or on the streets. Scavenging for food in trash barrels as she simultaneously carried on conversations with the President, she resembled a figure from a Hieronymus Bosch painting, a twentieth-century madwoman bearing witness to the failures of the present age.

Her life ended in a trash-strewn alley on West 40th Street in an area known appropriately as Hell's Kitchen. When her body was found, she was wearing a black, fake-fur coat, but her slacks had been ripped off. She had been raped and then stabbed multiple times. The warehouseman who found her body said, "I didn't even realize what it was at first. Then it registered. What I was looking at, this thing, was a human body. A woman. She was nude from the waist down. She was mutilated. Her head was bashed in. . . . There was blood everywhere."[6]

Like many homeless women, Phyllis Iannotta carried her possessions in a shopping bag. Next to her body, the contents of her bag had been scattered, the remnants of 22 years of work and 67 years of life. They consisted of two shabby sweaters, a ball of dirty white yarn, an empty box of Sloan's liniment, a vial of perfume, a bag of coffee, a can of Friskies turkey-and-giblet cat food, and a plastic spoon.

How Many Phyllis Iannottas Are There?

Since Phyllis Iannotta's death in 1981, the number of homeless people who are severely mentally ill has increased dramatically. In many cities such as New York, they are now an accepted part of the urban landscape and make up a significant percentage of the homeless who ride subways all night, sleep on sidewalks, or sleep in the parks. These mentally ill homeless people drift into the train and bus stations and even the airports. Mary Vierck is one of approximately 12 homeless people who live permanently at Kennedy International Airport; she worked as a secretary for 33 years but "was sent to the airport by Jesus Christ after a short-lived dalliance with a man named Joseph from Queens," and she is now waiting to be sent on her "next mission."[7] At Chicago's O'Hare Airport, some homeless women even brought in plants to decorate their corners.

Many other homeless people hide from the eyes of most citizens. They shuffle quietly through the streets by day, talking to their voices only when they think nobody is looking, and they live in shelters or abandoned buildings at night. Some shelters become known as havens for these mentally ill wanderers and take on the appearance of a hospital psychiatric ward. Also seldom seen are the mentally ill who live in the woods on the outskirts of cities, under bridges, and even in the tunnels that carry subway trains beneath cities.

How many people in the United States are homeless and severely mentally ill? The answer depends first on the total number of homeless persons and second on the definition used for "mentally ill"; both of these qualifiers have elicited considerable debate. In a 1984 study, the U.S. Department of Housing and Urban Development estimated that between 250,000 and 350,000 people in the United States were homeless. The Urban Institute, in its 1988 study, estimated the total number of the homeless to be between 567,000 and 600,000. The Census Bureau carried out a survey of public shelters on March 20, 1990, that identified 229,000 people in shelters or living visibly on the streets, but workers did not attempt to count those living in abandoned buildings, parked cars, or in other more-or-less hidden locations. Christopher Jencks, professor of sociology at Northwestern University, thoroughly analyzed the data from all these studies in his 1994 book *The Homeless*. He concluded that in

1987 "about 350,000 Americans were homeless" at any given time but that "any figure between 300,000 and 400,000 would be easy to defend."[8]

Jencks also noted, as have several other researchers, that the total number of homeless Americans appeared to increase during the 1980s. Based on the available data, Jencks estimated that in 1980 125,000 people were homeless and that this rose to 216,000 by 1984 and to 402,000 by 1988.[9] The number of public shelter beds for single adults grew at approximately the same rate during these years, from 35,000 in 1980 to 115,000 in 1988. Thus, the total number of homeless people in the United States appears to have increased between 1980 and 1988 by approximately 300 percent, whereas the total U.S. population increased by only 7.6 percent.

What percentage of the total homeless population is mentally ill? If the definition of "mentally ill" includes alcohol and drug addictions, then studies indicate that 75 percent or more of the homeless are mentally ill. If, however, only severe mental illness is the criterion, as defined in 1993 by the National Advisory Mental Health Council and listed in Chapter 1, then approximately 35 percent of homeless persons qualify.

Studies to establish the percentage of severely mentally ill people among the homeless population have yielded surprisingly consistent results. Studies done in the early 1980s in Philadelphia[10] and Boston[11] reported that 43 percent (Philadelphia) and 38 percent (Boston) of the men and women living in public shelters were severely mentally ill. Studies done in the late 1980s used more sophisticated sampling and diagnostic interview methodologies. The largest studies, each with samples of 200 or more homeless participants, were carried out in Baltimore,[12] Los Angeles,[13] and three California counties (Alameda, Orange, and Yolo)[14]; these studies reported rates for severe mental illness of 32 percent, 42 percent, and 33 percent respectively. Based on such studies, a Task Force of the American Psychiatric Association concluded in 1990 that the prevalence of severe and persistent mental illness (e.g., schizophrenia, schizoaffective disorders, and mood disorders) among homeless people "ranges from 28% to 37%."[15]

In some of these studies, the reported prevalence of psychiatric illnesses may be underestimated. For example, the Los Angeles study in which 42 percent of 328 homeless people were found on interview to be severely psychiatrically ill did not include another 66 who refused to participate, and it also did not sample those living on the streets or in outdoor areas. Paranoid schizophrenic sufferers, because of their mistrust of people, would be expected to be disproportionately represented among those who refused interviews. Other studies have also indicated a higher rate of severe psychiatric illnesses among homeless people who live on the streets and in other outdoor areas than among those who live in public shelters.[16]

Although no definitive study has proven the point, anecdotal evidence suggests that the number of homeless who are mentally ill has increased since the studies of the 1980s. For example, a 1991 survey of homeless shelters showed that in 17 of the 20 cities surveyed an upsurge in requests for shelter by psychiatrically ill street people had occurred in the previous 18 months.[17] In releasing the report, Boston mayor Raymond L. Flynn, president of the Conference of Mayors, observed, "Homeless shelters and city streets have become the 'de facto mental institutions' of the 1980s and 1990s."[18] And, a television station in San Francisco used prominent downtown billboards to advertise their series on the homeless: "You are now walking through America's newest mental institution."

It seems reasonable, then, to estimate that the prevalence of severe mental disorders among the homeless is approximately 35 percent, although this varies somewhat from city to city. Jencks's 1988 estimate of 402,000 homeless people in the United States would imply that approximately 141,000 in this group were severely mentally ill. In 1995, based on the increase in total population since 1988, this number would have risen to approximately 150,000 seriously mentally ill people. This is equivalent to the entire population of Hartford, Connecticut; Fort Lauderdale, Florida; Providence, Rhode Island; or Reno, Nevada.

What Is It Like to Be Homeless and Mentally Ill?

What do we know about the quality of life for these ill and homeless Americans? We know that they represent a broad spectrum of ages and educational backgrounds. A survey of homeless adolescents (ages 12 to 17) in Los Angeles reported that 31 percent were experiencing auditory hallucinations and other symptoms of psychiatric illness not attributable to drug use.[19] On the other end of the age spectrum, public shelters often are the only home for people in their 60s and 70s who have been discharged from state psychiatric hospitals.

The homeless who are mentally ill also cover a broad range of education. Rebecca Smith, a mentally ill 61-year-old woman who froze to death in a cardboard box on a New York street, became a media cause célèbre in 1982 when it became known that she had been the valedictorian of her college class. A sample of homeless adults in Los Angeles found that 48 percent of them had had some college education.[20] On the other hand, a survey of homeless individuals in Baltimore found that only 39 percent had graduated from high school,[21] and it is not uncommon to find some mentally ill homeless persons with IQs well below normal. Serious psychiatric disorders are indeed equal opportunity disorders.

Living in shelters or on the streets is likely to be difficult, even for a person whose brain is working normally. For those with a severe mental illness, this kind of life is often a living hell. One survey of 529 homeless people divided them into those who had been previously psychiatrically hospitalized and those who had not been so hospitalized. The previously hospitalized participants of the survey were 3 times more likely to obtain some of their food from garbage cans (28% vs. 9%) and much more likely to use garbage cans as their "primary food source" (8% vs. 1%) than the nonhospitalized interviewees. The previously hospitalized participants also were much more likely to have had an injury or accident within the past year (44% vs. 29%) and had a higher median number of "victimizations" (not further defined) within the past year (3% vs. 1%). All of these differences were statistically significant.[22]

There is also evidence that those who are homeless and mentally ill have a markedly elevated death rate from a variety of causes. This is not surprising since the homeless in general, even those who are not substance abusers, have a 3 times higher risk of death than the general population[23] and severely mentally ill people in general have a 2.4 times higher risk of death during any year.[24]

When homelessness and mental illnesses are combined, the results are predictable. As part of a study in England, investigators collected data for 18 months on 48 homeless people who were mentally ill. At the end of that time, 3 had died from physical causes (aortic aneurysm, heart attack, and suffocation during an epileptic fit), 1 had died in an accident, and 3 others had suddenly disappeared without taking any personal belongings with them. Depending on whether or not the missing participants were alive, the 18-month mortality rate was a minimum of 8 percent and a maximum of 15 percent.[25]

Freezing to death during bitter weather is all-too-common among the homeless in general and among the homeless who are mentally ill in particular. Usually, such deaths attract little attention, but on November 29, 1993, in Washington, DC, Yetta Adams was found frozen to death on a bench across the street from the headquarters of the Department of Housing and Urban Development (HUD). Ms. Adams suffered from schizophrenia and alcoholism and was living on the streets. The Secretary of HUD, Henry G. Cisneros, left his office to join the crowd and find out what had happened; later, he wrote, "Yetta Adams' death jarred me and all my colleagues at HUD, reminding us that our society is becoming an increasingly hostile environment for the homeless."[26]

Homeless people with brain disorders such as schizophrenia or mania frequently suffer fatal accidents caused by their impaired thought processes. One study of homeless mentally ill patients found:

> In 43 percent of the cases, patients showed the marked disorganization of mental illness and poor problem-solving skills. In an additional 30 percent, the subjects were not only disorganized but too paranoid to accept help. For instance, two of the patients had a place where they could live but were too paranoid and fearful to stay there.[27]

Such impaired thinking may be fatal. In Minneapolis, James Ludwig, diagnosed with paranoid schizophrenia and homeless, was killed by the police in 1990 when he refused to heed their command to stop and tried to run away. The police had been called to investigate a complaint of "a barefoot man playing in the dirt with a stick [and] acting strangely."[28] A highly publicized death arising from impaired thinking was that of Margaret King, a 36-year-old homeless woman who was found dead in 1995 in the outdoor lion exhibit at the National Zoo, Washington, DC. Ms. King suffered from schizophrenia and was said to believe that "she has a special relationship with God, either she is Jesus Christ or the sister of Jesus Christ, and that she receives direct messages from God."[29]

Because impaired thinking also makes self-protection difficult for the mentally ill, many of these homeless persons avoid using public shelters. According to a description of New York City's shelters:

> There is a hierarchy among the shelter's clients, and the visibly mentally ill are the lowest caste, untouchables among the outcast. . . . The mentally ill are often preyed upon by criminals who come to the shelter straight from prison. Those who receive Social Security disability checks become targets for muggers.[30]

For severely mentally ill homeless women, the consequences of impaired thinking are often more dire than they are for men. One study of the incidence of rape among women with schizophrenia reported it to be 22 percent, with two-thirds of those having been raped multiple times.[31] A study of homeless women in Baltimore found that "nearly a third of the women had been raped."[32] And a report on homeless women in San Francisco noted: "They're being raped and sexually assaulted at an alarming rate. . . . 'I know one woman who has been raped 17 times,' said Gregory Francis, vice president for programs at the Central City Hospitality House. 'She doesn't report it because it's just what happens out there' . . . To protect themselves from attack, homeless women have been known to wear 10 pairs of panty hose at once [and] bundle up in layers of clothing."[33]

Rape also exposes homeless mentally ill women to infection with the HIV virus that causes AIDS, especially since many of the men doing the raping are drug addicts among whom HIV infection is common. No study has been done to date of the HIV infection rate among homeless women who are severely mentally ill, but a recent study of HIV infection among severely mentally ill homeless men in a New York City shelter found that 19 percent of them were HIV positive.[34] Clinical AIDS will therefore become an increasing problem among the homeless mentally ill in the near future.

Murder is the most horrific cause of increased mortality among the psychiatrically impaired homeless. Although no formal study has been done on this, anecdotal evidence suggests that such deaths are not rare. In 1989, Van Mill, a 110-pound man with paranoid schizophrenia who was living in a tent in Des Moines, Iowa, was savagely beaten to death by three young men. After robbing and assaulting him, they threw him "into an empty wading pool at the park and at least one of them jumped up and down on his chest, crushing his small frame, police said."[35] In a case in Washington, DC, similar to that of Phyllis Iannotta, Ella Starks, a mentally ill woman who had been homeless for 10 years, was raped, "stabbed repeatedly, and died of asphyxiation when an umbrella was forced down her throat."[36]

The Relationship of the Homeless Mentally Ill to Deinstitutionalization

There is a causal relationship between the growing number of homeless people who are severely mentally ill and the deinstitutionalization of massive numbers of severely mentally ill patients. Some observers have denied this relationship and claimed "that deinstitutionalization has not caused homelessness."[37] Instead, they believe that social causes such as a lack of low-income housing, poverty, racism, and a lack of "well-paying industrial-sector jobs for unskilled and semiskilled workers"[38] are the real causes of the problem.

Douglas Mossman, a psychiatrist, and Michael I. Perlin, a lawyer, are proponents of this view. They assert, "Homelessness is, if nothing else, a condition of poverty, and poor individuals in general are at increased risk for episodes of psychiatric illness . . . ultimately, homelessness is a problem of poverty and resource distribution. . . . It thus seems clear that mental illness is not the primary cause of the plight of the homeless mentally ill."[39] Carl I. Cohen and Kenneth S. Thompson, both psychiatrists, also argue that focusing on mental illness "has obscured the social context of the emergence of mass homelessness in our country at this time."[40] Their solution to homelessness is "a future alliance between the homeless, the working class, and other socially concerned persons, including professionals, in support of new initiatives that would include governmental housing programs, improved health services, rejuvenated antipoverty programs, and community development projects."[41]

It seems evident that the arguments about the origins of the homeless mentally ill have taken on the same political hues as arguments about the origins of homelessness in general. Jonathan Kozol in *Rachel and Her Children*[42] and Peter Rossi in *Down and Out in America*,[43] among others, contend strongly that homelessness is primarily an economic and housing problem. Their reasoning has been countered by such researchers as Alice Baum and Donald Burnes in *A Nation in Denial*,[44] Richard White in *Rude Awakenings*,[45] and Christopher Jencks in *The Homeless*.[46]

Poverty and insufficient low-income housing certainly play a role in causing homelessness, but the question is how big a role? Such social inadequacies appear to be far less important sources of homelessness than mental illnesses and alcohol and drug abuse. In a study of the homeless in Los Angeles, 33 percent met criteria for alcoholism within the past year and another 30 percent had met criteria sometime during their lifetime.[47] A similar study in Baltimore found that 85 percent of men and 67 percent of women had abused alcohol or drugs at some time.[48] In another Los Angeles study, 50 percent of homeless participants acknowledged having used illegal drugs within the past month.[49] Furthermore, Jencks claimed that "a third of all homeless single adults use crack fairly regularly."[50] Other studies confirm this very high incidence of alcohol addiction and drug abuse among the homeless. Social theorists claim that homelessness leads to alcohol and drug abuse, while medical theorists claim that the alcohol and drug abuse produces homelessness.

With severe mental illnesses and homelessness, the pattern of cause and effect is clear. First, there is no evidence that homeless people who are mentally ill disproportionately represent lower socioeconomic groups. Second, surveys have shown that the homeless frequently have been previously hospitalized in psychiatric hospitals. Christopher Jencks, summarizing numerous studies, found that 22 to 24 percent of homeless persons reported former psychiatric hospitalization.[51] Among selected segments of the homeless population, such as drifters living specifically on the streets or in parks but not in shelters, the rate of previous psychiatric hospitalization is as high as 75 percent in New York[52] and 79 percent in Los Angeles.[53]

Finally, studies following up on patients discharged from psychiatric hospitals strongly suggest that homelessness is a consequence of severe mental illness. In Massachusetts, a study of 187 patients discharged from a public psychiatric hospital in 1983 found that 27 percent of them became homeless within 6 months of discharge.[54] In Ohio, a similar study of 132 patients found that 36 percent of them became homeless within 6 months after discharge.[55] Even more disturbing was that the Ohio study did not include for follow-up another 61 discharged patients who "were not medically cleared by hospital staff to participate in the study because of the severity of their psychotic behavior"; it is likely that an even higher proportion of this group became homeless. A similar figure for homelessness was cited in 1995 for New York City, where 38 percent of discharged psychiatric patients appeared to "have no known address within six months of their release."[56]

Perhaps the most ironic and poignant commentary on the causal relationship of severe mental illnesses and homelessness is the conversion into shelters for the homeless of buildings that originally served as units of public psychiatric hospitals. Keener Men's Shelter in New York City is a well-known example. For three quarters of a century, it was part of Manhattan State Hospital, serving patients with severe mental illnesses. Then, as more and more beds became vacant in the 1970s, the building was no longer needed and was turned over to the City of New York, which reopened it in 1981 as a public shelter for homeless men.

In 1982, Ellen Baxter and Kim Hopper described the Keener Shelter:

> Men lounge around in various stages of undress, in contact with the assortment of realities; among them are former hospital patients. By a stroke of grim irony, some of these ex-patients have come full circle back to the institution that had originally discharged them—this time for shelter, not treatment.[57]

In 1990, the Keener Shelter housed 800 homeless men. At least 40 percent of them were mentally ill, and many had previously been patients at Manhattan State Hospital. One man with schizophrenia had been living in the Keener Shelter for seven years, the same period of time he had previously been there when it had been a hospital. Despite being humanely and efficiently run by the Volunteers of America, the Keener Shelter is merely a shelter and cannot deliver the psychiatric care needed by many of its inhabitants. Nor is the Keener Shelter unique; a building on the grounds of New York's Creedmoor State Hospital was also used as a shelter in the 1980s, and a building on the grounds of St. Elizabeth's Hospital, the public psychiatric hospital in Washington, DC, has been used as an emergency shelter for homeless individuals in cold weather. For many of these homeless, it is like returning home.

Chapter 3

JAILS AND PRISONS

Deinstitutionalization doesn't work. We just switched places. Instead of being in hospitals the people are in jail. The whole system is topsy-turvy and the last person served is the mentally ill person.[1]

Jail official, Ohio

Confining George Wooten in the Denver County Jail in May 1984 was another indicator of the growing mental illness crisis. The 32-year-old Wooten had been jailed over 100 times, including 28 times in the previous 2½ years, for creating disturbances in the community. Wooten had been diagnosed with schizophrenia at age 17, and each time he used alcohol or sniffed glue or paint fumes, it exacerbated his schizophrenia and led to his disorderly behavior.

According to a newspaper account, "Wooten says he likes jailers and the place. He calls it home. . . . Eight years ago, the officers might have taken Wooten to a community mental health center, a place that was supposed to help the chronically mentally ill. But now they don't bother. . . . Police have become cynical about the whole approach. They have learned that 'two hours later [those arrested] are back on the street . . . the circle of sending the person to a mental health center doesn't work.'"[2]

Removing the Mentally Ill from Jails

The odyssey of repeated incarceration for severely ill people like George Wooten was common in the United States in the early 1800s although many Americans found such practices inhumane and uncivilized. Their sentiments found organized expression in the Boston Prison Discipline Society, which was founded in 1825 by the Reverend Louis Dwight, a Yale graduate and Congregationalist minister. Shocked by what he saw when he began taking Bibles to inmates in jails, he established the society to publicly advocate improved prison and jail conditions in general and hospitals for mentally ill prisoners in particular. According to the medical historian, Gerald Grob, Dwight's "insistence that mentally ill persons belonged in hospitals aroused a responsive chord, especially since his investigations demonstrated that large numbers of such persons were confined in degrading circumstances."[3]

Dwight's actions led the Massachusetts legislature to appoint a committee in 1827 to investigate conditions in the state's jails. The committee's report, which was directed to the State General Court, included documentation that many "lunatics and persons furiously mad" were being confined, often in inhumane and degrading conditions. In one jail, a man had been kept for nine years: "He had a wreath of rags around his body and another round his neck. . . . He had no bed, chair or bench . . . a heap of filthy straw, like the nest of swine, was in the corner. . . . The wretched lunatic was indulging [in] some delusive expectations of being soon released from this wretched abode."[4]

The committee report concluded: "The situation of these wretched beings calls very loudly for some redress. They seem to have been considered as out of the protection of laws. Less attention is paid to their cleanliness and comfort than to the wild beasts in their cages, which are kept for show."[5]

Among the specific recommendations of the committee was that all mentally ill inmates of jails and prisons should be transferred to the Massachusetts General Hospital and that confinement of mentally ill persons in the state's jails should be made illegal. Three years later, the Massachusetts General Court "overwhelmingly approved a bill providing for the erection of a state lunatic hospital for 120 patients"; this opened in 1833 as the State Lunatic Asylum at Worcester. When the hospital opened, "more than half of the 164 patients received during that year came from jails, almshouses, and houses of correction [prisons]."[6] One-third of these patients had been confined in these institutions for longer than 10 years.

Dorothea Dix, the most famous and successful psychiatric reformer in American history, picked up where Dwight had left off. In 1841, with the American asylum-building movement under way, Dix began a campaign that would focus national attention on the sad plight of the mentally ill in jails and prisons and would be directly responsible for the opening of at least 30 more state psychiatric hospitals.

At the time she began her crusade, Dix was a 39-year-old teacher who had been left a bequest by her grandmother, allowing her to give up teaching. Her father had been "shiftless, poverty stricken and irresponsible . . . fanatically religious, with a penchant for writing theological tracts in fits of 'inspiration,'"[7] and her childhood had therefore been very difficult. Her father may in fact have been mentally ill, which would account in part for her zeal to improve conditions for such sufferers.

Dix's crusade began in early 1841, when she agreed to teach a Sunday school class at the East Cambridge Jail outside Boston. While there, she noticed not only that there were insane prisoners among the inmates, but also that the insane prisoners had no heat in their cells. When she inquired about this, she was told by the jailer that it was because "the insane need no heat." Horrified, Dix reported her findings to her friends and set out to investigate other jails in Massachusetts to ascertain whether similar conditions prevailed. Over the next year, she visited dozens of jails and almshouses and then presented a report to the state legislature. It rang of reform and set the tone for Dorothea Dix's future work:

> I come to present the strong claims of suffering humanity. I come to place before the Legislature of Massachusetts the condition of the miserable, the desolate, the outcast. I come as the advocate of helpless, forgotten, insane and idiotic men and women . . . of beings wretched in our prisons, and more wretched in our Alms-Houses.
>
> I proceed, Gentleman, briefly to call your attention to the state of Insane Persons confined within this Commonwealth, in *cages, closets, cellars, stalls, pens: Chained, naked, beaten with rods,* and lashed into obedience![8]

After finishing her report in Massachusetts, Dix moved on to New Jersey, where she proceeded in the same fashion to visit jails and almshouses, then report to the state legislature and urge the building of public psychiatric hospitals in which insane persons could be treated humanely and receive treatment. By 1847, she had taken her crusade to many eastern states and visited 300 county jails, 18 prisons, and 500 almshouses. Her success in persuading state legislatures to build psychiatric hospitals was impressive, and she provided a major impetus to the reform movement.

The Reverend Louis Dwight and Dorothea Dix were remarkably successful in leading the effort to place mentally ill persons in public psychiatric hospitals rather than in jails and almshouses. By 1880, there were 75 public psychiatric hospitals in the United States for the total population of 50 million people. In 1880, the first complete census of "insane persons" in the United States was carried out. It was, in fact, a more complete census than has ever been carried out since and included letters to all physicians asking them to enumerate all "insane persons" in their community, a question about "insanity" on the census form that went to every household, and a canvassing of all hospitals, jails, and almshouses. A total of 91,959 "insane persons" were identified, of which 41,083 were living at home, 40,942 were in "hospitals and asylums for the insane," 9,302 were in almshouses, and *only 397 were in jails.* The total number of prisoners in all jails and prisons was 58,609, so that severely mentally ill inmates constituted *only 0.7 percent* of the population of jails and prisons.[9]

That was the situation in 1880.

Putting the Mentally Ill Back into Jails

The mentally ill began reappearing in America's jails and prisons in large numbers approximately 90 years after the 1880 census. In 1974 and 1975, for example, Glenn Swank and Darryl Winer assessed 545 inmates in the Denver County Jail and reported, "The number of psychotic persons encountered in the jail was striking, as was the number with a history of psychiatric hospitalization, particularly long-term (more than one month) or multiple hospitalizations. . . . Of the jail inmates with a history of long-term psychiatric hospitalization, many had been state mental hospital patients." They also noted a widespread belief among jail personnel "that there has been a marked increase in the number of severely mentally disturbed individuals entering the jail in recent years, but unfortunately there are no earlier data available for comparison. . . . The [jail] system seemed to have inherited responsibility for these persons by default rather than preference."[10]

A study of five California county jails carried out in 1975 by Arthur Bolton and Associates found that 6.7 percent of the inmates were severely mentally ill at the time of examination.[11] Gary Whitmer's 1980 study of 500 mentally ill people who had been charged with crimes emphasized the causal relationship between the person's mental illness and his or her crime, and he cited examples such as a man who had "smashed the plate-glass window of a retail store because he saw a dinosaur jumping out at him"; a woman who refused to pay her restaurant bill because she believed that "she was the reincarnation of Jesus Christ"; a man who harassed two other men whom he believed to be "CIA agents who had kidnapped his benefactress"; and a woman with paranoid delusions who went up to a man on the street and "struck the victim in the right buttocks" with a hat pin.[12] At the time of their arrests, only 6 percent of the mentally ill studied by Whitmer were involved in any treatment program leading him to conclude that the reforms brought about by deinstitutionalization had "forced a large number of those deinstitutionalized patients into the criminal justice system."

By the early 1980s, interest in the problem of the mentally ill in jails and prisons was growing, increasing as their numbers increased, and two methodologically sound studies of the problem were carried out. In Chicago, Linda Teplin, spurred by the observation that "mental health professionals speculate that the jails have become a repository for the severely mentally ill," interviewed 728 jail admissions using a structured psychiatric interview and found that 6.4 percent of them met diagnostic criteria for schizophrenia, mania, or major depression.[13] In Philadelphia, Edward Guy and his colleagues interviewed 96 randomly selected admissions to the jail and reported that 14.6 percent had schizophrenia or manic-depressive illness, which they labeled as "an alarmingly high incidence of mental illness among inmates of a city jail "[14]

A more inclusive but methodologically less rigorous study of mentally ill people in the nation's jails was carried out in 1992 by the Public Citizen Health Research Group and the National Alliance for the Mentally Ill.[15] Questionnaires were mailed to the directors of all 3,353 county and city jails in the United States asking them to estimate the percentage of inmates who on any given day "appeared to have a serious mental illness." This was further defined to include only inmates with schizophrenia or manic-depressive illness who were exhibiting symptoms such as auditory hallucinations, delusions, confused or illogical thinking, bizarre behavior, or marked mood swings. The jail directors were instructed *not* to include as mentally ill anyone who exhibited "suicidal thoughts or behavior" or "alcohol and drug abuse" unless the person also had other symptoms as previously described. No attempt was made to identify mentally ill inmates with more subtle symptoms of mental illness (e.g., an inmate with paranoid schizophrenia who did not discuss his delusional beliefs); the survey sought to count only those who were the most severely and overtly mentally ill.

Replies were received from 41 percent of the jails, which represented 62 percent of all jail inmates in the United States. Overall, the jail directors estimated that 7.2 percent of inmates appeared to have a serious mental illness, ranging from less than 3 percent in jails in Wyoming, Nevada, Idaho, and South Carolina to almost 11 percent in jails in Connecticut, Hawaii, and Colorado.

Studies of inmates with psychiatric disorders in state prisons have also been carried out, and the results agree with the results from the studies done in jails. In general, jails keep prisoners sentenced for one year or less, whereas prisons keep prisoners with longer sentences. Ron Jemelka and his colleagues reported that many such studies "used a field survey approach in which one or more key administrators in each prison system was asked to respond to a series of questions about the mentally ill in their facilities. These surveys have suggested that 6 to 8 percent of state prison populations have a serious psychiatric illness," but for a variety of reasons "facility surveys are likely to substantially underestimate the number of mentally ill offenders."[16]

When prison inmates have been actually interviewed, a higher percentage have been found to be severely mentally ill. In 1980, Frank James and his associates reported findings from interviews of 246 prisoners in Oklahoma; 10 percent of them were found to be acutely and severely disturbed.[17] In 1987, Henry Steadman and his colleagues published the results of interviews with 3,332 prison inmates in New York State; 8 percent of them were said to have "very substantial psychiatric and functional disabilities that clearly would warrant some type of mental health service."[18]

A 1988 study of 109 new admissions to the Washington State prison system, using a structured diagnostic interview, reported that 8.4 percent had schizophrenia, manic-depressive illness, or mania, while 1.9 percent more had schizophreniform disorder, and 10 percent met diagnostic criteria for depression.[19] A similar study of 1,070 prison inmates in Michigan found that 6.6 percent had schizophrenia or manic-depressive illness and 5.1 percent had major depression.[20] Considering all these studies, Jemelka et al. concluded that 10 to 15 percent of prisoners have a major thought disorder or mood disorder and "need the services usually associated with severe or chronic mental illness."[21]

Other studies have also been used to ascertain how frequently people with severe mental illnesses are put into jails and prisons. In 1991, a telephone survey was carried out of 1,401 randomly selected members of the National Alliance for the Mentally Ill, an advocacy and support group composed mostly of family members of persons with schizophrenia and manic-depressive illness. It was found that 40 percent of the mentally ill in this group had been arrested at some time in their lives and, at any given time, 1 percent of them were in jail or prison.[22]

Studies have also been done to ascertain arrest and incarceration rates for the homeless who are mentally ill. A 1985 study in Los Angeles of 232 people living in shelters and on the streets who had previously been psychiatrically hospitalized found that 76 percent of them had been arrested as adults.[23] This is similar to the 74 percent previous arrest rate reported for severely mentally ill inmates examined in the Los Angeles County Jail.[24] Such studies demonstrate a large overlap between mentally ill persons who are homeless and those who are in jail.

How many people with severe mental illnesses are in jails and prisons on any given day? If such illnesses are defined to include only schizophrenia, manic-depressive illness, and severe depression, then approximately 10 percent of all jail and prison inmates appear to meet these diagnostic criteria. The most recent data available in 1995 indicated there were 483,717 inmates in jails and 1,104,074 inmates in state and federal prisons in the United States, a total of 1,587,791 prisoners.[25] If 10 percent of them are severely mentally ill, that would be approximately 159,000 people. It is also likely that the mentally ill often rotate back and forth between being homeless and being in jails or prisons.

What Is It Like to Be Mentally Ill and in Jail or Prison?

Being in jail or prison when your brain is working normally is, at best, an unpleasant experience. Being in jail or prison when your brain is playing tricks on you is often brutal.

One reason for this is that jails and prisons are created for people who have broken laws. These institutions have rigid rules, both explicit and implicit, and a major purpose of incarceration is to teach inmates how to follow such rules. The system assumes that everybody can understand the rules and punishes anyone who breaks or ignores these structures. Because of illogical thinking, delusions, or auditory hallucinations, many of the mentally ill inmates cannot comprehend the rules of jails and prisons and this has predictable, and sometimes tragic, consequences. For example, a 27-year-old man with paranoid schizophrenia was severely beaten by guards in the Los Angeles County Jail because he "was violating jail rules requiring inmates to remain silent, place their hands in their pockets and keep their shirts tucked in" while waiting in line in the jail cafeteria. The beating produced permanent brain damage and the man was subsequently awarded compensation by a court.[26]

Illogical thinking, delusions, auditory hallucinations, and severe mood swings may also lead to bizarre behavior by severely mentally ill individuals in jails and prisons. Jail officials responded to the 1992 survey by the Public Citizen Health Research Group and National Alliance for the Mentally Ill with many examples of such behavior, including the following:[27]

He paced the floor screaming curses for three solid days, day and night.

He did considerable damage to the jail and never slept, continuously hollering and keeping all prisoners awake.

They often refuse to wear clothes; they throw food, play in toilets, yell, scream, masturbate, etc.

A man sets a fire in his room, using his mattress and blankets for fuel. During the investigation of the incident he says he set the fire in an attempt to drive the demons out of his room.

A newspaper in California described mentally ill inmates in a county jail "who try to escape by smearing themselves with their own feces and flushing themselves down the toilet."[28] Such bizarre behavior is disquieting to the other inmates, who frequently react with violence against the mentally ill. As one jail official succinctly phrased it: "The bad and the mad just don't mix."

The incidence of such abuse by inmates is very high, and is facilitated in some jails, such as the Los Angeles County Jail, by the policy of identifying the mentally ill with uniforms of a different color or with other conspicuous markers. Physical assaults against mentally ill inmates range from lacerations to brutal beatings. Jail officials acknowledge that abuse and assaults sometimes take place:[29]

All kinds of things can happen when a mental case is in jail. Some inmates have patience with mental cases. Others do not, especially if the mental case is loud and abusive. (Jail official in Texas)

Most of the mentally ill inmates we have handled in the past suffer damage mentally at the hands of the other inmates. We try to keep them separated but lack of room sometimes prohibits this. (Jail official in New Jersey)

A serious form of assault that sometimes occurs is attempted or actual rape. All inmates in jails and prisons are at risk for such attacks, but inmates who are confused by their illness and less able to defend themselves are more vulnerable.

Sometimes the rape is only threatened: "My brother, who was very delusional and obviously ill, was placed with the other prisoners. He said they pulled his pants down and threatened to rape him."

On other occasions, rapes do occur: "He was in the jail forensic program several times and on two different occasions he was taken from there and put into a cell with homosexuals who gang raped him."

The most severe forms of physical abuse can cause the deaths of inmates: In the Hinds County (Mississippi) Detention Center in 1994, a 43-year-old man with paranoid schizophrenia was beaten to death by an 18-year-old prisoner being held on charges of armed robbery and murder. The Hinds County Sheriff said that the death could not have been prevented, given "the design of the jail, inadequate resources, crowding, and the inability to isolate violent inmates."[30]

Suicide by mentally ill inmates is relatively common. Data collected from New York State jails between 1977 and 1982 showed that half of all inmates who committed suicide "had been previously hospitalized for treatment of a mental disorder."[31] A similar survey at the Los Angeles County Jail found that "71 percent had histories of mental illness or had been examined by jail mental health workers just before they killed themselves."[32] An analysis of suicide attempts in jails in Sacramento County, California, revealed that "almost all those attempting suicide had major psychiatric disorders . . . (major depression, schizophrenia and delusional disorders). . . . More than half were experiencing hallucinations or delusions at the time of the attempt. . . . More than 75 percent had histories of previous mental health treatment."[33]

For each successful suicide in jails, there are many others that are unsuccessful. A chief psychiatrist in the Los Angeles County Jail estimated that the ratio of failed attempts to deaths is approximately 20 to 1.[34] In some cases, the bizarreness of the suicidal behavior makes it difficult for jail officials to assess whether the person really meant to die or not—in New York, a woman swallowed four radio batteries, and in Montana, a man "tried to drown himself in the jail toilet." A guard in the Jefferson County Jail in Kentucky explained the system that some guards use in his jail to differentiate serious suicide attempts from suicide gestures: "If an inmate cuts his wrists, a guard checks the depth of the cut by inserting his thumbnail in the wound. Guards figure half a thumbnail or less is usually a fake."[35]

Another major problem for the mentally ill in jails and prisons is exposure to infectious diseases and neglect of their medical problems. Tuberculosis, some varieties of which are resistant to medications, spreads rapidly among jail and prison inmates. AIDS and venereal diseases can be a consequence of rape. People who are mentally ill frequently cannot describe their physical symptoms to jail and prison officials, and when they do so, the officials may ignore them. The consequences are sometimes fatal:

◇ A man with schizophrenia was arrested in Miami for disorderly conduct and taken to the Dade County Jail. He was observed to be "grossly psychotic" and to exhibit "bizarre behavior," including "shouting into the toilet bowl." He refused to eat and refused medication, gradually becoming quieter and withdrawn. On the fifteenth day in jail he was found dead; autopsy revealed pneumonia, which would have been easily treatable.[36]

◇ After taking an overdose of antipsychotic medication and attacking several people in a mall with a coffee mug, a man with schizophrenia was taken to the Missoula County Jail in Montana. He was placed in isolation and a few hours later began having seizures. He was noted to fall "repeatedly while trying to stand up" so he "was then put in leg irons and handcuffs, which were attached so the prisoner could not stand up." Approximately two hours later he was found to be comatose and resuscitation efforts failed.[37]

◇ A severely mentally ill woman, arrested in Buffalo for breaking the antenna off a car, was taken to the Erie County Holding Center. Nobody, including the woman, was aware that she was eight months pregnant. A few days later she gave birth in her jail cell and began screaming about an "animal" in her clothing. By the time medical help arrived the baby was dead.[38]

For the mentally ill, the effects of being in jail or prison are occasionally positive but more often negative. Interestingly, those who claim that it was positive, do so because they found prison to be the only place they could get psychiatric treatment. Family members occasionally claim that their mentally ill relative received better care in jail than in psychiatric hospitals. One woman reported that her son "preferred jail to being hospitalized. He said he was always treated with respect in jail. This was seldom the case during his many hospitalizations, he claims."[39]

Such cases are exceptions. Jails and prisons usually exacerbate psychiatric symptoms, both because the mentally ill are frequently placed in solitary confinement and because they often are not given the necessary medication to control their symptoms. A 1994 study of Ohio's prisons, for example, reported, "More than 20 percent of the 1,877 prisoners confined to punishment cells [solitary confinement] were mentally ill . . . [they are] abandoned in isolation units for violating prison rules they are incapable of comprehending. . . . [A mentally ill] woman of Marysville [Prison] has been in solitary confinement for almost six years."[40]

California is another state in which the mentally ill in state prisons suffer unnecessarily. California's prison system houses approximately 15,000 persons who are severely mentally ill and advertises itself as "one of the largest providers of mental health care in California." In 1995, a federal judge handed down a "blistering 345-page opinion" against the California Department of Corrections, citing "a rampant pattern of improper or inadequate care that nearly defies belief."[41] In one prison, mentally ill inmates were put in solitary confinement so frequently that it constituted "a deplorable, and clearly conscious, disregard for the serious mental health needs of inmates. . . . For these inmates, placing them in [solitary confinement] is the mental equivalent of putting an asthmatic in a place with little air to breathe." At another California prison, officials described a "grossly psychotic" inmate who had been in solitary confinement for a month, "smearing feces on the walls, stopping up toilets, being assaultive toward guards, [and] refusing to come out of his cell to take a shower."[42]

The Imprisoned Mentally Ill and Deinstitutionalization

Between 1980 and 1995, the total number of individuals incarcerated in American jails and prisons increased from 501,886 to 1,587,791, an increase of 216 percent. During this time, the general population increased by only 16 percent.[43] The vast majority of this increase has been fueled by changing demographics, more stringent mandatory sentencing laws, and the increasing availability of cocaine and other street drugs. Have the mentally ill, however, contributed more than their expected share to the increasing population of jails and prisons?

Several lines of evidence suggest the answer is yes. First, in 1939, Lionel Penrose, studying the relationship between mental disease and crime in European countries, showed that prison and psychiatric hospital populations were inversely correlated: As one rose, the other fell.[44] This has become known as the balloon theory—push in one part of a balloon and another part will bulge out. In 1991, George Palermo and his colleagues published an extensive analysis of the balloon theory utilizing data on U.S. mental hospitals, jails, and prisons for the 83 years between 1904 and 1987. They found the theory to be valid and concluded:

> The number of the mentally ill in American jails and prisons supports the thesis of progressive transinstitutionalism. The authors believe that the

statistical evidence derived from the national census data corroborates their clinical observation that jails have become a repository of pseudo-offenders—the mentally ill. Our opinion is that our results probably reflect the state of most United States jails.[45]

Observations by psychiatrists and by corrections officials also support a causal relationship between deinstitutionalization and the increasing number of former patients in jails and prisons. California was the first state to aggressively undertake deinstitutionalization, implementing the Lanterman-Petris-Short (LPS) Act in 1969, which made it much more difficult to involuntarily hospitalize, or keep in the hospital, persons who are mentally ill. In 1972, Marc Abramson, a psychiatrist in San Mateo County, published data showing that the number of mentally ill persons entering the criminal justice system doubled in the first year after the Lanterman-Petris-Short Act went into effect. Abramson said, "As a result of LPS, mentally disordered persons are being increasingly subjected to arrest and criminal prosecution."[46] Abramson also coined the term "criminalization of mentally disordered behavior" and in a remarkably prophetic statement said, "If the mental health system is forced to release mentally disordered persons into the community prematurely, there will be an increase in pressure for use of the criminal justice system to reinstitutionalize them. Those who castigate institutional psychiatry for its present and past deficiencies may be quite ignorant of what occurs when mentally disordered patients are forced into the criminal justice system."

Similar observations were made throughout California in the years following implementation of the Lanterman-Petris-Short Act. A 1973 study in Santa Clara County indicated the jail population had risen 300 percent in the four years after the closing of Agnews State Psychiatric Hospital, located in the same county.[47] In 1975, a study of five California jails by Arthur Bolton and Associates reported that the number of severely mentally ill prisoners had grown 300 percent over 10 years.[48] In California's prisons, the number of mentally ill inmates also rose sharply in the 1970s. One prison psychiatrist summarized the situation:

We are literally drowning in patients, running around trying to put our fingers in the bursting dikes, while hundreds of men continue to deteriorate psychiatrically before our eyes into serious psychoses. . . . The crisis stems from recent changes in the mental health laws allowing more mentally sick patients to be shifted away from the mental health department into the department of corrections. . . . Many more men are being sent to prison who have serious mental problems.[49]

A second approach to assessing the relationship between deinstitutionalization and the increasing number of mentally ill people in jails and prisons is to examine the reasons for incarceration. In the 1992 Public Citizen survey, investigators found that 29 *percent* of the jails sometimes incarcerate persons *who have no charges* against them but are merely waiting for psychiatric evaluation, the availability of a psychiatric hospital bed, or transportation to a psychiatric hospital. Such jailings are done under state laws permitting emergency detentions of individuals suspected of being mentally ill and are especially common in rural states such as Kentucky, Mississippi, Alaska, Montana, Wyoming, and New Mexico.

In Idaho, the incarceration of mentally ill persons who had broken no laws was standard practice until 1991, when the Idaho legislature made it illegal. Any persons requiring involuntary commitment were taken first to the local jail rather than to a hospital emergency room until they could be examined by a state-appointed psychologist. If the psychologist advised hospitalization, these people remained in jail until a psychiatric hospital bed became available. In 1990, Idaho state officials estimated that approximately 300 persons who had not been charged with any crime had been jailed that year for an average of five days each while awaiting psychiatric referral. This practice was true not only for the rural counties but also for Boise, the state capital, where the Ada County Jail detained 85 persons without charges even though there were two private hospitals with psychiatric beds a few blocks from the jail. One of them had even been built with a federal Community Mental Health Center construction grant. In many states, especially those with poorly developed public psychiatric services, this practice continues. A sheriff in Florida observed, "I have had mentally ill inmates in paper gowns in holding cells for close observation for up to six weeks before we could find a hospital bed for them."

Most severely mentally ill people in jail are there because they have been charged with a misdemeanor. A 1983 study by Edwin Valdiserri and his associates reported that mentally ill jail inmates were "four times more likely to have been incarcerated for less serious charges such as disorderly conduct and threats" compared with nonmentally ill inmates.[50] These inmates were 3 times more likely than those not mentally ill to have been charged with disorderly conduct, 5 times more likely to have been charged with trespassing, and 10 times more likely to have been charged with harassment. A more recent study at the Mental Health Unit of the King County Correctional Facility in Seattle found that 60 percent of the inmates had been jailed for misdemeanors and had been arrested on the average of six times in the previous three years.[51] Similar findings have been reported from other parts of the United States. In Madison, Wisconsin, the most common charges brought against the mentally ill who end up in jail are "lewd and lascivious behavior (such as urinating on a street corner), defrauding an innkeeper (eating a meal, then not paying for it), disorderly conduct (such as being too loud), menacing panhandling, criminal damage to property, loitering or petty theft."[52]

In examining records of these arrests, researchers often find a direct relationship between the person's mental illness and the behavior that led to apprehension. For example, a woman with schizophrenia in New Mexico was arrested for assault when she entered a department store and began rearranging the shelves because of her delusion that she worked there; when asked to leave, she struck a store manager and a police officer. A man with schizophrenia in Pennsylvania who was behaving bizarrely on the street was arrested for assault after he struck a teenager who was making fun of him. People who suffer from paranoid schizophrenia, in particular, are likely to be arrested for assault because they may mistakenly believe someone is following them or trying to hurt them and will strike out at that person.

Theft may involve anything from cans of soda (an Oregon man with schizophrenia was arrested for "stealing pop bottles to turn in for refund") to a yacht (a Kentucky man with manic-depressive illness stole a yacht at a dock, then drove it around the lake until it ran out of gas). One of the most common forms of theft involves going to a restaurant and running out at the end of the meal because the person has no money, a practice commonly referred to as "dine and dash."

Police frequently use disorderly conduct charges to arrest a mentally ill person when no other charge is available. The mother of a son with schizophrenia in Texas said that her son was frequently arrested for "just wanting to talk to normal (his word) people in the malls or street. . . . He would follow them and just keep talking. . . . [He] would not go away when they asked him to and they were afraid. . . . His looks were very unkempt, which added to their fear." A man with manic-depressive illness in Washington State remembers being arrested for disorderly conduct because "I played music on my stereo too loud" and his neighbors complained. A man with schizophrenia in Illinois was arrested for throwing a television set out the window, probably because he believed it was talking to him.

Alcohol- and drug-related charges are also common because alcohol and drug use among this population frequently occurs as a secondary problem among the mentally ill (e.g., a woman with manic-depressive illness in California was arrested for being drunk and disorderly on the street). There have been numerous arrests for driving while under the influence of alcohol or drugs; in some cases the person has not used either but, because of bizarre behavior, is assumed to have done so by the arresting officer.

Trespassing is another catchall charge police officers often use to remove mentally ill persons from the street. A man with schizophrenia and alcohol abuse in New Hampshire has been arrested 26 times, mostly on trespassing charges. A woman in Tennessee reported that her son with schizophrenia had been arrested and put in jail for holding a sign that says "Will Work For Food" and on another occasion for sleeping in a cemetery. In another scenario that frequently leads to arrest for trespassing, the mentally ill person has a delusion of owning a building; a man in Florida was arrested for refusing to leave a motel "that God had given him," and a man in Kansas entered a farmhouse and went to sleep because he believed he had won the farm as a prize from a cigarette company.

Local businesses often exert pressure on the police to get rid of "undersirables," including the mentally ill. This is especially true in tourist towns such as New Orleans, where the police have a well-known reputation for "cleaning the streets" by arresting all vagrants and homeless persons. A police official in Atlanta described how mentally ill homeless persons at the city's airport are routinely arrested, while a sheriff in South Carolina confided that "our problems usually stem from complaints from local business operators."

"Mercy bookings" by police who are trying to protect the mentally ill are also surprisingly common. This is especially true for women, who are easily victimized, even raped, on the streets. A sheriff in Arizona admitted that police officers "will find something to charge the person with and bring her to jail." A jail official in West Virginia, after describing how the local state psychiatric hospital routinely discharged severely disabled patients to the streets, said, "If the mental institutions will not hold them, *I will.*"

In Madison, Wisconsin, police arrested a mentally ill woman who was yelling on the streets and charged her with disorderly conduct. According to a police department spokesperson: "People called us because they were afraid she'd be assaulted . . . the woman was not exhibiting the dangerous behavior necessary for commitment to Mendota [State Hospital], she didn't want to go to a shelter and no one could force medication on her."[53] So the police arrested and jailed her for her own protection.

A Los Angeles police captain sounded the same theme:

You arrest somebody for a crime because you know at least they'll be put in some kind of facility where they'll get food and shelter. You don't invent a crime, but it's a discretionary decision. You might not arrest everybody for it, but you know that way they'll be safe and fed.[54]

Another member of the Los Angeles police force described frequent arrests of severely mentally ill homeless persons:

[They are] suffering from malnutrition, with dirt-encrusted skin and hair or bleeding from open wounds. . . . It's really, really pitiful. . . . You get people who are hallucinating, who haven't eaten for days. It's a massive cleanup effort. They get shelter, food, you get them back on their medications. . . . It's crisis intervention.[55]

Sometimes "mercy bookings" are initiated by mentally ill persons themselves to get into jail for shelter or food; a man in Florida admitted, that "I would commit a crime near the police station and turn myself in. . . . Jail would take me in and put me to work cleaning floors."

The mentally ill also are sometimes jailed because their families find it is the most expedient means of getting the person into needed treatment. As the public psychiatric system in the United States has progressively deteriorated, it has become common practice to give priority for psychiatric service to persons with criminal charges pending against them. Thus, for a family seeking treatment for an ill family member, having the person arrested may be the most efficient way to accomplish their goal.

This method of getting treatment is also used in states in which psychiatric hospitals are only available for people who are a danger to themselves or others. In the Public Citizen survey of jails, numerous family members confided that either the police or mental health officials had encouraged them in pressing charges against their family members to access psychiatric care for them. In Massachusetts, the mother of a man with schizophrenia wrote:

In our state a patient cannot get into a state hospital, even if willing, without being dangerous to self or others. . . . Rather than wait for the patient to become so psychotic that disaster occurs, many families bring charges against a patient for making threats or damaging property. We have done this.

Similarly, in suburban Philadelphia, the parents of a severely ill young man who had no insight into his illness, who had refused treatment, and whom psychiatrists refused to commit involuntarily to a hospital because they claimed he was not a danger to himself or others, was finally hospitalized after his parents called the police. The parents obtained a court order barring him from their home and, when he violated the order, had him arrested. The judge, who had suggested to the parents that they use this mechanism to get treatment for their son, then offered the son a choice of staying in jail or going to the hospital.[56] In these cases, jails become a transitional device to obtain psychiatric care from a failed treatment system.

The most direct approach for assessing the relationship between deinstitutionalization and the increasing number of mentally ill persons in jails and prisons is to ascertain how frequently former patients are arrested after discharge from psychiatric hospitals. Studies done prior to the beginning of deinstitutionalization did not find a higher arrest rate than for the general population. Virtually every study done since deinstitutionalization began has found the opposite.

Eight American studies of arrest rates of discharged psychiatric patients, done between 1965 and 1978, were analyzed by Judith Rabkin. "Each study found that arrest or conviction rates of former mental patients equaled or exceeded those of the general population in at least some crime categories when patients were considered as a homogeneous group." Rabkin concluded, "There has been a pronounced relative as well as absolute increase in arrests of mental patients."[57] Especially impressive was Larry Sosowsky's study of arrest rates of patients discharged from California's Napa State Hospital between 1972 and 1975, after the Lanterman-Petris-Short Act had taken effect. Compared with the general population, discharged patients with no previous arrest prior to hospitalization were arrested 2.9 times more frequently. For the category of "crimes against property" (e.g., shoplifting), the discharged patients were arrested 4.3 times more frequently. Discharged patients who had been arrested prior to their psychiatric hospitalization were arrested approximately 8 times more frequently than the general population.[58]

More recent studies have reported similar trends. John Belcher's study of 132 patients discharged from Columbus State Hospital in Ohio during 4 months in 1985 is particularly interesting. The patients were followed up at 1, 3, and 6 months to ascertain what had happened to them. By the end of 6 months, 17 percent of the 132 patients had been arrested. However, only 65 of the 132 discharged patients had diagnoses of schizophrenia, manic-depressive illness, or severe depression, and 21 of these (32 percent) were among those arrested and jailed. According to Belcher, "These 21 respondents were often threatening in their behaviors" and exhibited bizarre behavior "such as walking in the community without clothes and talking to themselves."[59] They also did not take medications needed to control their psychiatric symptoms and frequently abused alcohol or drugs. Significantly, all 21 of these former patients also became homeless during the 6-month follow-up period, again affirming the close connections between severe mental illnesses, homelessness, and incarceration.

It appears, then, that jails and prisons have increasingly become surrogate mental hospitals for many people with severe mental illnesses. In New York, the estimated population of 10,000 mentally ill inmates in the state's prisons "now surpasses [that of] the state's psychiatric hospitals."[60] In Austin, Texas, "the Travis County Jail has admitted so many prisoners with mental disabilities that its psychiatric population rivals that of Austin State Hospital."[61] In the Dallas County Jail, "On any given day you will find about 900 mentally ill and mentally retarded inmates [which] is more than twice the number housed in the nearest state mental hospital."[62] In Seattle "quite unintentionally, the jail has become King County's largest institution for the mentally ill."[63] In the San Diego County Jail, where "14 percent of the men and 25 percent of the women are on psychiatric medications," an assistant sheriff observes that "we've become the bottom-line mental health provider in the county."[64] And the Los Angeles County Jail, where approximately 3,300 of the 21,000 inmates "require mental health services on a daily basis," is now de facto "the largest mental institution in the country."[65]

Chapter 4

Walking Time Bombs: Violence and the Mentally Ill

Simply to release these seriously mentally ill persons who have, in addition, high proved potential for antisocial and violent acts does a tremendous disservice to these patients as well as to society. . . . These mentally ill persons cry out for treatment. . . .[1]

Dr. H. Richard Lamb, Psychiatrist,
University of Southern California

On the day before Halloween in 1985, a 25-year-old woman walked into a quiet shopping mall outside Philadelphia. She wore Army fatigues and a T-shirt that read "Kill Them All." She shot at everyone she saw, killing a 2-year-old girl, a 4-year-old boy, and a 64-year-old retired physician, and wounding seven others. Later she would say she was acting to save the world's energy supply.

The person doing the shooting was Sylvia Seegrist, who had a 10-year history of schizophrenia.[2] She had been psychiatrically hospitalized 12 times, including 5 times in the 3 years prior to the shootings, but had never been required to continue taking the medication that effectively controlled her symptoms. Her psychiatric records documented "hundreds of times" when she had said that "she felt like getting a gun and killing people." She had stabbed a psychologist and tried to strangle her mother. She had been found with a loaded pistol, which she said she intended to use to kill her parents. She was well known to the police and had been jailed for misdemeanors. The police were aware that she had tried to purchase a semiautomatic rifle a few months before the shootings and were also notified that she had a rifle and was acting bizarrely at a shooting range three days before the shootings.

Sylvia Seegrist had not always been psychotic and violent. She had been a "conscientious, hard-working student" who had taken accelerated math and science classes. She had played field hockey, liked horseback riding, and "played Monopoly by the hour with a neighborhood boy." She had planned to become a doctor. But that was before the onset of her schizophrenia at age 15.

During her trial, Sylvia's mother detailed the family's extensive efforts to get help for their daughter. It was apparent that the mental health system had failed, in part because the laws protected Sylvia's right to refuse treatment and medication. According to her mother: "We saw our daughter's illness progress, but were defenseless. It seemed to us that she had all rights except one. Because she denied her illness and resisted treatment, Sylvia did not have the right to get well."

What Is the Relationship of Mental Illness and Violence?

Researchers have been studying violent acts by people who are mentally ill for more than a century. In 1857, Dr. John Gray, one of the founders of what would become the American Psychiatric Association, published an analysis of 52 attempted or completed homicides by patients whom he had treated during a 7-year period at a large hospital in New York State. Gray noted: "Under the influence of the delusions and hallucinations peculiar to the disease, we meet with a tendency [to violence] so universal, so destructive to happiness, and so dangerous to society, how important is its careful study, with reference to the welfare both of the patient and the public!"[3]

For the hundred-year period between John Gray's study and the advent of deinstitutionalization, many mentally ill people—especially those with a tendency to violence—were confined to psychiatric hospitals for much of their lives. Sporadic reports of violent acts by mentally ill individuals appeared in psychiatric journals, newspapers, and magazines, but there are no suggestions that it was a major problem. A few studies were carried out of the arrest rates of patients who had been discharged from psychiatric hospitals; studies in 1922, 1930, 1938, and 1945 all found "that mentally ill persons had a lower arrest rate than the general population."[4] This in turn led to the oft-quoted claim that the mentally ill are no more dangerous than the general population, which was true prior to the era of deinstitutionalization because most potentially dangerous patients were kept in the hospitals.

Since deinstitutionalization began, every study that has been done has found a reversal of these arrest rates. Since the majority of the arrests are for nonviolent acts, however, high rates do not accurately measure violence, especially for severely ill persons, who may be arrested for reasons that have nothing to do with being violent. The most useful available studies of violent behavior focus on patients who have been discharged from hospitals or treated as outpatients, particular types of crimes, the incidence of violence among ill people living with their families, and violence by mentally ill respondents identified in general community surveys.

Several studies of patients discharged from psychiatric hospitals and of those being treated as outpatients have reported that violent crimes are elevated for these groups. Psychologist Judith Rabkin, summarizing studies done in the 1960s and 1970s of discharged patients, noted, "Arrest and conviction rates for the subcategory of violent crimes were found to exceed general population rates in every study in which they were measured."[5] For example, in a 6-year follow-up of 301 patients discharged between 1972 and 1975 from California's Napa State Hospital, the arrest rate for "violent crimes" was *10 times* the rate for the general population.[6]

More recent studies have pointed in the same direction. In a 1989 study of outpatients in a mental health center in Kansas City, the researchers reported that 25 percent of male psychiatric patients with a history of violence became violent again within one year following hospital discharge.[7] Swedish investigators, Per Lindqvist and Peter Allebeck, reported in 1990 that 644 individuals with schizophrenia, followed for 15 years after their initial psychiatric hospitalization, committed violent offenses at a rate four times higher than the general population, although "the violence recorded was almost exclusively of a minor nature" (e.g., threats of violence against officials).[8] And in an unpublished 1992 study, psychologist Henry Steadman and his colleagues found that "27 percent of released male and female patients report at least one violent act within a mean of four months after discharge" from a psychiatric hospital.[9]

The most careful study done to date on violent behavior by psychiatric outpatients was reported in 1992 by Bruce Link and his colleagues at the New York State Psychiatric Institute.[10] They compared 186 outpatients and 46 inpatients with 521 community residents who did not require any psychiatric care. The groups were matched on a wide variety of demographic characteristics, and violent behavior was measured in several ways (arrests, hitting others, fighting, weapon use within the past 5 years, and "hurting someone badly"). The psychiatric patients were further divided into first-contact patients, who had begun treatment within the past year; repeat-treatment patients, who had begun treatment more than a year previously and were currently being treated; and former patients, who had been treated in the past but not within the previous year.

The psychiatric patients engaged in significantly more violent behavior than the community residents. For the two most important indicators of violence, weapon use in the past 5 years and hurting someone badly, the psychiatric patients had rates approximately three times higher than the community residents. The study found only one demographic and socioeconomic variable that accounted for the differences in violent behavior between the two groups: the current level of psychotic symptoms. The sicker the patients, the more likely they were to have exhibited violent behavior. Although the study did not assess medication compliance, failure to take medication is a well-known cause of some exacerbation in psychiatric patients.

Similar findings were reported in a 1994 English study of 538 people with schizophrenia living in the Camberwell district of London. Men and women with psychiatric diagnoses other than schizophrenia, matched for age and sex with the study group, were used as control subjects. Compared with the controls, men with schizophrenia were found to have a 3.9 times greater risk, and women with schizophrenia a 5.3 times greater risk for conviction on charges of assault and serious violence.[11]

Two studies of violent behavior have been done on the mentally ill who present with certain characteristics or who commit certain types of crimes. Psychiatrist David Shore and his colleagues at the National Institute of Mental Health studied persons with schizophrenia who had gone to the White House to give the President advice, warn of impending danger, claim an imaginary reward, or request relief from imagined persecution (e.g., demand that the government remove a transistor supposedly implanted in the person's brain).[12] These schizophrenic men and women are labeled as "White House cases"; they are taken to St. Elizabeth's Hospital for psychiatric evaluation and then released. In following up 192 male White House cases 9 to 12 years after their discharge, Shore et al. found that persons who had not been arrested prior to their White House encounter had a subsequent arrest rate for violent crimes (assault, robbery, and murder) 1.6 times that of the general population. But, those with previous arrest records had a subsequent arrest rate for violent crimes 4.8 times that of the general population.

A somewhat different approach was taken by Daniel Martell, a psychologist, and Park Dietz, a psychiatrist, who studied 36 persons who had pushed or tried to push other people in front of subway trains in New York City.[13] Of the 36 offenders, 25 were referred for psychiatric evaluation, and data were available on 20 of them. Fourteen had a diagnosis of schizophrenia (8 had the paranoid subtype); one, schizoaffective disorder; one, manic-depressive illness; three, psychosis not otherwise specified; and one, antisocial personality disorder. Except for one episode that took place during an attempted robbery, all of the motives offered by these offenders reflected psychotic symptoms. Thus, mentally ill people appear to be responsible for many cases of this particular violent crime.

Another approach to studying violent behavior is to ascertain the incidence of violence among the mentally ill who are living with their families. In 1990, the National Alliance for the Mentally Ill (NAMI), a national advocacy and support group, conducted extensive telephone interviews with 1,401 randomly selected families in which a family member had a severe mental illness.[14] In almost all cases, the ill family member had a diagnosis of schizophrenia, manic-depressive illness, or major depression. In the preceding year, 11 percent of them had physically harmed another person, and 12 percent more had threatened to harm another person.

The study found a marked sex difference among those threatening harm (25% of males and 13% of females) but surprisingly little sex difference among those actually harming someone (12% of males and 10% of females). In an earlier survey of NAMI families, more than one-third had reported that their ill relative was assaultive and destructive in the home either sometimes or frequently.[15]

The results of the NAMI surveys are consistent with other reports of violence against family members. Straznickas and colleagues reported that among patients admitted to psychiatric hospitals who had physically attacked someone within the preceding two weeks, family members had been the object of the assault 56 percent of the time.[16] A similar study by Tardiff reported that family members had been the object of the assault 65 percent of the time.[17] Previous surveys of problems encountered by families with a severely mentally ill relative living at home have also reported threatening or assaultive behavior as a common problem.[18]

The results of the NAMI surveys are also consistent with anecdotal reports of violence against family members by the mentally ill. A frequent theme in these accounts is the association between the violence and the ill person's refusal to take medication; for example, in an article in the *New York Times* entitled "My Brother Might Kill Me," the author wrote that her brother's last several attacks all occurred after he refused medication.[19]

Finally, two studies have assessed violent behavior among persons with severe mental illnesses who were identified by surveys of the general population. As such, these subjects were not selected in any way by treatment criteria or by having been arrested.

The first study was the five-site Epidemiological Catchment Area (ECA) surveys, carried out between 1980 and 1983 by the National Institute of Mental Health.[20] The survey assessed violence in 426 individuals with severe mental illnesses and 7,379 individuals with no mental disorder by using four criteria: hitting or throwing things at a spouse or partner; hitting a son or daughter hard enough to cause bruises or injury; physically fighting with others; and using a weapon such as a stick, knife, or gun in a fight. A major shortcoming of the study was the lack of ratings for the severity of the violent behavior; hitting someone with a stick and killing someone with a gun were rated equally.

The study found that people with a severe mental illness living in the community reported having been violent on all four measures within the previous year much more frequently than those with no mental disorder. The frequency with which schizophrenic persons reported having used a weapon in a fight (21.5 times more often than persons with no psychiatric disorder) was especially noteworthy. In addition, the study found that almost one-third of the individuals with schizophrenia or schizophreniform disorder also met diagnostic criteria for drug or alcohol abuse or dependence and had a much higher rate of reported violence than did those without this cofactor. Higher rates of reported violence were found among respondents with drug or alcohol abuse or dependence but no severe mental illness than among those with severe mental illness alone.

The other random community survey, done in Sweden, included all people born in Stockholm in 1953 and still living there 30 years later.[21] The study focused on violent crimes committed by persons with a severe mental disorder. *Violent crimes* were defined as "all offenses involving the use of threat of physical violence (for example, assault, rape, robbery, unlawful threat, and molestation)," and *severe mental disorder* included schizophrenia, paranoid states, major affective disorders, and other psychoses. Compared with men and women with no psychiatric diagnoses, men with major mental disorders were found to be 4.2 times more likely and women with major mental disorders 27.5 times more likely to have been convicted of a violent crime.

As we have seen, it is clearly established that those who have a severe mental illness are, as a group, more likely to commit acts of violence than the general population. John Monahan, professor of law at the University of Virginia and the author of many studies in this field, concluded in a 1992 summary of this literature:

The data that have recently become available, fairly read, suggest the one conclusion I did not want to reach: Whether the measure is the prevalence of violence among the disordered or the prevalence of disorder among the violent, whether the sample is people who are selected for treatment as inmates or patients in institutions or people randomly chosen from the open community, and no matter how many social and demographic factors are statistically taken into account, there appears to be a relationship between mental disorder and violent behavior.[22]

At the same time, it should be explicitly noted that the mentally ill as a group account for only a small fraction of the violence in our communities. America is a violent society and within this broad landscape, the total contribution of the mentally ill is not large. *Alcohol and drug abuse far outweigh mental illness in contributing to the high incidence of violence in American society.*

Is there any way to estimate the magnitude of the contribution of mental illness to violence? Although there has been no scientific study of this question, we can roughly estimate the relationship of such illnesses to the homicide rate by using a study of published accounts of homicides committed by mentally ill persons in the Washington, DC, metropolitan area during 1992. This study found six local reports of such episodes resulting in 13 victims.[23]

Based on the 4.3 million population of the Washington, DC, metropolitan area and the fact that there were approximately 23,000 homicides nationally during 1992, it can be estimated that persons with mental illnesses were responsible for approximately 770 homicides during that year. Since many homicides are not reported in newspapers and others are not solved, a conservative national estimate of the total annual number of such crimes by the mentally ill would be approximately 1,000—approximately 4 percent of all homicides in the United States. In societies less violent than the United States, homicides by the mentally ill constitute a larger percentage of the total. In Iceland, in which only 47 homicides were reported over an 80-year period, mentally ill persons were responsible for 13 (28 percent) of them.[24]

Can We Predict Who Will Become Violent?

Studies of violence in the mentally ill suggest that only a small percentage become violent; the vast majority remain nonviolent despite their illness. Is there any way of identifying those who are prone to violence and thereby taking preventive measures?

There appear to be three primary predictors of violence and three other less well-defined predictors. The most important one is a history of past violence; this is the most significant predictor of violence no matter whether a person is mentally ill or not. In trying to predict future violent behavior, the person's history is the single most critical piece of information.

The second important predictor is drug and alcohol abuse, and this is also valid whether the person is mentally ill or not. In 1994, Jeanette Smith and Stephen Hucker reviewed studies of substance abuse in persons with schizophrenia and noted "a growing body of research suggesting a significant link between schizophrenia, substance abuse and violence."[25] An example of such studies was a Swedish report of 38 schizophrenic and violent persons in which 21 of the 38, or 55 percent, were definite or probable substance abusers.[26] From their review, Smith and Hucker concluded: "Schizophrenics appear to be particularly susceptible to the negative effects of substance abuse. These include psychiatric and social complications, with antisocial behavior, particularly violence emerging as one of the most worrying features."[27]

The third important predictor is the failure to take medication. There are several reasons those who are mentally ill often do not take medication including lack of insight, medication side effects, and a poor doctor-patient relationship (discussed in Chapter 8). In one study, only 50 percent of mentally ill patients were still taking prescribed antipsychotic medication one year after hospital discharge.[28]

Those who do not take prescribed medication appear to be much more likely to commit violent acts. In a study of psychiatric outpatients, "71 percent of the violent patients . . . had problems with medication compliance, compared with only 17 percent of those without hostile behaviors," and the correlation was highly significant ($p < .001$).[29] Similarly, in a study of inmates in a state forensic hospital, Smith found a highly significant correlation ($p < .001$) between failure to take medication and history of violent acts in the community.[30]

Another measure of failure to take prescribed antipsychotic medication is continuing prominent psychotic symptoms, because the medication usually reduces such symptoms. In Link et al.'s study of mentally ill persons living in the community, psychotic symptoms were highly correlated with fighting and hitting others and were "the only variable that accounts for differences in levels of violent illegal behavior between patients and never-treated community residents."[31]

A similar association of psychotic symptoms and violent acts was reported by psychiatrist Pamela Taylor in her English study of 121 men with psychosis who had committed crimes. She concluded:

Over 80 percent of the offenses of the psychotic [men] were probably attributable to their illness. . . . Within the psychotic group those driven to
offend by their delusions were most likely to have been seriously violent,
and psychotic symptoms probably accounted directly for most of the
very violent behavior.[32]

Studies of psychiatric inpatients have also consistently shown correla-
tions between insufficient medication and increased violent behavior.[33,34]

Anecdotal evidence also supports the belief that the failure to take medication is an important predictor of violent behavior. In the Public Citizen
Health Research Group—National Alliance for the Mentally Ill survey of
mentally ill persons in jails discussed in Chapter 3, many cases were identified in which a person committed a violent act as a direct consequence of
psychotic symptoms such as hallucinations and delusions related to failure
to take medication. For example, a man with schizophrenia had religious
delusions and robbed a church in Arizona "as a sort of revenge because this
particular church was not the 'true' religion." Released from jail, he immediately robbed the church again and turned himself in to the police saying
he had nothing to fear because "I am in the hands of the Lord."

An Arkansas man with paranoid schizophrenia believed that his father,
who lived in another state, was secretly spying on him. He therefore took
an old shotgun and staged a robbery of a grocery store in an effort, he
told police, to get his father to come out of hiding and show himself. In
Texas, a man with manic-depressive illness went to his bank to withdraw
some money. Because he had no identification, the bank refused to give
him money; incensed, he pulled out a pocketknife and threatened the
teller, resulting in an armed robbery charge. Another man, suffering from
schizoaffective disorder, robbed a bank in New York, then calmly sat
down on the front steps and waited for the police to arrive. A man with
manic-depressive illness in Tennessee stole a car "because the car was
green and I am green."[35] And in Rochester, New York, a man robbed a
bank using his pointed finger in his pocket as a "gun," then took the
money to the local zoo and threw it into the seal pit, "urging the animals
to return home." A New York Correctional Association report labeled
such violent acts "more pathetic expressions of mental illness than delib-
erate, premeditated crimes."[36]

In addition to a history of past violence, the abuse of drugs and alcohol,
and the failure to take medication, there are three other indicators of potential violent behavior, but their relative predictive importance is less certain. The first is neurological impairment. Research psychiatrist Menahem

Krakowski and his colleagues have carried out extensive neurological and neuropsychological testing of individuals with schizophrenia who were violent and compared them with those who were not violent. The violent group had a significantly higher number of neurological abnormalities such as abnormal reflexes, especially nonlocalized (or what are often called "soft") neurological signs.[37] Such findings suggest a nonspecific type of brain damage. Electroencephalographic (EEG) abnormalities did not differ between the violent and nonviolent groups.

Another factor that may have predictive value is the specific type of delusions, a common symptom in people with severe mental illnesses. Professionals have long assumed, based on common sense, that paranoid delusions are likely to predispose to violence. An example of this is the man who, while walking down a crowded city street, suddenly turned and struck a woman behind him because he believed she had a laser beam aimed at his testicles and was making him sterile.[38]

Emerging studies, however, suggest that the association between paranoid delusions and violence may be less straightforward. Pamela Taylor and her colleagues in England, through extensive studies, identified as more predictive of violence those delusions involving a belief that someone or something has taken control of the person's mind.[39] This is similar to findings reported by Bruce Link et al.: Strong predictors of violence in the mentally ill are the feeling that others are out to harm them and a feeling that their mind is dominated by forces beyond their control or that thoughts are being put into their head.[40]

The final factor that may predict violence is the specific type of hallucinations. Command hallucinations, in which voices tell the schizophrenic person what to do, may be compelling predictors of violence. Recent studies of their significance have been contradictory, and additional research is needed. It has also been claimed that hallucinations of noxious tastes or smells, especially when combined with paranoid delusions, predispose people with schizophrenia to violence.[41]

Utilizing all the studies done to date, can we predict who will become violent? Studies done in the 1970s reported that mental health professionals were unable to predict violence in their patients at more than a chance level. A recent reanalysis of those studies found flawed methodology in many of them and investigators concluded, "Clinical judgment has been undervalued in previous research."[42,43] Using only the three major predictive factors—a history of violence, the use of drugs and alcohol, and the failure to take medication—it seems likely that professionals could identify with reasonable accuracy many potentially violent persons. A major long-term study of risk assessment in the mentally ill, funded by the MacArthur Foundation and directed by Professor John Monahan, is now under way in Pittsburgh, Worcester, Massachusetts, and Kansas City, Missouri, and the preliminary results point strongly toward alcohol and drug abuse as being good predictors of violent behavior.[44] Much more research needs to be done.

Walking Time Bombs in the Community

There is overwhelming evidence that a small subgroup of the mentally ill have a propensity toward violence. It is also known that a persons' past history of violence, concurrent abuse of drugs and alcohol, and failure to take medications are risk factors for violent behavior. Thus, it might seem that people that with such risk factors would be targeted for specific treatment. This often is not the case.

The most complete study of this question was carried out at the Los Angeles County Jail by psychiatrist Richard Lamb, who followed up 85 persons who had been charged with serious crimes and who had been found incompetent to stand trial because of their mental illnesses.[45] The diagnosis for 71 of them had been schizophrenia, 6 had been diagnosed with major affective disorder, and the remaining 8 had received other diagnoses. The crimes for which they had been arrested on that occasion included 11 for murder or attempted murder, 14 for armed robbery, 19 for assault with a deadly weapon, 3 for rape, 10 for burglary, and 28 for other crimes. Seventy-three (86 percent) of them had prior psychiatric hospitalizations, including 12 who had previously been in forensic hospitals for the criminally mentally ill. Fifty-eight (68 percent) of them had been arrested for felonies and 20 (24 percent) for misdemeanors prior to their current arrest; thus only 7 of the 85 (8 percent) had not been previously arrested. Of the 78 who had prior arrests, 74 of them "had histories of serious physical violence against other persons ranging from assault to murder." By any measure, then, this was a group of very sick people, severely mentally ill individuals with a history of repeated violent acts and relapse of their psychiatric illnesses.

Based on their crimes and severity of mental illness, Lamb divided the 85 offenders into three groups: (1) 24 "psychotic habitual criminals" with long criminal records and occasional acts of violence; (2) 43 "psychotic sporadic offenders" with severe mental illnesses, less serious criminal acts, and occasional acts of violence; and (3) 13 "frequently violent psychotics" with severe mental illnesses and frequent violent acts. Five of the 85 cases did not fit in any of the groups. Lamb then ascertained what had happened to these persons at the end of two years.

After two years, only 34 percent of them were still incarcerated in hospitals or prisons. An additional 26 percent had been released to live in the community with follow-up mandated through a conservatorship, outpatient treatment, or probation; in most cases this arrangement was time-limited. The largest number—40 percent of the total group—had been released back into the community with no provision for postrelease follow-up or treatment. The average confinement, including both hospital and prison time, for those released without follow-up was only 14.4 months for the psychotic habitual offenders, 7.7 months for the psychotic sporadic offenders, and 13.1 months for the frequently violent psychotics. Most disturbing is that more than half (7 out of 13) of the members of the group of frequently violent psychotics, which Lamb assessed as "clearly highly dangerous individuals," were released with no provision for continuing treatment. Lamb concluded, "In most of these cases the problem is largely a failure on the part of society to take the necessary steps to protect itself and these patients."

There are suggestions that the situation in Los Angeles is not unusual. A study in Michigan of 687 people found not guilty by reason of insanity between 1976 and 1987 reported that only 21 percent were still hospitalized in 1993. In commenting on the study, the director of the Center of Forensic Psychiatry, which houses the most severely mentally ill accused of crimes, noted, "There are some ticking time bombs out there."[46]

There appears to be an increasing number of anecdotal accounts of tragedy following the release into the community of violence-prone people who have severe mental illnesses and are not being treated. The following examples are taken from media accounts:

◇ In 1988 in Brooklyn, Nick Gavrilou killed his elderly father and mother. Diagnosed with schizophrenia for 7 years, he had responded well to medication when he took it. He had beaten his parents on numerous occasions, including 3 months prior to the murders, when he had had to be subdued by "specially trained Emergency Service officers [who] used an electric shock gun, pressurized water and body shields." He was hospitalized for 3 weeks and released. He was psychiatrically evaluated for possible violent acts three more times in the 2 months before the murders.[47]

◇ In 1990 in Cambridge, Massachusetts, John F. Kappler, responding to voices in his head, drove his car onto a footpath, killing a young doctor who was jogging and seriously injuring a woman. Kappler, a fully trained anesthesiologist, had been diagnosed with schizophrenia and manic-depressive illness by various psychiatrists for over 20 years and had been hospitalized numerous times. He took medication irregularly. In 1975, he intentionally struck another car on a Los Angeles freeway. In 1980, "the voices told him to administer the wrong drug during surgery to a patient who suffered a cardiac arrest." In 1985, he was charged with attempted murder for allegedly turning off the life support system to another patient; at the time the District Attorney called him a "walking time bomb." Despite these acts, Kappler was not required to take medication and in fact even retained his license to practice medicine.[48]

◇ In 1991 in Grand Rapids, Michigan, Martin Speigl killed his father. Diagnosed with schizophrenia for 20 years, he had been originally hospitalized for threatening to blow up an airplane. He had been hospitalized at least six more times for violent acts, including attacking his father with a knife, and while hospitalized he had also "assaulted two patients without provocation." He routinely refused to take medication and had made numerous threats to kill people, including the President. One week prior to the murder, he had been "dropped off [at home] by a social worker" with no provision to guarantee that he would take his medication.[49]

◇ In 1993 in Fairfax, Virginia, Jeanette Harper killed the 71-year-old woman with whom she was living. Harper was a graduate of Duke University and a former teacher who had been diagnosed with schizophrenia and was "a gentle person when she took her medication." In 1986, she had shot to death a black man she did not know because "she feared all blacks were conspiring to murder her." She was released from the state psychiatric hospital in less than two years and mandated to take medication for only one more year. In 1991, she was evaluated psychiatrically for writing threatening letters to the governor's son. In 1992, she was again evaluated after she "rammed her car into the back of a tank truck . . . and then pretended she was in a coma when police tried to question her after a tussle on the highway." On the evening of the murder, she attacked the 71-year-old woman once, but a neighbor called the police who took Harper to a mental health center. The psychiatrist released her that same evening, whereupon she returned to the house and killed the woman.[50]

◇ In 1993 in Kansas City, Emmett Pulliam killed Lee Young, a neighbor. Pulliam had been diagnosed with schizophrenia for over 20 years. He killed his first wife and at various times was also convicted of "unlawful use of a weapon, assault, larceny, and abuse of family or children." In 1978, he robbed a bank, then "threw the money to the floor and took off most of his clothes," which he explained was "to attract the attention of President Jimmy Carter." In the week prior to the murder Pulliam "went around telling a lot of people he had to kill someone."[51]

With such failures to follow up and treat the mentally ill who have histories of violent behavior, people are likely to have decreasing confidence in psychiatrists and the mental health system. This lack of confidence, in turn, may strengthen community residents' resistance to the establishment of halfway houses or other facilities for mentally ill persons in their neighborhoods. Thus, even though only a small percentage of the mentally ill become violent, all could be penalized because of it. Diminished confidence may also incline juries to sentence mentally ill defendants to prisons, where they have a fixed sentence, rather than to psychiatric hospitals where psychiatrists have discretion regarding their release date. Although there are no recent studies quantifying these two trends, many professionals believe that both of them are occurring.

Violence, Mental Illness, and the Media

Acts of violence by a small number of the mentally ill severely stigmatize all such persons. An association between violent behavior and madness has existed in the mind of the public for hundreds of years; each such publicized incident reinforces this association.

Recent studies have confirmed that the association between violence and mental illness continues to be widespread. In a 1980 survey of college students' beliefs about people with schizophrenia, 52 percent believed that "aggression, hostility, [and] violence" were common or very common attributes, whereas only 9 percent said these attributes were uncommon or very uncommon.[52] A 1987 study of residents of Ohio revealed that "perceived dangerousness" was the single most important factor contributing to the stigma of mental illness.[53]

The media have both reflected and propagated this stereotype. In Canadian newspapers between 1977 and 1984 dangerousness and unpredictability were commonly attributed to the mentally ill.[54] Studies have found that newspaper stories tend to link mental illnesses to crime and that such stories are more likely to appear on the front page.[55] One study of prime-time television indicated that dangerousness and unpredictability were commonly attributed to TV characters who were mentally ill.[56]

Another study found that 72 percent of mentally ill characters on TV drama were portrayed as violent.[57]

Movies have linked mental illness to violence since the earliest days of the motion picture industry. *The Maniac Cook*, released in 1909, featured a prototypic psychiatrically ill homicidal character, and such productions have continued to emerge regularly from Hollywood studios over the years. Examples of this genre include *Psycho, Repulsion, Friday the 13th, Halloween, Nightmare on Elm Street, Silence of the Lambs*, and *Single White Female.*

Stigmatization and negative stereotypes lead to discrimination, and this creates major problems for the mentally ill and their families, making access to housing, jobs, social programs, and even psychiatric care more difficult. In fact, some say that the discrimination is worse than the disease itself. In recent years, the National Alliance for the Mentally Ill (NAMI) and the National Stigma Clearinghouse have made concerted efforts to combat this stigma and discrimination. The reality, however, is that there *is* an association between acts of violence and mental illness; insofar as this association continues, it will be difficult to reverse the public stereotype and to decrease discrimination.

There have always been occasional media accounts of violent acts by mentally ill persons. In the three decades following World War II, the most highly publicized cases were the 13 murders committed by Howard Unruh in Camden, New Jersey, in 1949; the 13 murders committed by Herbert Mullin in the San Francisco Bay area in 1972; and the multiple spree of rapes, robberies, and murders of Joseph Kallinger ("the Shoemaker") in the Philadelphia area in 1974. All three men were later diagnosed as having schizophrenia.

Beginning in the early 1980s, such stories have appeared more often. The killing of John Lennon by Mark Chapman and the shooting of President Ronald Reagan by John Hinckley received extensive publicity. So did the death of former civil rights activist and congressman Allard Lowenstein, killed by Dennis Sweeney, who was diagnosed with schizophrenia and who believed that Lowenstein "was part of a Jewish cabal that had tormented him for a decade in part by transmitting messages through his dental work."[58]

For the past 20 years, a constant stream of news stories have described violent acts committed by mentally ill persons. The most widely publicized cases involved homicides, but nonhomicidal violent acts have also received heavy coverage: Randall Husar, diagnosed with schizophrenia, used a hammer to attack the glass display case enclosing the U.S. Constitution and the Bill of Rights;[59] Michael Breen, said to be "muttering about earthquakes," punched Senator John Glenn in the face during a tree-planting ceremony;[60] Patrick Frank, diagnosed with schizophrenia, was indicted for setting fire to 17 churches that he claimed "were causing him to have homosexual urges";[61] Harry Veltman, diagnosed with schizophrenia, was sentenced to prison for sending threatening letters to Olympic skating champion Katarina Witt;[62] and Francisco Duran, diagnosed with schizophrenia, shot at the White House.[63]

The most highly publicized news stories have involved homicides with multiple victims. As previously described, Sylvia Seegrist shot 10 people at a Philadelphia shopping mall. James Brady, who believed that people were controlling him by a machine inside his body, killed 1 person and wounded 4 others in an Atlanta shopping mall.[64] Responding to command hallucinations from outer space, David Rice killed 4 members of a Seattle family.[65] Laurie Dann killed a boy and wounded 5 of his classmates in an Illinois elementary school.[66] At a Kentucky printing plant, Joseph Wesbecker, diagnosed with manic-depressive disorder, killed 7 coworkers and wounded 13 others.[67] Seeking revenge for "an evil conspiracy" against him, Gian Ferri killed 6 people and wounded 8 others at a law office in San Francisco.[68] In response to command hallucinations, James Swann killed 4 random pedestrians and wounded 10 others during a 2-month spree in Washington, DC.[69] John Salvi, diagnosed with schizophrenia, killed 2 and wounded 5 others in attacks on 2 Massachusetts abortion clinics.[70]

One of the most striking aspects of these accounts is how many of the mentally ill people were already known by psychiatric professionals and/or the police to be potentially dangerous. David Hassan killed four persons with his car two days after being released from a Los Angeles psychiatric hospital where he had been confined for "driving up and down the street trying to hit people."[71] James Brady, mentioned previously, had been labeled "homicidal and suicidal" at the Atlanta psychiatric hospital from which he was released one day prior to his shooting spree. In Rochester, New York, Gary Rosenberg, diagnosed with schizophrenia, killed two men only hours after being released from an emergency room where he had complained of voices telling him to kill others.[72]

John Smith, diagnosed with paranoid schizophrenia, killed the director of a soup kitchen in Jackson, Mississippi, after having been psychiatrically hospitalized 15 times, shooting at passersby once, and arrested 5 times for carrying a concealed weapon in the 15 months preceding the homicide.[73] In many instances, the mentally ill person's family had also sought unsuccessfully to get help for the person prior to the homicide. In

Los Angeles, the family of Betty Madeira, diagnosed with schizophrenia and identified as violent, had tried multiple times to have her committed to a psychiatric hospital before she stabbed to death her 78-year-old mother as the mother pleaded for help on the telephone.[74]

Another striking aspect of accounts of these homicides is that the perpetrators are almost never taking medication. James Becker, a Kentucky man diagnosed with schizophrenia but not taking his medication, killed his stepfather with a hunting bow.[75] In Michigan, Bartley Dobben, also diagnosed with schizophrenia but refusing to take medication, killed his two young sons.[76] Debra Jackson, a schizophrenic woman in Minnesota, killed her two young children after she stopped taking medication.[77] Although Gary Rimert was seriously ill, he took medication only occasionally; he stabbed to death his grandparents and two neighbors in South Carolina.[78] Keith Lodeger, diagnosed with schizophrenia and who "became uncontrollable when he did not take his medication," killed one child and wounded three others in an Ohio school.[79] In Baltimore, Clifton Williams, diagnosed with schizophrenia, was said to have "gone a long time without his medication" when he killed his mother with a circular saw as she slept.[80]

Are acts of violence by the mentally ill becoming more common? No formal study has been done on this question, but media stories suggest the answer is yes. For example, a study of local stories "of tragic events involving mentally ill individuals" in the Madison, Wisconsin, *Capital Times* during 1988 found that "six separate incidents resulted in four homicides, three suicides, seven victims wounded by gunshot, and one victim mauled by a polar bear" when a mentally ill man climbed into its den at the local zoo.[81]

I have kept a file with such accounts since the early 1980s. It is now four inches thick and has grown much more rapidly in the 1990s than it did in the 1980s. Even as I write this, the newspaper is covering two violent episodes. In one story, Mark Bechard, diagnosed with manic-depressive disorder—with a history of violent behavior and poor compliance with medication—is accused of stabbing and beating to death two elderly nuns and injuring two others in Maine.[82] In the other story, millionaire John duPont is charged with killing a former Olympic wrestler that duPont accused of "crawling through the walls and spying on him" and "masquerading around the house as his dog."[83]

Because of what is happening to services for the mentally ill, it would in fact be surprising if violence were not increasing. Severely ill patients are now being released from state psychiatric hospitals as deinstitutionalization is emptying the farthest back wards of patients who 10 years ago were deemed too disabled to live in the community. Simultaneously, community psychiatric services in almost all states have deteriorated. The combination of sicker patients with increasingly mediocre services leads to an inevitable, and often tragic, outcome.

What is perhaps most striking about media accounts, however, is how strongly they reinforce the public's association of violent acts with severe mental illnesses. As long as such stories continue to be reported, efforts to decrease stigma and discrimination against mentally ill persons will be problematic. John Lagos and his associates noted this as early as 1977 in an article entitled "Fear of the Mentally Ill: Empirical Support for the Common Man's Response."[84]

In 1981, the psychologist Henry Steadman similarly observed, "Recent research data on contemporary populations of ex-mental patients supports these public fears [of dangerousness] to an extent rarely acknowledged by mental health professionals. . . . It is [therefore] futile and inappropriate to badger the news and entertainment media with appeals to help destigmatize the mentally ill."[85]

In a similar vein, John Monahan recently added, "The data suggest that public education programs by advocates for the mentally disordered along the lines of 'people with mental illness are no more violent than the rest of us' may be doomed to failure. . . . And they should: the claim, it turns out, may well be untrue."[86]

We may ride to work on a bus that has a poster pleading for tolerance of mentally ill people who are "sick," not dangerous, and at the same time we may be looking at a newspaper headline that screams out the latest violent act of "mad felons."

Chapter 5

PSYCHIATRIC GHETTOS: COMMUNITIES AND FAMILIES

Deinstitutionalization has become a cruel embarrassment, a reform gone terribly wrong, threatening not only the former mental inmates but also the quality of life for all New Yorkers.[1]

Editorial, *New York Times*,
June 5, 1981

In the 1970s, the increasing number of mentally ill people who settled in Long Beach, New York, and other communities was an early indication of the emerging mental illness crisis. In Long Beach, a Long Island shore community of 34,000 residents, 712 former patients who had been discharged from state psychiatric hospitals were living in low-rent hotels using their supplemental security income (SSI) checks. The Administrator of the Long Beach Memorial Hospital noted: "Often they're brought in at night, confused and unable to communicate their problems. But we can't get their medical records. The clerk on duty at the hotel can't get into the cabinet because the manager's gone home with the key." At the Roman Catholic church, "where discharged patients reportedly have urinated on the floor during Mass and eaten the altar flowers," the assistant pastor observed: "It's a mind-blower. Most people in the parish accept these ex-patients, but it's not really a supportive community for them—they have no ties here."[2] By 1980, it had become such a politically sensitive issue that it was said, "When the governor goes out campaigning he avoids some places in Long Island because he would get nothing but anger and questions about why the patients are on the streets."[3]

Long Beach was representative of areas in many towns and cities that became psychiatric ghettos as patients were discharged from state hospitals without adequate provision for aftercare. In San Jose, California, "Businessmen reportedly purchased several abandoned sorority and fraternity houses close to San Jose State College and filled them with ex-patients"[4] from nearby Agnews State Hospital, which was being closed. Devine, Texas, with a population of only 3,928, opened approximately 20 board-and-care homes to house almost 500 patients being discharged from nearby San Antonio State Hospital. Portions of downtown Portland, Phoenix, Miami—indeed, virtually every American city—were taken over by ex-patients. A 1981 *Life* magazine story on the situation was titled "Emptying the Madhouse: The Mentally Ill Have Become Our Cities' Lost Souls."[5] Ten years later an article in the *Philadelphia Inquirer* summarized the situation: "The United States is in its third decade now of 'deinstitutionalizing' the mentally ill, which is a polite way of saying that it has quit warehousing them out of sight and started doing it in plain view."[6]

Ocean Grove, New Jersey: Deinstitutionalization in a Small Town

Ocean Grove, New Jersey, shows the effects of poorly planned deinstitutionalization on a small town. A sign at the town's entrance proclaims, "Welcome to Ocean Grove, A National Historic Site." The town was founded in 1869 by Methodist ministers for the purpose of "providing and maintaining the members and friends of the Methodist Church a proper, convenient and desirable permanent Camp Meeting ground and Christian seaside resort."[7] Its 6,600-seat Great Auditorium has hosted seven U.S. Presidents and is still used for Methodist services and other activities. Ocean Grove only occupies one square mile, yet it contains the highest concentration of Victorian houses in the United States—block after block of turreted roofs with cornices and railed porches. Ocean Pathway, stretching two blocks from the Great Auditorium to the ocean, was once labeled by the *National Geographic* as the "shortest, prettiest street in America."[8]

That was before deinstitutionalization came to Ocean Grove. With Marlboro State Psychiatric Hospital just 15 miles away, the old wooden hotels and Victorian boarding homes offered a convenient place for patients being released as New Jersey downsized its four state hospitals from over 22,000 patients in 1955 to just 3,400 in 1994. The number of discharged patients in Ocean Grove was not inordinate until the mid-1980s, when it began rising rapidly. By 1992, there were 426 licensed boarding home beds for discharged psychiatric patients and approximately 200 more that were unlicensed. The Grand Atlantic Hotel and Main Street House, standing next to each other in the center of town, together housed 101 discharged patients.

The majority of discharged psychiatric patients who came to Ocean Grove had been released from Marlboro. Others came from New Jersey's three other state psychiatric hospitals, Trenton, Ancora, and Greystone Park, some came from Veterans Administration Hospitals, and a few came from New York City, where one of the boarding home operators advertised for patients. By 1992, at least 600 former patients were living in Ocean Grove among its 5,600 other residents, thus constituting 10 percent of the population. Ocean Grove had become a "national historic site" not only for having a large concentration of Victorian homes, but also for having one of the largest concentrations of discharged psychiatric patients anywhere in the United States. An Ocean Grove resident observed in the *New York Times*, "They're turning this community into a mental ward."[9]

Once these severely ill individuals had been placed in Ocean Grove, the state appeared to forget them. Each patient had cost New Jersey approximately $70,000 per year while in Marlboro State Hospital, but by placing them in the community, the state effectively shifted the cost of their care to the federal government (a strategy described in Chapter 7). New Jersey has an active mental health lawyers group and is one of 15 states that does not have an outpatient commitment law (described in Chapter 8), so little effort was made to ensure that the discharged patients took their medication. And although the town of Ocean Grove had almost as many psychiatric patients as those remaining in Marlboro State Hospital, the state of New Jersey opened no outpatient clinic, day program, clubhouse, activity center, vocational training program, or rehabilitation facility in Ocean Grove. Except for a small drop-in center run by volunteers in a local church, the mentally ill in Ocean Grove had nothing to do except drink coffee, smoke cigarettes, watch television, and walk the streets. Some of them took medication regularly, but many did not. The results were predictable.

The effects of deinstitutionalization on the citizens of Ocean Grove can be measured by the stories they told:

◇ Residents referred to one street heavily used by discharged patients as "Thorazine Alley" because of its large volume of discarded "coffee containers, cigarette wrappers, paper pizza plates, empty Tiger Rose and Ripple bottles, beer cans, soda cans, candy wrappers, newspapers, magazines, balled-up Kleenex, and assorted bits of trash."

◇ Men and women were frequently seen urinating and defecating in public. Hedges planted in the 1890s along Ocean Pathway had to be removed because they were being regularly used as a bathroom.

◇ One woman noted, "My most unpleasant encounter was when jogging at the north end and coming upon a man with his trousers lowered, masturbating, on the Boardwalk at 7 in the morning."

◇ The mother of two small children said she was afraid to let them play in the yard. Another mother noted, "All the pleasures of visiting friends, playing together in the parks and bike riding are not permitted unless I escort them."

◇ At a Sunday service, a churchgoer had "witnessed . . . a young man making obscene gestures with his finger and giving obscene actions with his arm . . . to the minister during his sermon."

◇ A store owner had to lock his side door because of increased shoplifting. Another owner discovered a man exposing himself to customers. Still another store owner was beaten up by two mentally ill men.

◇ Owners of hotels and bed-and-breakfast establishments saw their tourism business decline sharply. One owner, forced into bankruptcy, said: "The overwhelming majority of guests which stay at my place have expressed their great dissatisfaction with the large number of severely mentally ill people in Ocean Grove. . . . They will not be returning." Property values in Ocean Grove decreased by approximately one-third.

◇ Prostitution was observed. Although this would be shocking in any small town, it was doubly so in a Methodist town noted for strictly following Sunday "Blue Laws" until 1979. Some children picked up used condoms as playthings, thinking that they were balloons.

◇ A former patient committed suicide by jumping from the fourth floor of a hotel. He had been discharged from Marlboro State Hospital just one week earlier. Another man sat on a roof for three hours threatening suicide until pulled off by the police. The local police experienced a sharp increase in ex-patient-related calls.

◇ A mentally ill man with diabetes was found on the streets in diabetic coma "two to three times a week . . . because he is not capable of, or is not supervised enough to take his regular dose of insulin." The emergency room at the local hospital had a major increase in psychiatric emergency visits.

◇ For people living in Ocean Grove, experiences such as these were lived day after day, month after month. As one resident summarized it: "This is not about a group brought in on a bus for a day at the beach. It's not about a movie where you leave the theater and go home when it's over. *This is never over.* It's inescapable. These people deserve our pity, our sympathy and our help. It's not their fault. But it's not our fault either! They deserve better, and so do we!"[10]

Founded specifically as a Christian community, Ocean Grove has a long tradition of tolerance and caring for those less fortunate than themselves. By the early 1990s, however, the town's tolerance level had been exceeded. What irritated the residents was not so much the presence of large numbers of mentally ill discharged patients, but rather that the state had made virtually no provision for their aftercare. It appeared that the Department of Human Services in Trenton, for reasons of funding, was focusing on only one goal and that was to empty the hospitals. Ocean Grove saw itself as being used as a human dump. Little or no thought was being given to the quality of the lives of the people being discharged, nor to the quality of the lives of those who would live around them. This, in a microcosm, was the failure of deinstitutionalization. It was also an important contributor to the mental illness crisis.

In retrospect, it is easy to see what should have been done. As I will discuss in later chapters, the state should have set up continuous treatment teams using the Program for Assertive Community Treatment (PACT) model or other aggressive case management techniques. This should have been complemented by the use of conservatorships or outpatient commitment provisions to ensure that the mentally ill who needed medications to remain well actually got them. The opening of a clubhouse, modeled after New York's Fountain House, would have provided an activity and job training center. Ocean Grove has a long tradition of volunteerism, and the mentally ill residents could have contributed significantly to the community's ongoing efforts toward beautification and maintenance of its historic Victorian houses. Since tourism is a major industry, job training could have provided those mentally ill residents who wished it with at least seasonal employment. And all of this could have been accomplished easily by using some of the funds New Jersey was saving by emptying its hospitals.

But none of that happened. Instead, in 1990 the town began a Neighborhood Watch program with 300 registered families and the Ocean Grove Community Patrol, in which 100 volunteers took turns patrolling the streets by automobile. By 1995, the Community Patrol had acquired three vehicles being discarded by the state police and was patrolling every day from 7 P.M. to 3 A.M. In 1992, citizens also instituted a walking patrol. Community residents also went public with their complaints through a Home Owners Association decrying the "dumping" of disproportionate numbers of mental patients into their community. State legislative hearings were held and legislation was passed increasing inspections of boarding homes for discharged psychiatric patients as well as setting limits for the concentration of the homes. Two of the largest facilities, the Grand Atlantic and Main Street House, were closed down and their residents relocated in other communities. By late 1995, the number of mentally ill residents in Ocean Grove had been reduced from 600 to approximately 200, and Governor Christine Whitman had publicly vowed to distribute future discharged psychiatric patients more equitably around the state and to provide outpatient services and rehabilitation. Ocean Grove residents watched skeptically.

Ocean Grove is not unique in New Jersey. The effects of the deinstitutionalization of the mentally ill can also be seen in other small towns such as Keansburg (population 11,000) and Red Bank (population 12,000). In Asbury Park (population 17,000), which is immediately adjacent to Ocean Grove, more than 1,000 discharged psychiatric patients are estimated to be living in 37 boarding homes and Residential Health Care Facilities. According to one published account, the town is a "psychiatric ghetto" in which a visitor gets "the palpable feeling . . . when strolling near or along the boardwalk on a winter's day, of being on the grounds of a state psychiatric institution. . . . Asbury Park seems like a discarded piece of another city that has washed up on the shore."[11]

The effects of deinstitutionalization can also be seen in larger New Jersey towns such as Long Branch and Atlantic City; in small cities such as East Orange, Camden, and Elizabeth; and in large cities such as Jersey City and Newark. Nor is New Jersey unique—a similar list of towns and cities that have been profoundly affected by deinstitutionalization can be drawn up for every state in the union.

New York, New York:
Deinstitutionalization in a Large City

In contrast to Ocean Grove, New York City is a megametropolis with almost 20 million people in the greater metropolitan area. Everything in New York is big, including the magnitude of the mental illness crisis.

Observing this has been especially difficult for many New Yorkers who pride themselves on their social consciousness and liberal social values. Much of the impetus toward deinstitutionalization nationally, in fact, arose from legal challenges initiated by the New York Civil Liberties Union.

From the earliest years of deinstitutionalization, many persons being discharged from New York's state and city psychiatric hospitals were not assimilated into the community. As early as 1974, it was said that "about 25 percent of the estimated 100,000 residents in welfare hotels were considered 'severely mentally dysfunctional' and most of these are ex-state hospital inpatients."[12] Between 1976 and 1980 "more than 40,000 state psychiatric patients were released in New York City,"[13] many of whom were placed into inadequate housing with little or no psychiatric aftercare. Inevitably, news items such as the following began to appear:

New York Times, Aug. 5, 1979. "21 Ex-Mental Patients Taken from 4 Private Homes." [Detectives removed residents from four homes in Queens where] dozens of other former mental patients have lived for years amid broken plumbing, rotting food and roaches. . . . The former patients in the homes were often poorly clothed, had at times gone without winter heat, and lived as virtual prisoners in the homes. . . . Last May the police found the decaying corpse of a former patient lying undisturbed in one home inhabited by six other residents.

Despite such reports, most New Yorkers continued to support deinstitutionalization, believing that occasional failures were amenable to the fine tuning of a fundamentally sound policy. In late 1979, a New York Times editorial appeared in response to the release of a man from Pilgrim State Hospital who went directly to his home and killed his wife, as he had threatened to do: "The entire program of deinstitutionalization—a sound and humane idea—is in danger of being discredited. . . . Clearly most mental patients are better off outside large state hospitals. Psychiatrists have learned that it is hard for them to regain their balance in a hospital setting."[14]

The opinion of many New Yorkers about deinstitutionalization changed in the 1980s, partly because of the increasing number of obviously disabled persons who were living on the streets, talking to unseen voices and eating from dumpsters. Representative of these unfortunates was Vito, "who wears a suit and lives in a coffinlike cardboard box," pictured on the front page of the New York Times with an outreach worker trying to give him a sandwich.[15] Also described was Antoine, who lived "amid a swathe of blankets and bottles on South Street, beneath the

Franklin D. Roosevelt Drive," and who was training "for the rigors of a mission to outer space." "'It's hard training for space,' he said. 'I'm tired of it.'" Another homeless man "lived near the World Trade Center because he believed it would be a good place to take off for outer space."[16] The growing number of such homeless was dramatic; during 1976, New York City police picked up approximately 1,000 "emotionally disturbed persons," also known as "EDPs," to be taken to hospitals for psychiatric evaluation, but in 1986 this number had swelled to 18,500, an 18-fold rise.[17] Some of this increase was due to greater use of cocaine and other drugs.

A second factor that changed the opinions of many New Yorkers about deinstitutionalization was the mounting number of local homicides and other violent acts committed by the mentally ill, most of whom were not receiving medications or other aftercare to control the symptoms of their illnesses. Such violent acts appeared to occur randomly in virtually every city setting. Three weeks after having been discharged from a psychiatric hospital, Mary Ventura pushed a woman into the path of a subway train.[18] Reuben Harris, diagnosed with schizophrenia, with 12 hospitalizations and a history of violent behavior, pushed another woman to her death in the same manner.[19] A few months later, Angel Coro, who had recently been released from a psychiatric hospital, plunged a hypodermic needle into the leg of a 6-year-old girl riding with her mother on the subway.[20] Afflicted by "delusions of grandeur" and "an obsession with nonexistent conspiracies," Colin Ferguson killed 5 people and wounded 18 others on a Long Island commuter train.[21] And on the Staten Island Ferry, Juan Gonzalez, who had been diagnosed with schizophrenia and psychiatrically evaluated for threatening to kill people four days earlier, killed two people and injured nine others with a sword.[22]

As more of the mentally ill were on the streets and in parks, episodes of violence increased. Police killed Louis Bertrain, who had experienced "a nervous breakdown after he slashed at pedestrians with a 12-inch blade on a crowded East Side street"; six months previously he had been arrested in Brooklyn for also menacing passersby with a knife.[23] In Central Park, a man, "muttering incoherently," used a baseball bat to brutally beat a young couple on their first date.[24] The following year, a woman walking her dogs in Central Park was stabbed to death by Kevin McKiever because he said she was "making noises" to bother him and that she may have been a witch. McKiever had previously stabbed another woman, was well known to city psychiatric services, and rarely took his medication.[25]

No place appeared to be safe from such random attacks. In a movie theater, "an apparently deranged man who had been muttering obscenities" jumped up in the middle of the movie, shouted "Don't laugh at me," then stabbed a stranger sitting nearby.[26] In a shoe store, Michael Vernon, diagnosed with schizophrenia but not taking his medication, shot five people to death because the store did not have the shoes he wanted in his size.[27] At the New York Technical College, Van Hull, who was "hearing voices," shot five people, killing one.[28] On Wall Street, Lois Lang, diagnosed with schizophrenia, killed the chairman of a foreign exchange firm and his receptionist because of Ms. Lang's delusional belief that she owned the firm and was owed money.[29] An NBC television employee at Rockefeller Center was killed by William Tager, who believed that television networks were purposefully sending "rays" and "vibrations" out of the television set to his brain.[30] And Steven Smith, who had been psychiatrically treated at Bellevue Hospital the previous month, raped and strangled a young physician in her office there.[31]

Even churches and homes were not immune to these senseless acts of violence. In the Bronx, Christopher Battiste, treated at city hospitals for severe mental illness twice in the previous two months, bludgeoned to death an 80-year-old woman on the steps of a church.[32] Jorge Delgado, who had been diagnosed with paranoid schizophrenia and previously hospitalized seven times, ran naked into St. Patrick's Cathedral, in Manhattan and killed an elderly usher with an iron prayer stand.[33] In Brooklyn Ghana Frazier stabbed his father to death when his father told him to take his medication. Ten years earlier, Mr. Frazier had dropped his 18-month-old nephew out of a fifth-floor window.[34] In Queens, Tatiana Belopolsky, said to be "chronically mentally ill," killed her elderly mother,[35] and Da Pei Wu killed his wife and two daughters because voices told him that they would be tortured if he did not kill them.[36]

New Yorkers reacted to these repeated violent acts in a predictable way. Columnist Bob Herbert, in discussing the Reuben Harris case, described the effect of these episodes:

> If you are a New Yorker the fear is there, somewhere, maybe buried deep beneath the surface of consciousness, or maybe right out there in the open, as loud and evident and nerve-racking as the screaming jackhammers, the endless emergency sirens and the careening, horn-blowing, red-light-running vehicles that are staples of New York's daily existence.
>
> The fear is that from out of the chaos some maniac will emerge to pointlessly, stupidly, inexplicably hurl you, blast you, cast you into oblivion.[37]

Some New Yorkers have suggested the need for stricter monitoring of mentally ill people with histories of violent behavior. Following the Harris case, the *New York Times* editorialized, under the headline "Amateur Hour at

Mental Health," that "strict guidelines are needed for schizophrenic patients with a history of stopping medication."[38] And in response to the Michael Vernon case, a *New York Times* op-ed piece suggested:

> The best way to try to prevent this from happening is what the mental health field calls court-mandated outpatient commitment—that is, the duty to take medication in exchange for the right to live in the community. It balances the public's right to safety with the patient's medical needs and right to live with the fewest restrictions possible.[39]

I will explore the ramifications of outpatient commitment in Chapter 8.

The problems of the homeless mentally ill and violent behavior by mentally ill persons came together in New York in two notorious cases—Joyce Brown and Larry Hogue. Brown had grown up in a middle-class New Jersey family, graduated from high school and business school, and worked for 10 years as a secretary. She then developed symptoms of mental illness and started using heroin and cocaine; the combined problems of illness and drugs got her psychiatrically hospitalized, then evicted by her sisters, and eventually evicted from a shelter, so that by 1986 she had become homeless and had taken up residence on a steam grate at the corner of East 65th Street and Second Avenue.[40]

Joyce Brown lived on the steam grate for a year and a half, urinating on the sidewalk and defecating in the gutter and on herself. She sometimes tore up money that passersby gave her, exploded in obscenities, ran unpredictably into traffic, and frequently wore little clothing despite cold weather. A city psychiatric outreach team tried five times to get her involuntarily hospitalized but each time she was released by psychiatrists as not being a danger to herself.

Joyce Brown's elevation to public consciousness and brief stardom occurred after New York's mayor Ed Koch observed her behavior on the street and, knowing that she needed treatment, asked accompanying mental health professionals to have her hospitalized. They explained to Koch that she could not be involuntarily hospitalized "because she did not present an 'imminent danger.' Koch was stunned and recalled thinking 'you're loony yourself.'"[41] Shortly thereafter, Koch proposed new, less restrictive guidelines to permit emergency psychiatric hospitalization for such people. Referring to civil libertarians who would contest the legality of his guidelines, Koch said: "If the crazies want to sue me, they have every right to sue, and by crazies I'm not talking about the people we're going to be helping. I'm talking about those who say, 'No, you have no right to intervene to help.'"[42]

Joyce Brown was picked up and involuntarily hospitalized under Koch's new guidelines, and the New York Civil Liberties Union immediately took the case to court. In hearings that resembled scenes from a Lewis Carroll story, Civil Liberties Union lawyers argued that other New Yorkers sometimes urinated on the sidewalk, that defecating on oneself was not really a threat to one's health, that running into traffic was akin to jaywalking, that tearing up money was a symbolic gesture of independence, and that Brown's obscene language was similar to that which can be heard in some movies. Judge Robert Lippmann, himself a former legal aid lawyer, ruled for the Civil Liberties Union, saying that "society, not Brown was sick." In ordering her release, Lippmann claimed that "the sight of her may improve us. By being an offense to aesthetic senses, she may spur the community to action."[43]

After several more rounds of highly publicized litigation, Joyce Brown was released. She then appeared on *Donahue* and addressed a forum at Harvard Law School, denying that she had been mentally ill and claiming that homelessness was simply caused by a lack of adequate housing. She was given a place to live and a temporary job, but within a few weeks she returned to live on the streets and continued to be there when last reported. Watching this vaudeville of jurisprudence, many New Yorkers questioned where deinstitutionalization had taken us and shared the musings of their mayor in wondering just *who* truly was psychotic.

By the early 1990s, the traditional sympathy expressed in the New York media for street people had significantly subsided. Random acts of violence by homeless mentally ill persons continued to be reported and the *Manhattan Spirit* editorialized:

> Longtime New Yorkers say that it is the single biggest change in the City they inhabit, the looming fear that the person who stops you on the street to insist you give him change, or who calls the park bench you sit on home, may be well beyond the reach of reason, beyond intimidation, in the grip of some vision that could spur him or her to attack whomever is unlucky enough to be nearby.
>
> "It used to be that if someone was following you or harassing you, you could just stare him down and make him go away," said one New York native. "Now, you never know if that person is just insane."[44]

D. J. Jaffe, a spokesman for the local Friends and Advocates of the Mentally Ill, was quoted in the same article as saying that for a mentally ill person "it's harder to get into Bellevue [psychiatric hospital] than into Harvard."

It was another *Manhattan Spirit* cover story in 1992 that labeled Larry Hogue as "The Wild Man of West 96th Street."[45] Hogue, who was diagnosed with manic-depressive illness and who also abused crack cocaine, had lived in doorways on West 96th Street since 1985 and had terrorized the neighborhood. Among other acts, he was said to have thrown stones through the stained glass windows of a church, broken car windows, set fires beneath cars, jumped on the hood of moving cars, threatened to roast and eat the dog of one resident, masturbated in front of children, and on one occasion was convicted of pushing a schoolgirl into the path of a moving truck. He had been hospitalized more than 30 times but failed to take medication each time he was discharged; crack cocaine further exacerbated his psychosis. Although for at least two years there were news reports describing attempts to get Hogue hospitalized for a longer period, compared with the tribulations of Joyce Brown four years earlier, the media expressed little sympathy for Hogue. Even more striking was that the neighborhood that Hogue had terrorized and that had fought to get him off the street had been viewed as an area particularly liberal and sympathetic to homeless people.

Joyce Brown, Larry Hogue, and the other thousands of homeless mentally ill individuals have had a profound effect on the quality of life in New York and other cities. A woman writing in *The Wall Street Journal* said, "A simple visit to the local elementary school, post office or grocery store, for instance, can be a Dantean journey through the dark underside of our society."[46] Another woman, writing in the *New York Times*, described "a child being wheeled in a carriage on Broadway [who] was slapped by a deranged man. . . . My husband encountered a deranged man who tried to bite his leg. . . . We have, sadly, grown accustomed to the images of madness on our streets and the menacing life that lives on them and now owns them."[47]

George Will, in a column in the *Washington Post* discussing the Joyce Brown case, noted:

> We are focusing exclusively on the individual, and in terms of his or her rights. But the community, too, has rights, needs and responsibilities that, if attended to, will leave the homeless better off. . . . Society needs order and hence has a right to a minimally civilized ambience in public spaces.[48]

And Gary Maier, a psychiatrist at Mendota State Hospital in Wisconsin, eloquently expressed a similar theme:

The gatekeepers of the chronic mentally ill must recognize that a failure to assess not just the rights of mentally ill persons, but also their ability to achieve a minimum standard of acceptable behavior in the community, will further erode public confidence in the professionals who govern patient care. . . . When the personal freedom of the mentally ill is given priority over all other considerations, the tyranny of some will jeopardize the autonomy of all.[49]

New Tasks for Police on the Streets

Although there is scant documentation, it is evident that the mental illness crisis has had major effects on many public services. Public transportation, including terminals such as train and bus stations as well as subways and buses themselves, have become homes for many mentally ill persons. Public libraries and museums frequently serve as unofficial day centers for ill persons looking for a warm, safe place. Hospital emergency rooms and ambulance services have reported serving many more severely mentally ill patients since deinstitutionalization was implemented. City and county social service and housing agencies have seen caseloads rise dramatically and have had to learn to deal with clients whose illnesses make filling out forms much more difficult than the already complicated norm. But no public service has been as profoundly affected by this crisis as the task of policing the streets.

From the very onset of deinstitutionalization, police departments reported an increase in mental-illness-related calls. Upper Darby Township in suburban Philadelphia, which had 133 officers to serve a population of 100,000, reported "that mental-illness-related incidents increased 227.6% from 1975 to 1979, whereas felonies increased only 5.6% and the total number of incidents, excluding these categories, decreased by 9%."[50] When police officers were asked to explain the increase, they said: "It's harder to get people into the hospital now, and once they're in, they don't stay long. You can turn around the next day and see someone back on the street." The authors of this study concluded, "Families, friends, and others in the community call on the police to act as agents of social control for mentally ill individuals whose behavior, although disruptive, does not meet criteria for involuntary civil commitment."

Police departments throughout the United States have reported similar findings. In New York City, as noted previously (reference note 16), the number of mentally ill persons taken to a hospital for evaluation by the police increased from approximately 1,000 per year in 1976 to 18,500 in 1986. Also in New York, calls to 911 about "emotionally disturbed persons" increased from 20,843 in 1980 to 46,845 in 1988.[51] In Los Angeles, the Police Department's Mental Evaluation Unit handled 3,059 cases and 12,613 calls in 1987, but in 1993 it handled 4,136 cases and 54,737 calls.[52] A recent survey of California law enforcement agencies found that during a three-month period 29 percent of police officers and sheriff deputies had had to handle a "mental health crisis," whereas only 28 percent of them had had to respond to a robbery call.[53] Similarly in Cincinnati and Hamilton County, Ohio, "during a one-month period, almost 60 percent of the officers had responded to at least one call involving a presumably mentally ill person, and 42 percent had responded to more than one such call."[54] Some of these calls were caused by the widespread use of crack cocaine, PCP, and other street drugs that may cause bizarre and assaultive behavior, but the majority appear to have been a direct effect of deinstitutionalization.

The sharp increase in such calls has substantially altered the job of being a police officer. The Los Angeles Police Department's Mental Evaluation Unit reported that 15 percent of all persons brought to the unit for evaluation "were nude at the time of their arrest."[55] City, county, and local police reports regularly include cases describing disordered behavior. For example, in 1993 the *Burt County [Nebraska] Plaindealer* described a confrontation between Darrel Conger and a police officer:

> It is alleged that he struck both Lyons police officer Steven Stillman and his patrol car with a shovel. He also is accused of injuring Alex Williams with a hammer and of striking vehicles belonging to Williams and Tom Johnson. . . . Conger suffers from bipolar disorder, also known as manic depressive illness, which caused him to be delusional on the day of the Lyons incident.[56]

The time that police officers must spend on cases involving mentally ill persons is impressive. In cities such as New York, a police officer must wait with the mentally ill person in the hospital emergency room until that person has been seen. According to a 1989 account, "Police officers frequently end up waiting 12 hours or more until a doctor can decide whether to admit the patient."[57] Committing this much time for mental illness cases can leave a police unit dangerously shorthanded for other tasks. Consequently, many police officers take mentally ill persons to jail rather than to the hospital.

In a small community with few police officers, a single mentally ill person can tie up most of the available resources for several hours. In 1994 in

Whitefish, Montana, an armed woman with a psychiatric history "stood in her bedroom doorway with a weapon in each hand for eight hours without moving. . . . Whitefish police and six members of the sheriff's tactical weapons team entered the house and stood watch during the night. Three negotiators, two from the Kalispell Police Department and one from the FBI, tried to talk to the woman, but she had not spoken during the standoff. . . . Authorities were bringing a shield called a body bunker from Missoula and were considering using it to try to disarm the woman."[58]

In addition to utilizing human resources, police cases involving the mentally ill are often expensive. A person who was threatening to jump from a bridge in New York was stopped by a coordinated rescue team that included "at least 20 police officers and supervisors, half a dozen emergency vehicles, several highway units, and a helicopter. A harbor unit and a hostage negotiating team were also alerted."[59] Such costs should be taken into consideration when computing the total costs of de-institutionalization.

The most serious confrontations occur between police officers and mentally ill people who are armed. In these situations, New York police use Emergency Service Unit vehicles equipped with "electric stun guns, fire extinguishers converted to water cannons, Mace, mesh restraining blankets, Velcro body cuffs, plastic shields, high intensity lights, and shepherd's crooks and other poles and restraining bars."[60] Such confrontations can terminate peacefully with apprehension or violently with an attempted suicide, an attack on the police, or an attack by the police. All three outcomes frequently involve fatalities.

Anecdotal accounts suggest that fatal encounters between police and the mentally ill have risen sharply in recent years. This change likely reflects the number of mentally ill persons who are not receiving medication or other treatment and the easy availability of guns in most states. Police officers are often victims:

◇ In 1992, in Jackson, Mississippi, David Smith, diagnosed with paranoid schizophrenia, killed Officer Rickey Joe Simmons.[61]

◇ Donald Polcyn, diagnosed with paranoid schizophrenia, killed Officer Ervid Clemmons in 1993, in Minneapolis, Minnesota.[62]

◇ In Great Falls, Montana, in 1993, Bobby McDonald, diagnosed with paranoid schizophrenia, killed Officer Shane Chadwick.[63]

◇ In 1994, Stephen Mercer, diagnosed with schizophrenia, killed Sheriff's Lieutenant Bill Sibrava. Mercer was also killed in this

Albuquerque, New Mexico, shootout as was his father, a former state senator and candidate for governor.[64]

◇ In Huntsville, Alabama, David Zmyewski, diagnosed with paranoid schizophrenia, killed Deputy Sheriff Thomas Lewis and wounded Deputy Billy Thrower. Zmyewski was also killed in the 1994 incident.[65]

◇ In 1995, George Page, diagnosed with manic-depressive illness, killed Officer Steven Ames of Winston-Salem, North Carolina.[66]

In most of these cases, the attacker had been well known to the police, had a previous history of violence, and was not taking medication at the time. For example, Bobby McDonald had had two previous encounters with police before moving to Montana; in one of them "he reportedly was carrying 26 concealed weapons, some held by metal bands to his legs."

The media also frequently report confrontations that end with fatal outcomes to the mentally ill person:

◇ Gaithersburg, Maryland, police officers, in 1991, killed David Sipple, a manic-depressive man, after he lunged at them with a knife.[67]

◇ In 1992, police in Brooklyn, New York, killed Earl Black, who was ill with schizophrenia, after he lunged at them with a knife.[68]

◇ Sheriff's deputies, of Hemet, California, in 1994, killed Troy Dederick, diagnosed with manic-depressive illness after he approached them with a machete.[69]

◇ In 1995, in Plano, Texas, police killed Michael Clement, a 15-year-old boy with autism, after he lunged at them with a knife.[70]

◇ In 1995, police in Spokane, Washington, killed Blaine Dalrymple, a paranoid schizophrenic man, after he lunged at them with broken glass.[71]

◇ Tampa, Florida, police, in a 1995 incident, killed Leon Williams, diagnosed with paranoid schizophrenia, after he attacked them because he thought that he was being attacked.[72]

◇ In 1995, police shot Mark Pederson, diagnosed with schizophrenia, in his home in Simi Valley, California, after he lunged at them with a knife. His mother said that he had stopped taking his medication.[73]

Police officers and sheriff's deputies vary widely in the training they receive on how to handle the mentally ill. Adequate training would undoubtedly reduce the risk of tragic outcomes in these confrontations. Such episodes are inevitable, however, when approximately 2.2 million mentally ill people who are not being treated are living in the community at any given time.

Family Tragedies

Caring for someone who is mentally ill and living at home can be extremely difficult, especially if the person's symptoms are prominent because medication either is not effective or the person does not take it. One mother said, "It is like asking a family member to take care of someone who needs dialysis; it's a very special need."[74] Mothers and fathers, while retaining the parental role, must sometimes take on the tasks of case manager, psychotherapist, money manager, cook, janitor, laundry worker, landlord, disciplinarian, medication-dispenser, or best friend.

This intensive involvement with the ill person necessarily detracts from time available for other family members, resulting in strained relationships and the dissolution of marriages. Nobody has yet estimated the number of families and marriages that have fallen apart because of deinstitutionalization and the inability to get a severely mentally ill family member rehospitalized, but anecdotal data suggest it is legion. Brothers and sisters often become angry and resentful because the mentally ill sibling places inordinate demands on a family's emotional and financial resources. Wendy Kelley, the vice president of a chapter of the Alliance for the Mentally Ill, recalled that when her sister developed schizophrenia "suddenly both my brother and I felt there was no time for us; everyone was consumed by what was going on with my sister."[75]

One of the most difficult experiences for families with a mentally ill member is watching the person deteriorate psychiatrically without being able to do anything about it because of stringent involuntary commitment laws. Chris Shermeister, in an article in the *Sheboygan Press*, described visits to his brother David's apartment and his unsuccessful attempts to get the Sheboygan (Wisconsin) Mental Health Center to have David hospitalized:

> Weeks earlier I had phoned the Sheboygan Mental Health Center and described what I had seen during a previous visit to David's apartment. I urged them to inspect the deplorable living conditions David was subjected to.
>
> I reiterated with urgency the fact that David was not medicated and was not able to provide for himself; that he was not cognizant of personal hygiene; that there was no toilet paper or toilet seat; that his laundry lay molding in a half-filled bathtub; that he was, in my opinion, slowly starving (he had lost over 40 pounds in four months and was bone thin); that

he was perpetually without money and that I had every reason to suspect that he was being preyed upon.

The entire flat was littered with filth. Garbage and debris were everywhere. It reeked.

David always had kept himself and his surroundings clean and orderly. He would never choose to live so wretchedly. I choked back tears; my gut wrenched at the lonely misery I saw there.

He offered me popcorn, the only food he had on that day. I turned my face from him and sobbed. It was like seeing him helplessly condemned to a hell—an innocent soul that I loved and was powerless to retrieve.[76]

Consider also the effects on family members of seeing their ill relative become homeless. In Miami, Meg Livergood stopped for a red light and saw crossing in front of her car "the repulsive vision of a tall, hunched-over woman with a snarled nest of hair . . . legs blotched and swollen, carrying a bundle wrapped in a piece of cloth, hobo style," then realized that it was her mentally ill and homeless sister.[77] In New York, Elizabeth Swados passed a homeless man with "tinsel in his filthy hair" and with "his face smeared black," then realized that it was her ill brother.[78] In Washington, DC, a young woman whom I know, rushing through National Airport to catch a flight back to college, suddenly confronted her homeless, mentally ill mother who had been missing for two years and had been living at the airport. The effects of such encounters on people's lives must be counted among the consequences of deinstitutionalization.

Family members who become threatening or violent have the most profound effect on their families. One mother who had been the object of an attack, summarized the psychological as well as physical trauma: "The thought of being attacked and physically harmed by another is frightening in itself, but when the attacker is your own flesh and blood, it is additional, unspeakable trauma upon trauma as your whole being sways between love and fear."[79] Newspaper headlines alone suggest that deinstitutionalization has brought a reign of terror to some families:

◇ "Couple Lives in Fear of Schizophrenic Son's Return," *Tulsa World*, June 24, 1984.

◇ "My Brother Might Kill Me," *New York Times*, May 6, 1987.

◇ "Families Under Siege: A Mental Health Crisis," *Philadelphia Inquirer*, September 10, 1989.

◇ "A Brush with Madness. A Tormented Artist Is Free. His Parents Are in Terror. A Surreal Case of Justice," *Washington Post*, May 12, 1993.

The story lines are remarkably the same: A family member with schizo-phrenia or manic-depressive illness who does not take medication and be-comes violent toward the family, the unsuccessful attempts by the family to get the person involuntarily treated, and the consequent terror.

An extreme and tragic version of this scenario took place in Chester County, South Carolina, on December 19, 1988.[80] Malcoum Tate, diag-nosed with severe paranoid schizophrenia, had terrorized his family for 16 years with erratic and violent behavior. He had told his sister that he would kill her small daughter, N'Zinga: "I'm going to have to kill N'Zinga because God's telling me that she's the devil." He also threatened other family members: "Y'all are evil. I'm going to have to do something. Y'all ain't doing right, all y'all should be dead. And that might be my mission—what God put me here to do. That's my mission." And "some night he'd creep into his mother's room while she slept and stand over her bed until she felt his presence and opened her eyes." Then he would "laugh that crazy laugh" and walk out of the room.

Malcoum Tate's mother and sister did everything they could to get treatment for him. "We had asked and begged and pleaded for some-body to do something," they said later. Their unsuccessful efforts were well documented by local police and mental health authorities. Mal-coum Tate was repeatedly arrested and released and hospitalized and released, the last two admissions each lasting less than one week despite abundant evidence of his history of violence and dangerousness. And once discharged, he never took the medication he needed to control the symptoms of his schizophrenia.

Finally, on the night of December 19, 1988, Malcoum Tate's mother and sister drove him south from their home into the country. There his sister shot him to death by the side of the road, then wept. She is now serving life in prison for the crime.

Chapter 6

LOOKING BACKWARD:
WHERE WE HAVE BEEN

*Perhaps now would be a good time to rethink the whole idea of deinstitu-
tionalization. The idea doesn't need to be abandoned, but clearly it needs to
be refined.*[1]

Editorial, *Cleveland Plain Dealer,*

June 5, 1994

The first psychiatric hospital in the United States opened in 1773 in
Williamsburg, Virginia, as the Eastern Lunatic Asylum. Although Virginia
then had a population of almost half a million people, the hospital contained only 20 beds; even those were not completely filled until after
1800. It was not until 1816 that a second psychiatric hospital opened.
That hospital, in Baltimore, was soon followed by others in Philadelphia,
Boston, and New York, and the era of hospital confinement for the mentally ill had begun. It would last for 150 years.

Humane considerations were a major motivating force behind the
building of public psychiatric hospitals. There was considerable resistance among state legislators to allocating funds for their construction
because of the cost. Supporters of the hospitals such as Dorothea Dix invoked images of the mentally ill living on the streets, in almshouses, and
in jails. An 1824 report to the New York State Legislature described the
common practice of community officials "passing on" mentally ill persons
from town to town, often leaving them in town squares in the middle of
the night.[2] It was a nineteenth-century version of the *Narrenschiff*, the

Ship of Fools that sailed from port to port with human cargo that nobody wanted.

Throughout the middle years of the nineteenth century, public psychiatric hospitals stressed humane care for patients. This was an era of "moral treatment" in which most hospitals had only a few hundred patients, the use of restraints and seclusion was kept to a minimum, and adequate food and exercise were stressed. Kindness, firmness, and structure were the guiding forces of "moral treatment." As late as 1880, there were only 41,000 people in psychiatric hospitals in the United States and the largest, Willard Asylum for the Insane in upstate New York, had 1,513 patients.

The era of "moral treatment" was rapidly forgotten as public psychiatric hospitals in the United States became overwhelmed with patients. Between 1880 and 1955, the number of inpatients rose from 41,000 to 559,000, more than thirteenfold increase, whereas the total population of the United States grew slightly more than threefold. By 1955, psychiatric hospitals such as New York's Rockland State Hospital with over 9,000 patients and Pilgrim State Hospital with over 14,000 patients were virtual small cities unto themselves. Hospitals that had originally been built as humane asylums had become on the best of days merely human warehouses. On the difficult days, they became much worse than that.

Milestones: An Ohio Example

If I were to select a single event to mark the beginning of the deinstitutionalization era in the United States, it might be the appointment in mid-1944 of a grand jury to investigate conditions in Cleveland State Hospital. The investigation was prompted by a series of articles in the *Cleveland Press* that had started on October 7, 1943. Using headlines such as "Mental Patients Here Beaten and Shackled" and "Mental Patients Given Bad Food, Little Meat," the articles documented hospital practices such as "the beating and shackling of patients," "the inadequacy and revolting nature of the food, the overcrowding, the low salaries, [and] the neglect of treatment."[3] It was alleged that four women patients had been put into seclusion rooms "and left there unattended until all four came down with pneumonia. Their unconscious bodies and high temperatures were discovered only on the day of their death." Thirteen patients with tuberculosis were put into rooms "having neither sunlight nor ventilation. It was demonstrated that during at least one two-week period no medical officer, except the superintendent on a routine tour, had seen these desperately ill people." And for those patients who died, "it was shown that rats, in a makeshift basement morgue, ate away the face of an aged patient while his body awaited burial."

The sources of their allegations were conscientious objectors who had been assigned to work in the hospital in lieu of military service during World War II. More than 3,000 pacifists—mostly Quakers, Mennonites, and Methodists—were working in public psychiatric hospitals throughout the United States. They were shocked by the conditions they found, and in Cleveland they approached a newspaper reporter with their stories. State mental health authorities initially denied the allegations, but the stories kept coming. In 1944, the governor asked a grand jury to investigate the situation; it not only substantiated the allegations, but also added new ones:

> The Grand Jury is shocked beyond words that a so-called civilized society would allow fellow human beings to be mistreated as they are at the Cleveland State Hospital. No enlightened community dare tolerate the conditions that exist at this institution. . . .
>
> Cleveland State Hospital is not a hospital; it is a custodial institution in which we have incarcerated the sick. It presents a case history of brutality and social criminal neglect. Patients have died shortly after receiving violent attacks from the hands of attendants or other patients, made possible only by the lack of proper supervision. In other cases patients have died under circumstances which are highly suspicious.
>
> Frequent active assaults have resulted in broken bones, lacerations, bruises and a consequent deterioration of the mind. Favorite weapons have been the buckles of heavy straps, the loaded end of heavy key-rings, metal plated shoes and wet towels which leave no marks after choking.
>
> Violent patients have been used for "strong-arm" purposes by attendants who persist in running the hospital as a penal institution. The atmosphere reeks with the false notion that the mentally ill are criminals and sub-humans who should be denied all human rights and scientific medical care.[4]

As a direct consequence of the newspaper articles and grand jury investigation, the superintendent of Cleveland State Hospital was fired, money was added to the hospital's budget, and reform began. It was the first major victory for the reform-minded conscientious objectors and spurred them to start collecting information on conditions in hospitals in other states. In 1945, when the war was over, the conscientious objectors took their reports and sought to organize a national movement for hospital reform. Prominent citizens agreed to support them including Pearl Buck, Henry R. Luce, Reinhold Niebuhr, J. Robert Oppenheimer, Eleanor Roosevelt, and

Bess Truman. Luce, the owner of *Time* and *Life,* was especially important because he provided the reformers with a national forum. On May 6, 1946, *Life* magazine carried a 12-page story entitled "Bedlam 1946: Most U.S. Mental Hospitals Are a Shame and a Disgrace."[5] Accompanied by pictures of hospital dayrooms filled with dozens of naked patients, the article became the prototype for Albert Deutsch's *The Shame of the States,*[6] Mike Gorman's *Oklahoma Attacks Its Snake Pits,*[7] and other exposés that soon followed.

Following their successful efforts in Cleveland, the reformers enlisted two important members of Congress—Senator Claude Pepper of Florida and Representative Percy Priest of Tennessee—as national sponsors for their efforts. Priest was chairman of the House Public Health Subcommittee, and Pepper was chairman of the Senate Subcommittee on Health and Education; in late 1945 and early 1946 both subcommittees held hearings that led to the creation of the National Institute of Mental Health. Ten years later, Rep. Priest introduced legislation entitled "The Mental Health Study Act of 1955" and held hearings before his Subcommittee on Health and Science, leading to the creation of the Joint Commission on Mental Illness and Health. The frightful conditions at Cleveland State Hospital and the work of the conscientious objectors in exposing those conditions continued to be cited for many years by those who advocated closing down such hospitals and moving patients into the community.

Fifty years after the grand jury investigation of conditions in Cleveland State Hospital that effectively initiated the era of deinstitutionalization, another report was issued on conditions for mental patients in Ohio. The 1994 report was the work of a court-appointed team of experts who investigated conditions for mentally ill inmates of Ohio's prisons. The *Cleveland Plain Dealer* characterized the report as reading "like a Charles Dickens novel: tales of naked men and women languishing in fetid cells, sometimes without heat or hot water, or being punished 'for behavior that appears to be entirely the result of their mental illness.' "[8] The report cited hundreds of patients "abandoned in isolation units for violating prison rules they were incapable of comprehending. . . . More than 20 percent of the 1,877 prisoners confined to punishment cells were mentally ill. . . . Many were grossly psychotic and extremely dysfunctional . . . including an unidentified woman at Marysville [prison] who has been in solitary confinement for almost six years." Another man, "on suicide watch although no one was watching him, had been completely naked and cold for four days and had not one stitch of covering or bedding and no possessions." "Investigators found numerous allegations that prisoners were physically assaulted in response to psychotic outbursts."

In 1944, there had been 2,200 patients in Cleveland State Hospital; in 1994 the number was only 140. Ninety-four percent of the patients had been deinstitutionalized and the beds had been closed down. Conversely, in 1994 there were 41,156 prisoners in the Ohio state prison system. The 1994 prison report noted that there had been "an explosion in the number of mentally ill inmates" and specifically blamed "'repetitive incarceration' of nonviolent offenders on scant mental health services in their home counties, a problem that worsened after Ohio closed most of its state mental hospitals."[9]

A Deinstitutionalization Balance Sheet

The 1944 and 1994 Ohio reports are useful milestones for assessing the outcome of deinstitutionalization. At the time of the first report, most men, women, and children with severe psychiatric illnesses were living in state psychiatric hospitals. At the time of the second report, most such people were living in community settings of one kind or another. Is it possible to weigh the benefits and liabilities of this massive 50-year shift of the mentally ill?

Among the most important benefits of deinstitutionalization is that the vast majority of patients say they are happier living outside hospitals than inside hospitals. In a recent study of 53 patients discharged from a Rhode Island state hospital and followed up a mean of 7.5 years after discharge, "94 percent expressed a preference for life in the community."[10] These patients, however, had been discharged into "well-staffed structured community residential treatment settings such as group homes or intensely supervised apartments," and patients discharged into less favorable living situations probably would express a lower level of satisfaction. Benefits of community living frequently cited by patients include more autonomy, more privacy, and more contact with their family and friends.[11] Yet despite their apparently successful placement in well-staffed community living facilities, 55 percent of these patients required rehospitalization at least once.

How should these obvious benefits of deinstitutionalization for the majority be weighted against the equally obvious failings for a substantial minority, as outlined in the preceding chapters? How many Thomas McGuires, Phyllis Iannottas, George Wootens, Sylvia Seegrists, Larry Hogues, and Malcom Tates do there need to be to offset the patients who have benefited? How should one assess the lives of the approximately 150,000 mentally ill homeless, or the 159,000 incarcerated in jails and prisons on any given day? How many episodes of violence by the few should be considered as the price that must be paid for freedom for the many? How should the deterioration of community life for many citizens in towns and cities be compared with the freedom of mentally ill individuals to live as they wish and take medication if they please? And how can we weigh the effects on the families of severely ill family members who are not taking their medication, are out of control, and are threatening them? How big does the mental illness crisis have to be before there is a consensus that it is too big?

Despite the benefits of deinstitutionalization for the majority of previous residents in public psychiatric hospitals, a growing number of people have concluded that the human price that has been paid for deinstitutionalization, as it has been carried out, has been too high. For example, Seymour Kaplan, one of the pioneers of deinstitutionalization in New York, said that "it was the gravest error he had ever made."[12] Donald Langsley, another pioneer of deinstitutionalization, similarly recalled that "those of us who were once so enthusiastic now weep a little as we look backwards at what has happened to the promising child of the 1960s and early 1970s."[13] For anyone who is regularly exposed to the failures of deinstitutionalization and the current crisis, it is difficult not to share such sentiments.

In thinking about the failures of deinstitutionalization, keep in mind that deinstitutionalization was implemented as a policy in the United States although virtually no studies had been done on it. The only study of deinstitutionalization done prior to 1963 (and which was cited by virtually every advocate for this policy) was John Wing's English study of 20 hospitalized patients with chronic schizophrenia who were selected because they were high functioning and able to work; most of them did well when moved from the hospital to community settings.[14] It seems incredible that a policy that has led to the effective deinstitutionalization of three-quarters of a million people, 92 percent of all patients in American public psychiatric hospitals, was launched on the basis of a single study of 20 selected patients, but that is in fact the case. As late as 1981, a review of studies of deinstitutionalization identified only five outcome studies that had been done up to that time, and three of those were said to be methodologically flawed.[15] It is doubtful that ever, in the history of modern medicine, has such a profound change in treatment for so many sick people been implemented with so little scientific justification.

An important consideration in the assessment of deinstitutionalization is paternalism versus personal autonomy. This issue was eloquently discussed by one of the panels that the National Institute of Mental Health convened in 1989 to create a national plan to improve services for people with severe mental disorders. The panel noted:

> The institutionalization of severely mentally ill people, particularly in hospital back wards, constituted a form of societal paternalism in which many persons suffered bleak, meaningless lives. With deinstitutionalization and the lack of a community support system, many former patients and others with severe mental illnesses have been given nearly absolute individual liberty but at a very high price. Now that patients can be committed to treatment services only if they are extremely and imminently dangerous to themselves or society, our society allows individuals incapable of realistic planning to struggle through life and wander the streets. Like ships without rudders, homeless people with severe mental illness are free, but at significant risk to life and without much hope of happiness.
>
> One could argue that in the name of individual liberty we have created a system that is a much greater danger to life and the pursuit of happiness than the one it replaced. Furthermore, by moving from one extreme societal response to another in the care of severely mentally ill people, we have avoided the very difficult policy question regarding the appropriate balance between absolute liberty and paternalism. . . . What is the appropriate balance between liberty and paternalism that will maximize individual and societal rights to physical safety and well-being?[16]

Another assessment of deinstitutionalization is to say it was fundamentally a good idea that was carried too far. Richard Lamb, a psychiatrist at the University of Southern California, has convincingly expounded this position, including the corollary that some individuals with severe mental illnesses *are* better off living long-term in hospitals that offer true asylum rather than living in the community.[17] Even Robert Okin, one of the strongest advocates for deinstitutionalization and the architect of its implementation in Massachusetts, acknowledged, "Studies in 7 states over the past 15 years have demonstrated that 60 percent of state hospital patients could be cared for in the community if proper services were provided."[18] If Okin is correct, that means 40 percent of the patients cannot be cared for in the community. Since 92 percent of the patients who were in public psychiatric hospitals have been deinstitutionalized, we have therefore discharged thousands of patients who should have remained in hospitals. These are, presumably, the people who have ended up homeless, who are in jails and prison, who are responsible for acts of violence, and who have contributed heavily to the deterioration of life in communities and within their families.

A final assessment of deinstitutionalization is to say that it has never really been tried. This is accurate insofar as we now understand what services mentally ill persons need to successfully live in the community and recognize that such services, in most cases, have not been provided. Psychiatrist, John Talbot, past president of the American Psychiatric Association, has been an articulate spokesperson for this position, arguing that deinstitutionalization has in fact merely consisted of "transinstitutionalization" and "detreatmentization." Talbot defines "transinstitutionalization" as occurring when "the chronic mentally ill patient [has] his locus of living and care transferred from a single lousy institution to multiple wretched ones,"[19] such as run-down nursing homes or large group homes. "Detreatmentization" occurs when someone becomes severely ill for the first time and cannot obtain needed hospital treatment because the hospital beds have been closed.[20]

What Do the Mentally Ill Need?

What would be required to solve the mental illness crisis? To answer this question, it is first necessary to identify the needs of the ill and to ascertain why these needs are not being met. The following vignettes describe real people, although necessarily disguised to prevent identification:

◇ Janice P., a successful physician, has manic-depressive illness. She has insurance coverage and can afford to supplement it as necessary to obtain the best care available. The private psychiatrist who treats her is a skilled psychopharmacologist who balances her lithium, carbemazepine, and other ancillary medications as her illness waxes and wanes. He has also taught her how to minimize stress and to recognize the signs of an impending relapse. Prior to the availability of medication, Ms. P. would have spent long periods in psychiatric hospitals. She has never required hospitalization, however, and is receiving good care. Ms. P. is an example of someone for whom the present system is working well.

◇ Severe depression caused Anthony T. to take early retirement. He is a former factory worker who lives on a pension and receives psychiatric care at a mental health center staffed predominantly by social workers. Because he is not insightful or highly verbal, he is not considered to be a good candidate for psychotherapy. Both psychiatrists at the center are poorly trained and have only used tricyclic antidepressants on Mr. T.'s illness. One of them suggested a trial of fluoxetine (Prozac), a newer antidepressant, but it would have cost Mr. T. $70 per month. His retirement income makes him ineligible for Medicaid. Because of economic and ideological problems, the treatment system is only partially meeting Mr. T.'s needs.

◇ A college graduate with paranoid schizophrenia, Stephen A., has lived in public shelters or rooming houses for the past eight years. He changes residences and cities frequently to try to escape the CIA, which he believes is following him and directing pain-causing rays at his body. He has no insight into his illness and all attempts to reason him out of his delusions have been futile. On two occasions, his parents attempted to have him involuntarily hospitalized, but on both occasions he was assisted by public defenders who successfully convinced the judge that he was not a danger to himself or others and therefore did not meet criteria for involuntary treatment. The treatment system is failing Mr. A. predominantly for legal reasons.

◇ Saundra S., a sixth-grade dropout, has schizoaffective disorder and epilepsy. She takes medication irregularly and lives alternately in shelters, on the streets, or with boyfriends. Because she can be abusive and occasionally physically assaultive toward professionals who try to help her, responsibility for her care is shunted from agency to agency on a regular basis. The treatment system is failing Ms. S. for economic, legal, and ideological reasons.

◇ Dually diagnosed with manic-depressive illness and alcohol and drug abuse, Tony C. is a high school graduate who was trained as an electrician. When he is high, he often gets into trouble and has been jailed on seven different occasions. Although he has lost his license, he often drives while intoxicated. When drinking or using drugs, he does not take his lithium, thereby causing frequent recurrences of mania and exacerbating his problems. For one year he had a court-appointed conservator who controlled his funds, living situation, and medication, but because he did so well, the judge said that the conservatorship was no longer necessary. The treatment system is failing Mr. C. for economic and legal reasons.

These five men and women are representatives of the 5.6 million people with severe mental illnesses in the United States. A small number of them, like Janice P., are being well served by private or public providers. The majority of them are not being well served for three major reasons. First, the economics of the funding system includes virtually no incentives for treating people like Anthony T., Saundra S., or Tony C.; indeed, there are even economic disincentives for doing so. Second, the legal system has major impediments to providing involuntary treatment for individuals like Stephen A., Saundra S., or Tony C. And third, the ideological mixing of "mental health" with mental illness makes it difficult to find professionals who are interested in, much less trained, to treat patients such as Anthony T. and Saundra S. Each of these problems—economic, legal, and ideological—will be examined in detail to ascertain how they might be solved. And if we can solve them, then we will have confronted the mental illness crisis.

Chapter 7

New Initiatives in Funding

We got into much of the current mess by acting on the best of intentions without foreseeing the worst of unintended effects.[1]

JOSEPH A. CALIFANO, former Secretary of the
United States Department of Health, Education, and Welfare

Economic factors are the single largest cause of the mental illness crisis and the failure of deinstitutionalization. Contrary to popular belief, however, the most important economic factor is not that too little money has been allocated, although that is a problem in some states. Rather, what has led to the present crisis is the shifting of costs by state and local governments to the federal government, especially to federal Medicaid. The consequences of this policy have put mentally ill persons onto the streets and into jails, have produced uncoordinated care and revolving-door readmissions, and have led to the transinstitutionalization of hundreds of thousands of mentally ill individuals from state psychiatric hospitals to nursing homes and other institutions, many of which are more restrictive and offer worse care than the hospitals from which these patients were discharged.

A $38 Billion Federal Carrot: How Medicaid et al. Are Driving the System

To understand how cost-shifting to the federal government produces malignant effects on people with severe psychiatric disorders, you must first understand the workings of the pertinent federal programs.

Medicaid

Officially known as Title XIX of the Social Security Act, Medicaid was enacted in 1965 as an attempt by the federal government to help state and local governments pay for acute medical care costs of low-income individuals, especially, in the words of President Lyndon B. Johnson, "poor mamas and babies." It is financed jointly by federal, state, and, in some states, local funds. In 1995, the federal share of total Medicaid costs averaged 56 percent, ranging from a minimum of 50 percent in wealthier states to 80 percent in the poorest state, Mississippi.

States have had limited discretion in managing Medicaid programs. They have been mandated to cover persons receiving Aid to Families with Dependent Children (AFDC), Supplemental Security Income (SSI), and certain other categories of indigent persons. States could also, if they wished, extend Medicaid coverage to other individuals with incomes above the poverty level. Similarly, states have been mandated to cover specific medical services such as inpatient and outpatient care in general hospitals, emergency room services, nursing home care, and physician services, but states could also, if they wished, cover optional services such as case management, rehabilitation, home health care, and services by nonphysicians.

States varied widely on Medicaid spending because of the variable portion of the state's share, which was based on the state's per capita wealth, variable number of people covered, and variable services covered. The highest Medicaid-use states have been Connecticut, New York, and New Hampshire, which spent more than three times more state funds on Medicaid per capita than did the lowest Medicaid-use states, Mississippi, West Virginia, and California.[2] Medicaid has thus been a federal bank account from which states could withdraw unlimited money as long as the states were willing to contribute matching funds.

The growth of the Medicaid program in recent years has been startling. During the 1980s, Medicaid grew at approximately 10 percent each year. Beginning in 1988, however, the growth rate increased sharply, more than doubling between 1988 and 1994, from $51.3 billion to $135.4 billion.[3] This increase contributed significantly to the federal deficit and led directly to proposals for modifying the Medicaid program.

Medicaid costs have also increased sharply for state budgets because of the required state matching funds. Money that states spend on Medicaid matching funds, however, is usually offset by money saved. For example, if a 50-year-old patient is in a state psychiatric hospital, the state pays most of the hospital cost. When that same person is transferred to a nursing home, federal Medicaid pays 50 to 80 percent of the cost (depending on the state) and the state pays the remainder. Even though the state's Medicaid costs have increased, these costs have been offset by decreased costs for the psychiatric hospital. Medicaid has thus been a major mechanism by which states have transferred medical, including psychiatric, costs to the federal government.

As early as 1980, Medicaid was recognized as "the largest single mental health program in the country."[4] Estimates suggest "that about 15 percent of total Medicaid dollars are spent on mental illness."[5] The total 1994 Medicaid program of $135.4 billion was funded 58 percent ($78.1 billion) by the federal government and 42 percent ($57.3 billion) by state governments, which means that approximately $11.7 billion federal Medicaid funds and $8.6 billion state Medicaid funds were spent on services for the mentally ill (Table 7.1). The majority of these funds paid for the residents in nursing homes, in intermediate care facilities, and on the psychiatric wards of general hospitals. Most of these funds went for the care of people with severe mental illnesses as defined in Chapter 1, although an unknown portion also went for the care of patients with substance abuse and other disorders not included under the definition. Mentally ill persons in state

TABLE 7.1

Federal Dollars for Support and Services for Persons with
Mental Disorders (not including mental retardation) in 1994

Program	1994 Total Program Dollars (billions)	Percentage of Recipients with Mental Disorders (not including mental retardation)	Federal Dollars (billions) for Support of Persons with Mental Disorders
Medicaid	$135.4 of which 78.1 is federal dollars	15%	$11.7
Medicare	161.9	3	4.9
SSI (disabled only)	18.6	30.2	5.6
SSDI	37.7	25.5	9.6
Food stamps	23.7	6	1.4
HUD section 202 housing	—	—	1.0
Mental health block grant	0.3	100	0.3
Veterans Administration			
a) mental health services	—	—	1.3
b) disability benefits	17.3	13	2.2
Total			$38.0

psychiatric hospitals were not eligible for Medicaid coverage unless they were under age 22 or over age 65. According to a 1995 analysis done by the National Association of State Mental Health Program Directors: "In many states Medicaid now supports about one-third of the community mental health programs and has been almost the only source of new revenue for the public mental health system during the last five years. It is sometimes the sole funding source for community support and rehabilitative services"[6] for the mentally ill.

States have become highly inventive in finding ways to shift the burden of state health and mental health costs to the federal Medicaid program. For example, in 1993 in North Carolina, the four state psychiatric hospitals transferred $100 million to the state Medicaid program. These funds were counted as a state contribution to Medicaid, thus qualifying North Carolina for $200 million in federal Medicaid funds. When the federal funds were received, the original $100 million was returned to the state hospitals, and North Carolina was legally entitled to use the $200 million for whatever it wished. Such fiscal maneuvers, although technically legal, led one federal official to observe that "the Medellin drug cartel could learn a lot about money laundering from the states."[7] Devising new ways to shift additional state costs to the federal Medicaid program became a major focus of activity in state departments of health and mental health.

Medicaid has been a fiscally open-ended federal and state program originally devised for "poor mamas and babies," a group that by 1995 accounted for only 27 percent of Medicaid expenditures. Medicaid, instead, became the major source of funds for elderly and disabled residents of nursing homes and other long-term care facilities and was the single largest source of funds for services for the severely mentally ill.

Medicare

Officially known as Title XVIII of the Social Security Act, Medicare was enacted in 1965 to cover medical costs for elderly and disabled Americans. Part A of Medicare pays for costs of hospitals, skilled nursing facilities following hospitalization, hospices, and some home health care. Part B of Medicare, for which eligible participants must pay a monthly premium that in 1995 was $46.10 per month, pays for the services of physicians and some nonphysician health providers. Medicare is funded entirely by the federal government, and its cost has increased approximately 10 percent per year in recent years; in 1994 these costs totaled $161.9 billion.

It has been estimated that approximately 3 percent of Medicare costs go for coverage of psychiatric disorders;[8] in 1994 this totaled $4.9 billion (Table 7.1). Benefits include up to 190 lifetime days of hospitalization in psychiatric hospitals, up to 90 annual days of hospitalization in the psychiatric units of general hospitals, some partial hospitalization, and some outpatient services provided by psychiatrists, psychologists, and social workers.

Supplemental Security Income

The Supplemental Security Income (SSI) program provides income support for low-income elderly, blind, or disabled adults and blind or disabled children. It was established in 1972, replacing the Old Age Assistance (OAA) and the Aid to the Permanently and Totally Disabled (APTD) programs. The mentally ill had been covered by the APTD program since 1962. Eligibility for SSI is established using national standards both on the basis of the person's disability (physical, mental, and inability to work) and low income (must have less than $2,000 in assets). Once approved for SSI, the person has been automatically eligible for Medicaid benefits and food stamps. In 1995, the federal SSI payment was $458 per month for a disabled individual living alone. Total federal SSI costs in 1994 were $22.2 billion.[9] In addition, 27 states provided a state supplemental payment, which in five states (Alaska, California, Connecticut, Massachusetts, and Wisconsin) was more than $100 per month; the total cost of state SSI supplements in 1994 as $3.7 billion. There are no restrictions on how recipients spend their SSI funds.

The SSI program has grown steadily since the first payments were made in 1974, but the disabled subgroup has grown especially rapidly. Between 1974 and 1994, during which time the general population increased 22 percent, the total number of people receiving monthly SSI checks increased by 96 percent, from 3,248,949 to 6,377,111, while the number receiving SSI because of disability increased by 273 percent, from 1,285,201 to 4,790,658.[10]

Among the causes of SSI disability, mental disorders other than mental retardation is the single largest diagnostic category, accounting for 30.2 percent of all SSI disabilities in 1994. This is followed by mental retardation (27.6 percent), diseases of the nervous system and sense organs (9.5 percent), diseases of the musculoskeletal system (6.7 percent), and diseases of the circulatory system (5.0 percent). Thus the three largest categories of diseases entitling persons to disability payments under SSI—mental disorders, mental retardation, and diseases of the nervous system and sense organs—are all disorders of the brain. Together, they account for 67.3 percent of all SSI disabilities, or $12.7 billion in federal SSI disability costs.

Information on the diagnostic causes of SSI disability has been available since 1976 and shows a progressive increase in the percentage of SSI disabilities due to mental disorders. In 1976, 18.4 percent of SSI disabilities were attributable to mental disorders other than mental retardation, and by 1986 this had increased to 22.6 percent. Since 1986, the percentage has climbed at the rate of 1 percent per year, reaching 30.2 percent in 1994. During these same years, the percentage of SSI disabilities due to mental retardation has remained essentially unchanged. In 1994, the total number of people who received SSI disability payments because of mental disorders was 970,400, and they received $5.6 billion out of the total $18.6 billion paid to all SSI disability recipients (Table 7.1).

There are several reasons the number of mentally ill recipients of SSI has increased so rapidly. Deinstitutionalization has been a major factor, because the vast majority of patients discharged from state psychiatric hospitals apply for and are approved for SSI. The criteria to determine disability have also become more liberal in recent years, especially the 1990 Supreme Court ruling in *Zebley v. Sullivan*, in which the qualifying criteria for SSI for children with mental disabilities were made much more lenient.[11] Finally, there has been an attempt in at least some cities and counties to move recipients of general assistance or welfare from these programs to SSI. Since general assistance and welfare utilize significant amounts of state and local funds, moving such persons to federal SSI effectively shifts the cost of their support to the federal government.[12]

Disability Insurance Trust Fund

The Disability Insurance Trust fund, which is part of the Old-Age, Survivors, and Disability Insurance (OASDI) program, is commonly referred to as SSDI. It began in 1956 as a program to provide income maintenance to workers who had become disabled and whose disability was expected to last indefinitely. In contrast to SSI, in which a work history is not necessary, persons qualifying for SSDI income maintenance must have been employed long enough to qualify for Social Security benefits. SSDI recipients received up to $661 per month in 1994, depending on how long they had been employed. If their SSDI payment was less than the $458 they were eligible for under SSI, they received a supplemental check from SSI, bringing their total monthly payment up to $458. SSDI recipients automatically become eligible for Medicare benefits two years after their SSDI begins. The SSDI program is administered by the federal government and financed primarily through contributions from employees and employers.

SSDI, like SSI, has grown rapidly. Between 1988 and 1994 total SSDI benefits increased 96 percent from $19.2 billion to $37.7 billion. The largest diagnostic category of SSDI disability was mental disorders other than mental retardation, which in 1994 accounted for 25.5 percent of all SSDI recipients. The next largest diagnostic categories for SSDI recipients were disorders of the musculoskeletal system (20.9 percent), circulatory system (13.6 percent), nervous system and sense organs (10.0 percent), and injuries (6.1 percent). The total SSDI payments from the Disability Insurance Trust Fund in 1994 were $37.7 billion. A total of 989,300 SSDI recipients were disabled due to mental disorders and received income support totaling $9.6 billion (Table 7.1).

If SSI and SSDI, both income maintenance programs, are combined, the total amount of federal funds going to persons with mental disorders other than mental retardation in 1994 was $15.2 billion, which constituted 27 percent of all SSI and SSDI disability payments.

Food Stamps

Established in 1964, the Food Stamp Program provides coupons redeemable for food at retail grocery stores to low-income individuals and families. Income and assets determine the amount of coupons a person can obtain. Recipients of SSI are automatically eligible for food stamps. The program is completely paid for with federal funds, except that state funds are used for some administrative costs. The Food Stamp Program has grown rapidly in recent years, more than doubling in size from $11.1 billion in 1988 to $23.7 billion in 1994.

A 1993 survey of food stamp users reported that 20.3 percent of them were receiving SSI.[13] Since approximately 30 percent of SSI recipients are mentally ill, then approximately 6 percent of all food stamp recipients are probably also mentally ill. In 1994, the value of these food stamps would have been $1.4 billion out of the $23.7 billion total program (Table 7.1).

Federal Housing Programs

The federal Department of Housing and Urban Development (HUD) supports subsidized housing under Sections 8, 202, and 811 housing programs. Section 8 programs serve the largest number of mentally ill

Americans, and these programs have been especially important for many deinstitutionalized patients from public psychiatric hospitals who have nowhere to live. Estimates of the HUD funds used to support housing for the mentally ill in 1994 are approximately $1 billion[14] (Table 7.1).

Federal Community Mental Health Block Grant

In 1982, a series of categorical federal programs for persons with mental illnesses were consolidated into a single Community Mental Health Services block grant. The grant has been given annually to each state after the state has submitted a plan for its use to the federal government. In fiscal year 1994, the mental illness block grants totaled $275 million, an amount that had been virtually unchanged in recent years. A separate block grant covered substance abuse services.

Veterans Administration

The federal Veterans Administration (VA) provides medical, including psychiatric, care to those among the nation's 26 million veterans who have disabilities or who are indigent. Most of the direct services are delivered in 171 VA hospitals, of which 26 are primarily psychiatric hospitals. According to VA data for 1993, the total expenditures for VA mental health services was $1.3 billion,[15] a substantial but unknown portion of which was for substance (drug and alcohol) abuse services. The VA also provides disability payments to veterans and their survivors; in 85 percent of cases the disability is service-connected and in the remainder it is non-service-connected. In 1994, the VA paid a total of $17.3 billion in such benefit payments.[16] According to VA data, 13 percent, or $2.2 billion, was for psychiatric disabilities.[17] It is common practice in many states to try and identify all veterans receiving state and local psychiatric services and then to encourage them to apply for federal veterans' benefits, thereby decreasing the state's costs.

Total federal dollars going to support the mentally ill, as shown in Table 7.1, reached approximately $38 billion in 1994. Although data are not available to ascertain exactly what proportion goes to persons with *severe* mental illnesses, as defined in Chapter 1, it certainly is the vast majority. In 1955, prior to the implementation of the federal programs just discussed, states were responsible for virtually 100 percent of the cost of this care. The billions of federal dollars now being spent each year is thus a late twentieth-century windfall for the states, which had had primary fiscal responsibility for these services for more than one hundred years.

TABLE 7.2
Percentage Fiscal Contribution for Support and
Services for Persons with Mental Illnesses

	Federal	State and Local
1963	2%	98%
1985	38	62
1994	62	38

What percentages of the costs of mental illnesses are now being paid by federal, state, and local governments? Previous calculations suggested that in 1963 state and local governments paid 98 percent of the total cost, with the federal government paying approximately 2 percent. By 1985, this fiscal responsibility had shifted to 62 percent state and local and 38 percent federal.[18] In 1994, the federal government paid out $38 billion for the care of the mentally ill. Adding all available data,[19] including $8.6 billion in Medicaid matching funds and $0.94 billion in supplemental SSI payments contributed by the states, it appears that total state and local expenditures for mental illnesses in 1994 were approximately $22.9 billion. Therefore in 1994, state and local governments contributed 38 percent of the total cost of mental illnesses, while the federal government contributed 62 percent, exactly reversing the percentages of nine years previously. This is shown in Table 7.2.

The Consequences of Cost-Shifting

What have been the effects of this massive shift in fiscal responsibility over the past three decades? There have been five main consequences, which I will discuss in detail in the following five sections of this chapter.

Inappropriate Discharge

Cost-shifting has been the primary reason for the inappropriate discharge of many patients. It is widely assumed that the introduction of antipsychotic drugs in the 1950s was the most important factor in deinstitutionalization. Chlorpromazine (Thorazine) became available in 1954, and within one year it had been given to over 2 million patients. In 1955, New York State and California became the first states to make chlorpromazine available in all state psychiatric hospitals.

When we look at deinstitutionalization statistics, however, it is apparent that the initial decreases in the patient censuses of state psychiatric hospitals were modest. A 1962 study of reduction in patient censuses in New York State between 1955 and 1961 reported:

> [The decreases] have continued at a rate of 1 percent to 1½ percent per year in our state, and careful review of the data indicates that this rate may be expected to continue. . . . Statistical evidence is lacking for a massive acceleration of the process of shrinkage. Much of the limitation appears to be inherent in the drug therapy with which the process was begun.[20]

Overall in the United States the state psychiatric hospital census decreased only 4 percent between 1955 and 1960 (from 558,922 to 535,540) and an additional 11 percent between 1960 and 1965 (to 475,202). In fact, if deinstitutionalization had continued at the same rate as in the years 1955 to 1965, when the availability of antipsychotic drugs was the main driving force, there would have been approximately 225,000 individuals in state psychiatric hospitals in 1994 *assuming there was no increase in the general population* (Figure 7.1). Allowing for the population increase that has taken place, there would have been approximately 350,000 patients in state psychiatric hospitals in 1994 instead of the 72,000 that were there.

Following the enactment of Medicaid and Medicare in 1965, the pace of deinstitutionalization accelerated significantly. In addition to Medicaid and Medicare, in 1962 the mentally disabled were made eligible for income support under APTD, the predecessor of SSI, and in 1964 the Food Stamps Program was implemented. Federal dollars were therefore available for income support, medical and psychiatric care, and food supplements for the mentally ill who were being discharged from state psychiatric hospitals. While in state hospitals, patients were the fiscal responsibility of the states, but by discharging them, the states effectively shifted the majority of that responsibility to the federal government. The state psychiatric hospital census therefore decreased 29 percent between 1965 and 1970 (from 475,202 to 337,619), 43 percent between 1970 and 1975 (to 193,436), and 32 percent more between 1975 and 1980 (to 132,164).

The observation that the introduction of federal programs was the most important factor driving deinstitutionalization is not a new one. As early as 1981, Paul Lerman, a social worker at Rutgers University, published a monograph under a contract with the National Institute of Mental Health in which he noted:

> The acceleration of deinstitutionalization over the past two decades is primarily linked to States taking advantage of legislative amendments and

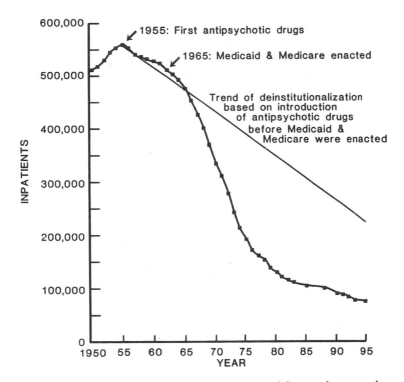

FIGURE 7.1   Number of inpatients in public mental hospitals 1950 through 1995.

broad regulatory interpretations of welfare, medical assistance, and social services titles of the Social Security Act. . . . Deinstitutionalization has been an emergent byproduct of expanded uses of the welfare state.[21]

Four years later William Gronfein, an economist also at Rutgers University, published an analysis of Medicaid availability and the rate of deinstitutionalization from 1973 to 1975 and concluded:

Clearly, then, Medicaid payments are very strongly associated with the amount of deinstitutionalization experienced by a state in the early 1970s. A correlational analysis of this type does not, of course, permit us to draw causal conclusions. Nonetheless, the data are consistent with a model in which Medicaid funds are used as a way of transferring costs from the states to the federal government, and in which one of the influences on the degree to which state hospital systems declined in the early 1970s was a state's involvement in the Medicaid program.[22]

State incentives for cost-shifting to the federal government reside almost exclusively in the discharge of patients from state hospitals, who then become eligible for SSI, Medicaid, food stamps, and other federal benefits. States gain nothing by ensuring that patients receive follow-up care following their hospitalization because readmission of the patients can be deflected to the psychiatric wards of general hospitals, where federal Medicaid will cover much of the costs. The $38 billion federal carrot thus provides a strong incentive for states to discharge patients from state psychiatric hospitals whether or not the patients are ready to go and whether or not aftercare services are available. Consequently, many discharged patients have ended up on the streets, in public shelters, in jails, or in prisons.

Transinstitutionalization

Federal dollars have created transinstitutionalization. Because of incentives created by federal programs, hundreds of thousands of patients who have technically been *de*institutionalized by being discharged from state psychiatric hospitals have in reality merely been *trans*institutionalized to nursing homes and other similar institutions where federal funds pay most of the costs. When the federal government set up Medicaid and other federal programs for the mentally ill, the architects specifically excluded most payments to state psychiatric hospitals and other "institutions for the treatment of mental diseases," (IMDs), because the federal government did not intend to take over what had been a state responsibility. IMDs were defined as "institutions or residences in which more than 16 individuals reside, at least half of whom have a primary psychiatric diagnosis." States accepted the IMD exclusion as a challenge to their diagnostic creativity and proceeded to transfer massive numbers of patients from state hospitals to nursing homes.

A survey of nursing homes conducted in 1985 by the National Center for Health Statistics reported that 348,313 out of 1,491,400 nursing home residents, or 23 percent, had a mental disorder.[23] Because nursing homes tend to underdiagnose these disorders in their residents to keep under the 50 percent limit specified by the IMD exclusion, many observers believe that the percentage of mentally ill individuals in nursing homes is substantially higher than 23 percent. It has been claimed that "nursing homes are now the largest single setting for the institutional care of the mentally ill."[24]

To shift additional costs to federal programs, many states have created other long-term institutions for the treatment of mentally ill patients. For example, Iowa houses them in "residential care facilities." In 1994, the state had 183 such facilities, with 6,683 residents, the largest facility having 216 beds. Many of these are former county poorhouses with a facelift and a new name. Some of them look remarkably like the wards of state psychiatric hospitals. The main difference is that the cost of care for mentally ill residents in these facilities is borne largely by federal dollars, whereas the cost of care in the state hospitals is borne largely by state dollars.

A major problem with this use of nursing homes and similar institutions is that most of them do not have staff trained to work with mentally ill patients and therefore offer only custodial care. Most of the care in nursing homes is provided by aides who are poorly trained, poorly paid, and stay for only short periods. The psychiatrist John Talbott observed in 1981, "No nursing home in the country employs a full time psychiatrist, and few offer any form of psychiatric rehabilitation."[25] Another major problem with these alternative institutions is that they are even less frequently inspected than are psychiatric hospitals.

Transinstitutionalization is a product of cost-shifting by the states to make more mentally ill patients eligible for federal support and reimbursement. As state psychiatric hospitals improved in quality in the 1970s and 1980s, it became increasingly common to discharge patients from relatively good hospitals with active rehabilitation programs and transinstitutionalize them to nursing homes or similar institutions with markedly inferior psychiatric care and no rehabilitation at all. States saved state funds, but transinstitutionalized patients paid a substantial price in substandard care.

Psychiatric Treatment in General Hospitals

Federal dollars have moved psychiatric inpatient care from public psychiatric hospitals to general hospitals. Because Medicaid pays for psychiatric care in general hospitals but not in psychiatric hospitals, there has been a massive shift in psychiatric inpatient care from public psychiatric hospitals to general hospitals, often with adverse consequences. In 1969, there were 17,808 inpatient beds in psychiatric wards of general hospitals. By 1990, this number had increased to 38,327,[26] and studies suggest that an additional 60,000 psychiatric inpatient beds are scattered on nonpsychiatric wards of general hospitals. This would mean a fivefold increase in psychiatric beds in general hospitals during the same years when there was a fourfold reduction of psychiatric beds in state and county hospitals. According to data published in 1993 by Charles Kiesler and Celeste Simpkins, researchers at the University of Missouri and Vanderbilt

University, "over 60 percent of all psychiatric inpatient episodes take place in general hospitals."[27]

Although moving inpatient care from public psychiatric hospitals to general hospitals may seem theoretically reasonable, in fact it is usually more expensive and has caused major problems for the most severely ill patients. Costs in general hospitals are often $200 per day or more higher than the costs in public psychiatric hospitals. These additional costs are of little consequence to the states since federal Medicaid dollars are paying the majority of the bill; the *states'* costs are lower and that is the limit of their concern.

There is also evidence that general hospitals admit psychiatric patients with less severe illnesses but turn away those who are more seriously ill. Kiesler and Simpkins reported that between 1980 and 1985 the number of patients with depression and other affective disorders in general hospitals doubled, whereas the number of patients with schizophrenia decreased by 8 percent.[28] A study by Carla White and her colleagues in the Department of Psychiatry at the University of Massachusetts at Worcester, also found that admissions to general hospitals were easily obtained for patients with symptoms such as depression but were much more difficult to obtain for patients with schizophrenia or with such characteristics as assaultive behavior, involuntary status, or homelessness.[29] Thus federal Medicaid dollars have effectively replaced psychiatric beds in public hospitals with psychiatric beds in general hospitals except that the latter often will not admit the patients who need treatment the most. Consider the following:

William M., age 47, had spent 19 years in Fairview State Hospital in Pennsylvania. He was discharged from the hospital to live in a boarding house in Philadelphia. For the first month he did well, but then stopped taking the antipsychotic medication that controlled the symptoms of his illness. "He became floridly psychotic, unkempt, malodorous, out of touch with reality, and extremely paranoid about being poisoned. His resulting physical problems included infestations of lice and maggots." He moved from his boarding house to live on the streets. Attempts to get him rehospitalized at Fairview were unsuccessful, because Pennsylvania had a rule that if the patient had been out of the hospital for more than 30 days he could not be readmitted without first being hospitalized in the psychiatric unit of a general hospital. But no hospital would take him because he had no fixed address and no money. Several weeks later "William M. was found dead behind a Philadelphia crisis center, his feet bitten by rats."[30]

Uncoordinated Provision of Care

Federal dollars have contributed substantially to disjointed, uncoordinated care for mentally ill individuals. Prior to the 1960s, when federal funds for psychiatric care became available, the public psychiatric care system was almost completely run by the states, often in partnership with local counties or cities. Since that time, the public psychiatric care system has become a hodgepodge of categorical programs funded by myriad federal, state, and local sources. The primary question that drives the system is not "what does the patient need?" but rather "what will federal programs pay for?" Workers in state departments of mental health spend an extraordinary number of hours defining and redefining federal mandates so that they can fit additional costs into federal boxes and send them off to Washington for reimbursement. One observer remarked, "A whole industry of consultants has sprung up to teach states how to claim every last federal dollar."[31] The result is the most expensive, yet least coordinated, system of public psychiatric services in the Western world.

The complexity of funding systems for public psychiatric services is illustrated in Figure 7.2 by a schematic representation of funding sources for the state of Iowa.[32] Iowa is an atypical state insofar as more funds for mental illness services come directly from county general funds. Except for that, the various funding streams pictured in Figure 7.2 resemble those in other states. Because of this bewildering complexity, directors of public psychiatric services for cities, counties, and states must combine the skills of an accountant, entrepreneur, and corporate executive to determine which expenses should be charged to which funding source.

The clinical needs of psychiatric patients demand continuity of care whenever possible, yet the present funding system virtually precludes continuity. Because Medicaid will pay for inpatient care in general hospitals but not in state psychiatric hospitals, the majority of psychiatric admissions now go to general hospitals. In some places, such as Salem, Oregon, patients are admitted to a general hospital that is, literally, across the street from the state psychiatric hospital even though a patient may have had 10 or more previous admissions to the state hospital and be well known to its professional staff. The following is an example:

Because of severe schizoaffective disorder, Rebecca J., age 56, had spent 25 years in a New York State psychiatric hospital. She lived in a group home in the community but required rehospitalization for several weeks approximately once a year when she relapsed despite taking medications.

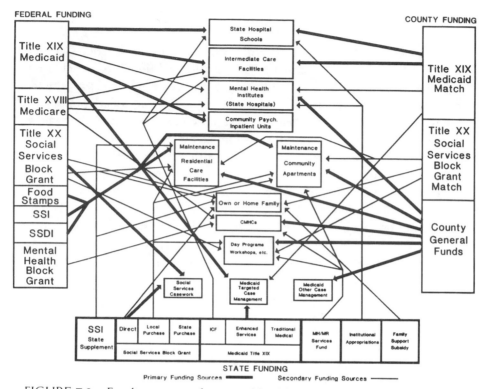

FIGURE 7.2   Funding sources for mental health programs in Iowa.

As a result of the reduction in state hospital beds and attempts by the state to shift readmissions for fiscal reasons, these rehospitalizations increasingly took place on the psychiatric wards of general hospitals that varied widely in quality. In 1994, she was admitted to a new hospital because the general hospital where she usually went was full. The new hospital was inadequately staffed to provide care for patients as sick as Rebecca J. In addition, the psychiatrist was poorly trained and had access to only a small fraction of Rebecca J.'s complex and voluminous past history. During her 6-week hospitalization, Rebecca J. lost 10 pounds because the nursing staff did not help her eat, had virtually all her clothing and personal effects lost or stolen, became toxic from her lithium medication which was not noticed until she was semicomatose, and was prematurely discharged while she was still so psychotic that she had to be rehospitalized in another hospital less than 24 hours later. Meanwhile, less than a mile away in the state psychiatric hospital where she had spent many years, a bed sat empty on a ward with nursing staff and a psychiatrist who knew her case well and with her case records readily available in a file cabinet.

Except for a brief psychiatric summary, patients' records are not usually sent from one hospital to another, a major impediment to providing good care. In large cities, a severely psychiatrically ill patient who also has medical problems may be admitted to 6, 8, or even 10 different area hospitals in a period of a few years. Under such circumstances, continuity of care is impossible and even quality care becomes problematic.

When psychiatric patients are discharged from hospitals, follow-up is often minimal. As early as 1969, it was reported that 40 percent of these patients being discharged from state hospitals "were not referred for further treatment, care, or rehabilitation."[33] Nineteen years later, in 1988, a national survey of 915 inpatient psychiatric facilities reported that 46 percent of the facilities "provided patient follow-up of one week or less. . . . Transitional care services for mentally ill patients leaving the hospital were uneven and disappointing. . . . Financial barriers appear to play a critical role."[34] The major problem is that state or local mental health authorities have little fiscal incentive to provide follow-up care; if individuals relapse, they can simply be readmitted to the psychiatric ward of a general hospital where the federal government will pay most of the cost.

The consequences of lack of follow-up are relapse and readmission. Studies have shown that without medications 53 percent of severely mentally ill patients relapse within 10 months[35] and 85 percent relapse within 5 years.[36] Such relapses often lead to readmissions to hospitals. Thus "in Chicago 30 percent of the patients discharged from [state] facilities must be rehospitalized within 30 days"[37] and in New York "nearly 40 percent of all psychiatric patients discharged from hospitals are rehospitalized within six months."[38] Another study in New York found that 24 percent of the psychiatric patients being readmitted to the hospital already had 10 or more previous admissions.[39]

The most complete study of psychiatric hospital readmissions in the United States was carried out by Jeffrey Geller, a psychiatrist, who asked 196 state psychiatric hospitals to identify the patient admitted to their hospital in 1987 who had had the most previous admissions.[40] The average number of admissions was 31, with a range from 5 to 121. All except 16 percent of the multiple recidivists had been diagnosed with schizophrenia, schizoaffective disorder, or manic-depressive illness. And since the mean age of the group was only 42.2 years, they presumably have many more admissions in their future. Here is a typical example:

Alan P. was admitted to St. Elizabeth's Hospital in Washington, DC, for the 27th time in 12 years with a diagnosis of chronic schizophrenia. He invariably responded well to medication within three weeks. He was then discharged to live in the community, given medication for two weeks and strong admonitions to keep his outpatient appointment at a local community mental health center. He had no insight into his illness or need for medication, however, and usually discarded the pills in a trash can en route to his boarding house. Slowly over the ensuing weeks, his behavior became increasingly bizarre as his psychosis returned. The community mental health center simply crossed his name off its list when he failed to come for his scheduled appointment. His most recent admission had been precipitated by an arrest for disorderly conduct; he had alarmed tourists by standing in the pool in front of the Lincoln Memorial and picking apart dead pigeons.[41]

In addition to readmissions, the failure to follow up psychiatric patients after discharge from hospitals also leads to homelessness, incarceration in jails or prisons, and episodes of violence. In fact it is now common to find people who cycle between hospitals, the streets, and jail almost continuously. Among the many people identified in the 1992 survey of mentally ill individuals in jail, we identified a man with schizophrenia who had been jailed twice and hospitalized 36 times; a manic-depressive woman who had been jailed three times and hospitalized 29 times; a man with manic-depressive illness who had been jailed 35 times and hospitalized 20 times; a man with schizophrenia who had been jailed and hospitalized between 25 and 30 times each; another who had been jailed 30 times and hospitalized four times; and a man with manic-depressive illness who had been jailed 82 times and hospitalized three times.[42] All of them had also lived for varying periods in public shelters and on the streets. For such people, the cycle must be like that of medieval pilgrims who go on, year after year, enduring hardships in hopes of attaining grace. Within the public psychiatric care system as it is currently organized, grace is in very short supply.

Not only is such a system inhumane for those with brain diseases, it is also expensive. As early as 1984 researchers calculated the costs of care for "Sylvia Frumkin," the pseudonymous protagonist of Susan Sheehan's prizewinning *Is There No Place on Earth for Me?*[43] For her 27 admissions over 18 years, the cost of hospitalizations, halfway houses, and foster homes was $636,000, and that cost did not include outpatient medication costs, emergency room services, general health care, social services, law enforcement services needed to return her to the hospital, legal services, court costs, lost wages, or even the direct care costs incurred by Ms. Frumkin's family.[44] More recently, a study of psychiatric rehospitalizations in New York State calculated that "the average cost per rehospitalized patient" was $36,750.[45] Multiplying such costs by the number of patients rehospitalized shows clearly where a large percentage of the money in the psychiatric care system is going.

The present disjointed funding system for public psychiatric services virtually guarantees disjointed care. The fiscal incentive for states is to discharge patients, but there is no incentive to follow them up. A state mental health official illustrated the system's inevitable outcome with a story about a farmer driving his chickens to market:

> The farmer has too many chickens for the roosts in his truck, just as the state has too many mentally ill for the jails or the surviving state hospitals.
>
> The clever farmer beats on the truck sides to keep half the birds in the air. The state shuffles the insane between institutions.
>
> It's clumsy, but it saves the farmer the cost of a new truck. And as for the chickens, they get eaten anyway.[46]

Labeling Children as Disabled

Federal dollars have markedly increased the labeling of children as disabled and forced some parents to give up custody of their children to get psychiatric services for them. Our public psychiatric services for mentally ill children have never been very good, but federal dollars appear to have made them considerably worse. The number of children who have been labeled as psychiatrically disabled so they could be qualified for federal SSI payments, and the number of children whose parents have had to give up custody to qualify for federal funds is alarming.

Children with psychiatric disorders have qualified for SSI payments since the original legislation was passed in 1972, but eligibility was strict and largely confined to children with mental retardation, psychosis of childhood, and organic brain syndrome. In 1990, however, the Social Security Administration markedly broadened the list of mental impairments that qualified children for SSI, including attention deficit hyperactivity disorder, psychoactive substance dependence disorders, and personality disorders. Also in 1990, the United States Supreme Court ruled in *Sullivan v. Zebley* that children's eligibility for SSI should be based not only on their diagnoses, but also on their ability to perform "age-appropriate activities" including social, communication, cognitive, and motor skills.[47]

These two actions have *quadrupled* SSI awards to children for mental impairments, increasing from 1,900 per month in 1989 to 8,700 per month in 1993. The approval rate for children's applications increased from 38 percent to 56 percent. By the end of 1993, the number of children who were receiving SSI had increased from 296,300 to 770,500 over four years and constituted almost 20 percent of all SSI recipients.

The rapid increase in the number of children receiving federal SSI payments was noted by the House of Representatives, which asked the General Accounting Office (GAO) to investigate. The GAO report noted that from 1991 to 1993, 22 percent of all awards to children for mental impairments went to children with "behavioral problems." Theoretically, any child with behavioral problems or substance abuse problems and who is unable to perform "age-appropriate activities" might qualify for the SSI payment of $458 per month. There are even disability criteria for "emotional disorders of infants" whose ability to perform "age-appropriate activities" is assessed by their responsiveness to stimuli.

State and local governments have enthusiastically embraced this open-ended SSI subsidy seeing it as an opportunity to shift more costs to the federal government. Some of the children being approved for SSI come from families receiving public assistance, funded partly by state and local government, and the public assistance payment is stopped as soon as SSI begins. In New York City, the "Board of Education and the Human Resources Administration have cooperated on a joint project to get every special education student receiving welfare onto SSI." Once on SSI, the child can theoretically remain on it for life. Stories of SSI abuse are accumulating rapidly, including "a family in Arkansas with all nine kids on SSI" and "another family with 11 children on SSI"[48] receiving $4,000 a month. There are even allegations that "mothers have called the agency trying to get their unborn children on SSI."[49]

The equally problematic children's custody issue dates to 1980, when Congress enacted the federal Adoption Assistance and Foster Care Act, also known as Title IV-E of the Social Security Act. The Foster Care Act was intended to provide federal funds for permanent housing for abused and abandoned foster children, thus reversing "foster care drift"; it was not designed or intended to provide for children with severe mental illnesses other than abused or abandoned foster children. To qualify for federal dollars for residential care for these children, states were required either to take custody of the children or to have a "voluntary placement agreement" signed by the parents or a judge. Such agreements are time-limited and require periodic court review; thus, they are administratively cumbersome, and most states elected to simply take custody of such children as the easier alternative.

Within two years after the passage of the act, some state mental health officials realized that they could use it to get federal funds to support residential care for *any* mentally ill child simply by taking state custody of the child. All that was required was for the child's mother and father to be willing to give up custody. Before taking custody, the state bore most of the cost for residential services for the children; after taking custody, most of the cost was effectively shifted to the federal government.

By the late 1980s, cost-shifting by taking custody had become widespread. A 1988 survey of parents of severely mentally ill children found that 25 percent of the respondents had been asked by the state to give up custody as a condition for receiving residential services for their child; one-third of the parents had in fact given up custody.[50] A 1990 survey of states reported that 28 of 45 states (62 percent) that responded used custody transfer to save state funds, and there were suggestions that the true percentage was higher;[51] Tennessee and Georgia have been especially aggressive in demanding that parents give up custody. Overall, it appears that between 50,000 and 100,000 parents have been required by the states to give up custody of their children as a condition for receiving residential services.

Single Responsibility Funding and Block Grants

The only logical solution to cost-shifting and the economic causes of the mental illness crisis is single responsibility funding. As long as fiscal responsibility for different programs is divided between the federal and state governments, both sides will continue their efforts to shift costs to the other to the detriment of the individuals being served.

Proposing single responsibility funding raises the question, Which level of government should have the single responsibility—federal, state, or city/county? During the colonial period and the initial years of the United States, the care of mentally ill and other disabled persons was assumed to be a local, usually town or city, responsibility. In the early 1800s, this gradually shifted to the state level, although not without many arguments, and it remained a state responsibility until the 1960s. Since that time, fiscal responsibility for mentally ill persons has increasingly shifted from being a state to being primarily a federal responsibility.

To assure consistent standards of care, one can make a theoretical argument for fixing responsibility for mental illness services at the federal level, as is done in some European countries. Whether this system is feasible in a heterogeneous nation of 265 million people, spread out from Point Barrow to Key West, is more debatable.

Probably the strongest reason for not fixing responsibility at the federal level, however, is that the federal government, in effect, has had this responsibility for the past decade, during which the mental illness crisis has grown steadily worse, not better. In addition, the federal government's record of failed oversight and inept management of the federally funded Community Mental Health Center program,[52] beginning in the late 1960s, should by itself disqualify the federal government from any consideration for having the primary responsibility.

States are probably the most logical level of government to take responsibility for public psychiatric services except where the states are very large. California (31.2 million), New York (18.2 million), Texas (18.0 million), Florida (13.7 million), Pennsylvania (12.1 million), Illinois (11.7 million), and Ohio (11.1 million) are almost certainly too large to manage these programs centrally from the state capital. Some of the large states have recognized this. Ohio has set up regional Community Service Boards, California has decentralized public mental health programs from Sacramento to the counties, and New York has proposed giving block grants to the counties to create Integrated Delivery Systems. For large counties (e.g., Los Angeles County, with 9.2 million residents), however, even this is probably larger than can reasonably be administered from a single locus.

On the other end of the spectrum are states that have less than a million people each: Alaska, Delaware, Montana, North Dakota, South Dakota, Vermont, and Wyoming. There is an optimal economy of scale for financing and administering public mental illness services, and it may well be economical for contiguous states with small populations to combine resources for facilities such as a forensic hospital for the criminally insane, tertiary care diagnostic facilities, or inpatient units for severely ill children. This joint sharing of resources is also desirable—and frequently done—in sparsely populated but contiguous counties in states that decentralize services to the county level.

Accountability is key: Responsibility for public mental illness services should be legally and firmly fixed at a single level of government so that the governor, county executive, or mayor can be held accountable for these services. If mentally ill homeless people are overrunning the local parks, everybody should know whom to call. If the mentally ill are overflowing the local jails, everybody should know whom to call. If there is an epidemic of violent episodes by sick people who are not being treated, everybody should know whom to call.

No level of government can take true responsibility for services without also having responsibility for the funds with which to deliver those services. That does not mean that taxes collected only at the state or local level should be used to fund public mental illness services. Rather it means that taxes collected at all levels of government for this purpose must be allocated to the level of government that has the responsibility.

The Canadian health care system is a good example of this principle. Primary responsibility for health services, including services for mentally ill persons, is fixed at the provincial level. The provinces vary widely in population from Ontario (9.8 million) to Prince Edward Island (130,000). The money for supporting health, including mental health, care comes from both federal (40 percent) and provincial and local (60 percent) taxes. The federal share is given to the provinces contingent on the provincial plan being comprehensive, offering services to all residents, and being portable (i.e., residents are entitled to full benefits even when temporarily absent from their home province). There are significant differences among the health plans from province to province, so that it is more accurate to say that Canada has 10 provincial health care systems than that it has a single system. Residents receive health services from physicians and hospitals that then bill the provincial government. Administrative costs and paperwork in this single-source funding system are substantially less than in the United States.

How do the mentally ill fare in a single source funding system such as is used in Canada? The limited available data suggest that public mental illness services are, on the average, significantly better in Canada than in the United States.[53] A few states, such as New Hampshire, offer public psychiatric services that are competitive with most Canadian provinces, but on average the Canadian system offers substantially better psychiatric care than the American system. (The major problem at this time with Canadian psychiatric services is not their availability or organization, but rather legal limitations in using involuntary hospitalization and medication for ill persons with impaired insight; this problem will be discussed in Chapter 8.)

The Medicaid block grant, or Medigrant, under consideration by Congress can be seen as a possible step toward single responsibility funding and the improvement of public services for the mentally ill. Under the provisions of this block grant, the Medicaid payments that the federal government has been giving to the states as federal matching funds would be divided among the states using a complex formula that includes projected population growth. The states would receive these funds not as matching funds but as an outright grant. States should still be legally obligated to provide services to their disabled, including severely mentally ill, citizens, and treatment outcomes must be measured and monitored, but the states should have broad flexibility to shape the services as they wish.

Although some public officials, mental health professionals, families with mentally ill members, and recipients of services have enthusiastically supported the proposal as a means to improve public psychiatric services, others have strongly opposed it. Among the chief arguments are that funds would be reduced, that states would siphon off Medicaid funds for use on non-health-related projects, and that state officials are not competent to run such programs.

The Medicaid block grant would reduce the federal fiscal share of Medicaid by reducing the annual growth of federal funds from more than 10 percent per year to approximately 5 percent. High-Medicare user states, such as New York, would in fact lose considerable funding over time. It would be difficult to find an economist, however, who believes that the federal economy can sustain an annual 10 percent or more rate of Medicaid growth for very many years. In theory, the greater flexibility that states would have to organize services more efficiently should offset the decrease in annual growth, but whether this would in fact take place remains to be seen. Federal-state arguments regarding who should be responsible for what services have a long and honorable history in the United States. A federal study of the effectiveness of block grants given to the states under President Reagan reported that they were working remarkably well as long as the states had had prior experience with similar programs and there was "accountability for results."[54] Without such accountability, Medicaid block grants would ultimately fail to improve services.

The Potential Advantages of Single Responsibility Funding

Single responsibility funding, if combined with accountability (discussed in this chapter) and prioritization of services (see Chapter 9), can fundamentally alter and markedly improve services for persons with psychiatric illnesses. Combining state and local funds with federal Medicaid dollars in a single decision-making process, as the Medicaid block grant accomplishes, would be a major step forward.

What are the potential advantages of single responsibility funding? First, it would change the basic incentive system of deinstitutionalization. States would no longer have an incentive to transfer patients from state psychiatric hospitals to nursing homes, since the cost of their care in both places would come from the same funds. There would also be no fiscal advantage in hospitalizing people on psychiatric wards of general hospitals rather than in state psychiatric hospitals; decisions on where to hospitalize could be based on where the person would get the best and most cost-effective care as well as on considerations of geographic convenience.

Without the bureaucratic limitations of Medicaid regulations, psychiatric hospitalization would change markedly with a shift toward crisis intervention in the community. This has already happened under the cost-reduction incentives of managed care but would accelerate quickly. The Louisville Homecare Project, carried out under Benjamin Pasamanick from 1961 to 1964, demonstrated that approximately three-quarters of persons with schizophrenia can be successfully treated at home using daily visits by public health nurses *and* guaranteed medication compliance. The project was hailed as a landmark by the director of the National Institute of Mental Health, who said it "provides specific scientific evidence that many schizophrenics . . . need not be hospitalized if they are adequately treated in their home communities."[55] Yet in the 30 years since this demonstration, homecare has been virtually unused both because Medicaid did not cover it and because of the failure to address the medication compliance issue.

Single responsibility funding would also accelerate the development of other alternatives to hospitalization. In the early 1970s, the Southwest Denver Mental Health Services contracted with six private homes to each take one or two acutely mentally ill persons for up to three weeks at a time. Each home was assigned a coordinator from the mental health center, and the home sponsors met regularly "to learn from each other and from the [mental health center] staff."[56] Psychiatric nurses were on 24-hour call, antipsychotic medications were readily available, and psychiatrists made home visits as needed. At that time, Southwest Denver Mental Health Services was strongly oriented toward home visits, with two-thirds of all initial psychiatric evaluations taking place in the home. The Southwest Denver crisis homes program resulted in a dramatic decrease in hospitalization and was considered to be very successful. However, because such services were not covered by Medicaid, it was not replicated and eventually died.

Other alternatives to psychiatric hospitalization for the acutely ill include crisis residences with 24-hour nursing coverage and hospitalization during days only (day hospitalization) or during nights only (night hospitalization). All of these have been proven to be effective as an alternative to full hospitalization for some people but have not been widely used because of limitations on Medicaid reimbursement.

Changes would also take place in institutional practices for patients requiring long-term hospitalization. Currently, most of these patients are placed in nursing homes because that is what Medicaid reimburses. Without such fiscal constraints, alternatives to nursing homes would develop, including homecare with visiting nurses, contracted care in private homes, and community residences with 24-hour nursing coverage. It is also likely that for a small group of the markedly disabled, long-term care in state psychiatric hospitals, and in residential facilities on the grounds of the hospitals, is the most humane and cost-effective way to provide care. Under single responsibility funding, all such decisions could be made on the basis of what is clinically most appropriate for the mentally ill person, not on the basis of what is reimbursable through Medicaid.

Single responsibility funding would also improve outpatient services. Medication maintenance is a fundamental need for those with severe psychiatric disorders, but many also require help with housing, social rehabilitation, and vocational rehabilitation. Under the current Hydra-like mental health financing system, funding for clinical care, housing, and rehabilitation are separate and virtually impossible to combine into a single program.

There are proven models for outpatient psychiatric care that integrate most of the clinical, housing, and rehabilitation needs of the mentally ill. Because of the current funding system, these models have not been widely replicated, but under single responsibility funding they could be. Examples of such models are the Program in Assertive Community Treatment (PACT) model, the Fountain House clubhouse model, and the Fairweather Lodge model.

PACT programs, also referred to as continuous treatment teams, are based on a program that developed in Madison, Wisconsin, in 1972. A team of approximately 8 to 10 mental illness professionals and paraprofessionals take full responsibility for approximately 100 to 150 patients with severe mental illnesses. Full responsibility means 24-hour, 7-day-a-week, on-call coverage by a team member with attention to clinical, housing, and rehabilitation needs. Most of the contacts between treatment team members and those who are mentally ill take place in the patients' homes, workplaces, or elsewhere in the community, not in the professionals' offices. Medication is usually delivered rather than requiring the person to come to a clinic to obtain it. Care is assertive insofar as PACT team members actively seek out these patients for follow-up care.

PACT programs have proven to be both clinically effective and cost-effective. Randomized trials of the PACT model have been carried out in England and Australia as well as in the United States and have shown that persons treated using this model have much lower rates of hospitalization; both the mentally ill and their families are highly satisfied with it.[57] A detailed cost analysis reported that in 1994 it cost $29,965 per person per year for treatment and maintenance in a PACT program; of this, $9,259 was for direct psychiatric treatment, $3,716 for medical care and human services, and the remainder for maintenance, community expenses (e.g., law enforcement), and family expenses.[58]

Despite over 20 years of experience and multiple studies of cost-effectiveness, in 1993 there were only approximately 100 replications of the complete PACT model program in the United States, the majority in Wisconsin and Michigan.[59] This includes programs that have modified the PACT model to meet the clinical needs of specific psychiatric populations, such as New Hampshire's PACT programs for persons dually diagnosed with mental illnesses and substance abuse.[60]

The main reason for the lack of further dissemination of PACT programs is difficulties in funding the program under Medicaid. To get even partial Medicaid reimbursement, it is necessary to write standards for the proposed program, then get the standards approved by both the state and federal government, a process that takes a minimum of one year. Once approved, the PACT team must keep voluminous records to ensure partial Medicaid reimbursement. The funding process discourages all but those who are most committed to setting up such teams.

The Fountain House clubhouse model was developed in New York City in 1948. A clubhouse is a community facility open 7 days a week, in which members, as they are called, congregate for social and educational activities. Medications are not given out, but members are strongly encouraged to take them as prescribed. Since all members have been mentally ill, no stigma accrues to that status. Vocational rehabilitation is an integral component, with all members being expected to participate on work teams that maintain the clubhouse by preparing lunch, cleaning, or answering telephones. Many members also participate in formal vocational training programs, and clubhouses have proven to be one of the most successful models for job rehabilitation. Most clubhouses are also associated with housing programs in which members share apartments or homes.

Clubhouses have been proven to be highly effective; they are also cost-effective. Hospitalization rates are dramatically lower and employment rates significantly higher in clubhouse members compared with controls.[61] Despite this proven track record, in 1995 there were only approximately 200 clubhouses in the United States, and many of these did not follow the complete clubhouse model. Clubhouses were most widely available in Massachusetts and Virginia, where the state department of mental health had specifically made an attempt to develop them. Clubhouses have not become more widespread primarily because they do not fit into existing Medicaid reimbursement categories, which exclude most vocational or educational rehabilitation activities. According to Kenneth Dudek, the Executive Director of Fountain House, "the limitations of Medicaid are the major reason why clubhouses have not become more widespread."[62]

A third proven model that integrates housing and rehabilitation needs for the mentally ill is the Fairweather Lodge model, originally developed by George Fairweather in 1963 at the Palo Alto Veterans Administration Hospital.[63] Each lodge consists of six to eight severely ill persons who live together in a house and jointly operate a business. The guiding principle is empowerment of people to take responsibility for their lives through participation in a cohesive, problem-solving group.

The businesses operated by Fairweather Lodges include janitorial and lawn services, house painting, furniture building, shoe repair, and catering. A home coordinator is available to supervise the lodge but does not live there. Residents are expected to continue taking medications prescribed for them. The lodge combines a residence, work group, and social network for members and works best for those who have been hospitalized for long periods.

Decrease in hospitalizations for lodge residents is dramatic. A Michigan study showed that residents had been rehospitalized for only 20 days a year, compared with an expected 189 days a year based on their previous record. The projected savings for the state of Michigan was estimated to be $2 million per year.[64] Similarly, a Texas study showed that lodge members had a 92 percent employment rate and were very satisfied with their program.[65] Most lodges have not become self-supporting, as originally hoped, but costs per member in a Texas survey averaged only $10 a day.

Despite impressive data on effectiveness and cost savings, the Fairweather Lodge program has not been widely replicated. In 1967 and again in 1975, the National Institute of Mental Health provided funds to promote the dissemination of the lodge model. All 255 state mental hospitals in the United States were directly contacted and told about the program. Despite these efforts, by 1995 only approximately 90 lodges were operative, the majority of them in Michigan and Texas. Funding for them has been difficult since Medicaid covers only the clinical costs, not the vocational or rehabilitative, aspects.

Another advantage of single responsibility funding with decision-making fixed at the state or, in some states, county level is the possibility of much greater innovation in human resources. Under the federal

Medicaid program, a multiplicity of regulations have governed the training and degrees a professional must have for services to be Medicaid reimbursable. States should have the responsibility for such regulations and the authority to approve changes in strategies.

An example of a new strategy that was discontinued because of Medicaid regulations was the use of nurses in the Louisville Homecare Project to treat the mentally ill in their homes. In 1994 in the United States, there were 18,901 nurses with certification in psychiatric and mental health nursing. Although these nurses are widely used on psychiatric inpatient wards, in most other countries they are used far more widely for providing outpatient psychiatric services. In 1995, there were only 248 advanced practice psychiatric nurses in the United States; such nurses have a master's degree in psychiatric nursing, have completed a supervised clinical internship, and have passed a national credentialing examination.[66] An advanced practice psychiatric nurse who has also had training in psychopharmacology may prescribe medication in some states. In the state of Washington, which has been a leader in the use of advanced practice psychiatric nurses, a few of them specialize in the outpatient treatment of mentally ill patients with schizophrenia and manic-depressive illness.

Because of Medicaid restrictions, physician assistants have also been markedly underutilized for outpatient psychiatric services. In 1995, there were approximately 25,000 physician assistants in the United States, concentrated in North Carolina, New York, Pennsylvania, and Florida. Fewer than 200 of them were specialized in psychiatry, and most of those were employed by psychiatric hospitals to do physical examinations on inpatients.[67] Since physician assistants can prescribe medications, they are an underused potential resource for delivering outpatient psychiatric services in either a clinic or homecare setting.

Still another underused human resource comprises the mentally ill themselves, or *consumers* as some prefer to be called. Since 1986 in Denver, the mentally ill who are stable on medication have been trained in a 6-month training program to be case managers for other ill people.[68] As consumer case managers or consumer providers, as they are more often called, they have been hired by many mental health centers in Colorado. Having previously been on the receiving end of psychiatric services, these workers bring special insights and empathic skills to their tasks. The consumer provider training program has been replicated in Texas, Massachusetts, Pennsylvania, and Washington, but like all such innovations, its development has been severely constrained by Medicaid's failure to reimburse for such services. A study of families in which consumer case managers were providing services to their ill relative found a high degree of satisfaction with the services.[69]

Single responsibility funding under which the state has decision-making and regulatory authority opens up a wide range of innovations for delivering psychiatric services. Once the strings of federal Medicaid regulations have been cut, changes in services and human resources become possible. And it is only through encouraging such innovation that we will learn how to deliver quality psychiatric services in the most cost-effective manner.

Managed Care or Mangled Care

Even before President Clinton proposed national health care reform in 1993, it had become evident that something was going to have to change in the organization of American medicine. Health costs had reached 12 percent of the nation's gross domestic product in 1990 and were projected to go to 18 percent by the year 2000. States spent approximately $100 billion on health costs in 1991, and this figure was projected to reach $244 billion by 2000. For many businesses, employee health costs were escalating rapidly and consuming an increasing share of profits.

The "managed care" solution to rising health care costs came from the business community. With managed care, employees must go through a gatekeeper to get reimbursed for most medical care. In its simplest form, managed care is a process of getting prior approval for a hospitalization, operation, or consultation with a specialist. In its more complex form, a managed care company assumes responsibility for managing medical services for a group of employees or Medicaid patients and then contracts with physicians and other medical providers for services. The contract may be on a fee-for-service basis or an annual per person capitated fee.

Businesses using managed care companies have achieved impressive health care savings, including savings on mental health benefits. IBM decreased mental health spending from $521 per employee per year in 1990 to $375 in 1993, and Alcan Aluminum, from $170 in 1991 to $71 in 1993.[70] The vast majority of employees whose mental health benefits have been affected under managed care were using these services for psychotherapy or for the treatment of alcohol and drug abuse problems. Savings came from limiting hospitalizations and restricting the duration of psychotherapy. Managed care companies sprouted and grew virtually overnight, with the largest share of mental health benefits contracts going to Value Behavioral Health, Merit Behavioral Care (formerly

Medco), Human Affairs International, U.S. Behavioral Healthcare, and Green Spring Health Services (which merged with Charter Medical Corporation to form Magellan Health Services).

Many such companies are subsidiaries of insurance (e.g., Aetna), pharmaceutical (e.g., Merck), or other large corporations and the managed care companies continue to merge, buy each other out, and change their names on a frequent basis. Mental health benefits may be managed separately from general health benefits (a "carve-out") or they may be managed together (an "integrated" or "carve-in" system). By 1995, managed care companies had assumed responsibility for mental health benefits for 58 percent of all Americans covered by health insurance.

States, faced with rapidly rising Medicaid costs for general health services, observed the savings of private sector companies using managed care, and many decided to go the same route for state residents on Medicaid. Because of extensive federal Medicaid regulations, however, the states first had to obtain waivers from the federal government setting aside selected Medicaid regulations such as one guaranteeing that Medicaid recipients will have a "free choice of providers." Under most managed care systems, patients do not have this free choice. Arizona was the first state to obtain a Medicaid waiver from the federal government. The waiver process was streamlined in 1993, and by early 1996 a total of 43 states had obtained waivers and applications from almost all the others were pending.

Since mental health services constituted a significant and rising percentage of state Medicaid expenditures, many states decided to put Medicaid mental health expenditures under managed care as well. By late 1995, Arizona, Utah, Massachusetts, Washington, Tennessee, Oregon, Colorado, Iowa, and Nebraska had either implemented such programs or were planning to do so. Most of these Medicaid managed care programs for mental health services were set up separately from the Medicaid general health programs (carve-outs), although in Oregon and initially in Tennessee, the two were integrated (a carve-in).

Should managed care be expected to work effectively for people with severe mental illnesses? Managed care demonstrated its potential to reduce mental health costs for private sector companies, but employees in those settings are predominantly healthy and few have severe mental illnesses. Medicaid beneficiaries, by contrast, frequently have severe mental illnesses such as schizophrenia, manic-depressive illness, and severe depression. Many of them remain sick for years and need social and rehabilitative services as well as psychiatric care. Just because managed care has proven effective in reducing mental health costs in the private sector does not necessarily mean that it can do so for state Medicaid recipients.

In the late 1980s, two major studies were carried out assessing the effectiveness of managed care for people with severe mental illnesses. In Minneapolis in 1987, 739 Medicaid recipients with severe mental illnesses were randomly assigned to a prepaid managed care program or to a traditional fee-for-service program. The patients in the prepaid managed care plan had significantly shorter hospital stays (1.6 vs. 4.3 days, $p < .01$) but were more likely to be refused emergency services ($p < .06$). In addition, a subsample was restudied two years later and those who had been in the managed care plan had a significantly *lower* level of function ($p < .02$) as measured by the Global Assessment Scale.[71]

For a similar study in Rochester, New York, in 1987, investigators randomly assigned mentally ill patients to a capitated managed care program or to a traditional fee-for-service program. At the end of two years, the persons in the capitated managed care program had spent significantly less time hospitalized ($p < .01$) and therefore had had lower mental health care costs (14 percent in the first year, 8 percent in the second year). However, there were no differences between the two groups in psychiatric symptoms, level of function, or life satisfaction measurements.[72]

By 1989, then, experience with managed care for the mentally ill suggested that managed care can reduce hospitalization days and therefore costs. There were also suggestions, however, that managed care had liabilities with this patient population, including "the tendency for capitation programs to encourage underservice in order to reduce the economic exposure of providers."[73] A 1989 assessment of mental health managed care capitation programs concluded:

> Capitation is both more difficult to establish and less likely to yield beneficial outcomes than had initially been hoped. . . . Our experience to date with capitated mental health care, however, suggests that simply borrowing existing models of prepaid care may well prove detrimental to the mentally ill and certainly will not capture the full benefits that capitation ought to produce.[74]

Since 1989, many states have begun capitated and other forms of managed care programs for hundreds of thousands of severely ill people on Medicaid. Although no formal evaluation of these programs has yet been published, there are suggestions that the earlier warnings have validity. Apparent problems have included the profit motive overriding concerns about quality of care, poor continuity of care, skimming the easy patients and dumping the most difficult patients from the managed care system, and failing to give priority to those who are sickest.

The Profit Motive

The profit motive in managed care companies should not be underestimated. Managed care is big business, as shown by the size of state mental health managed care contracts for Medicaid patients in Iowa ($100 million), Maricopa County, Arizona ($130 million), Massachusetts ($168 million), Nebraska ($173 million), and Tennessee ($200 million). The directors of managed care mental health companies are very well compensated, and the chief operating officers (CEOs) of the parent corporations receive extraordinary compensation in salaries, bonuses, and stock options. In 1994, for example, Ronald Compton, CEO of Aetna Insurance, the owner of Human Affairs International which managed some mental health contracts for the military CHAMPUS program, received total compensation of $1.1 million; Robert Patricelli, CEO of Value Health Inc., the owner of Value Behavioral Health which managed public mental health contracts in Massachusetts, received total compensation of $1.2 million; E. Mac Crawford, CEO of Magellan Health Services, the owner of Green Spring Health Services which managed public mental health contracts in Tennessee, received total compensation of $1.4 million; P. Roy Vagelos, MD, the CEO of Merck and Company, the owner of Medco Behavioral Care (which later became Merit Behavioral Care) which managed public mental health contracts in Iowa, received total compensation of $3.5 million; William W. McGuire, MD, the CEO of United Healthcare, the owner of U.S. Behavioral Healthcare which managed public mental health contracts in Washington, received total compensation of $6.1 million.[75] *The Wall Street Journal* characterized mental health managed care companies in 1995 as "a $2 billion industry, with plenty of potential for additional growth. . . . Such managed care firms are extremely profitable, boasting [profit] margins of 15 percent and more even after heavy expenditures on case managers and computer systems."[76] This profit margin is in addition to high administrative costs, which were, for example, 21.9 percent in 1994 for United Healthcare.[77]

Reports of the profit motive overriding concerns about quality of care have surfaced frequently. These have included a failure to hospitalize severely ill patients and the use of the least expensive medications even when a trial of more costly medications, such as clozapine or risperidone, is clearly indicated. Under the contract between Merit Behavioral Care and the state of Iowa, Merit earns an average "commission" of $880 for each adult who applies for but is denied admission to a psychiatric inpatient unit.[78] It has also been alleged in Iowa that Merit "has a practice of calling the hospital *daily* to question if the stay is a 'medical necessity' . . .

Even if the person attempted suicide the day before, Medco [now Merit] representatives can call the next day to question whether the person *still* meets the criteria of medical necessity."[79] According to an editorial in the *Des Moines Register*, "Iowa psychiatrists . . . told of several instances in which suicidal, dangerous or severely psychotic patients were denied hospitalization. One report involved a mother who had just tried to kill her two children."[80]

In Rhode Island in 1995, United Behavioral Systems, a managed care company owned by United Healthcare, was fined $100,000 for allegedly paying incentive bonuses to the company's medical director, a psychiatrist, contingent on the company's profits. The profits, in turn, were generated by denial of psychiatric care. According to a news account "the complaints mostly involved delays or denials of hospitalization for seriously mentally ill patients. . . . Incentive payments range from 50 percent to 200 percent of the incentive target."[81]

Massachusetts is another state in which mental illness services for Medicaid recipients have been said to be grossly inadequate under managed care companies. A 1995 warning from the state Division of Medical Assistance expressed "serious concern" that mentally ill adults and children were being neglected and accused the HMOs of spending only $4 to $5 per member per month although the HMOs were being compensated at $22 per member per month.[82] Such reports recall a 1988 caution from a corporate executive regarding tendencies of managed care companies to minimize treatment for severe mental illnesses:

> Unfortunately, a lot of managed care activity is simply ratcheting down of costs with little or no attention to quality patient care. Many HMOs see their mental health component as a "soft" area in their budgets which can be cut back to virtually nothing.[83]

Continuity of Care

Continuity of care is another problem for mental health managed care, although theoretically, it should be one of the advantages. Continuity is extremely important for the mentally ill both because of the complexity of their illnesses and because many such patients find it difficult to relate to an ever-changing panoply of case managers and other mental health professionals. To reduce costs, many mental health managed care companies have hired less expensive and less experienced employees and bypassed local providers who had been providing the care. Low wages guarantee frequent turnover of staff.

An extreme example of this lack of continuity was the situation in Phoenix in 1995; ComCare, which provided managed care in that city, hired psychiatrists from "rent-a-doc" companies. Such psychiatrists, who came to Phoenix from other places and stayed for as little as three weeks, exemplified *non*continuity of care. According to a newspaper account, "other employees tell of patients seeing, say, six doctors in six months. . . . It sure seems clear that rent-a-docs are another sign of a public mental-health system in dangerous disarray."[84] This lack of continuity of care under managed care is further exacerbated by the fact that Medicaid waivers and managed care cover only certain segments of the mental health system, usually omitting altogether state psychiatric hospitals.

Skimming for Profit

A third problem with mental health managed care of Medicaid patients is that some companies try to select in only the least ill patients (skimming) and to select out the most severely ill (dumping). Medicare utilization of general health services illustrates this issue; in 1993 "19 percent of [Medicare] enrollees cost Medicare nothing, and 53 percent cost less than $500 each."[85] The vast majority of Medicare costs were accounted for by the other 28 percent of enrollees. Therefore, to maximize profits a mental health managed care company should logically enroll as many low-service-users and as few high-service-users as possible. Since severely mentally ill patients are high-service-users, it is not surprising that managed care companies try to exclude them. As described by Richard Surles, Executive Vice President of Merit Behavioral Care: "Right now the Medicaid managed care mindset is not oriented toward case finding and presumptive eligibility for people who are outside the system. You don't go looking for people who are going to be the highest risk unless you want to go bankrupt."[86]

For the difficult-to-manage and high-service-user mentally ill who do become registered under managed care systems, there are always ways to unregister them. Studies of heavy users of psychiatric services have shown that 10 to 30 percent of severely mentally ill patients utilize 50 to 80 percent of the services.[87] Excluding such high users makes managed care much more profitable. In some states, persons who require involuntary hospitalization automatically go to the state psychiatric hospitals and are effectively removed from managed care. The mentally ill who are arrested go to jails and/or into the state forensic system, which also effectively removes them from managed care. Still another form of creative case management is to provide especially difficult patients with free bus tickets to the next state.

Denying Priority Services

A final problem with managed care mental health companies is their failure to give priority services to the most severely mentally ill patients, whom they are unable to dump from the system. This has been a major point of contention for many years with American public psychiatry in general (see Chapter 9). Since the mental health professionals in positions of leadership in the managed care companies previously worked in American public and private psychiatry, it is not surprising that they are continuing to make the same mistakes. A 1989 statement by Saul Feldman, Chairman and Chief Operating Officer of U.S. Behavioral Healthcare, illustrates such thinking:

> To provide care for that [severely mentally ill] population at the expense of providing it to people who are neurotic or who have less persistent mental disorders, or even the worried well seems to me will only increase the number of chronically mentally ill. . . . Mental health problems generally don't go away and if they are not treated they get worse. If there are no resources and no services to treat people to prevent mental illness . . . what we may be doing in effect is creating a whole new army of chronically mentally ill people because we're not spending money on preventing chronic mental illness; we're spending all the money on people who are already chronically mentally ill.[88]

The idea that the failure to treat "people who are neurotic" or "the worried well" will lead to an increase in severe mental illness has been completely discredited. The very name mental health managed care companies have chosen—Behavioral Healthcare—suggests that their main interest is in managing health care users with behavioral problems, not severe mental illnesses.

There are multiple reasons to suspect that mental health managed care may not work for people with severe mental illnesses. So far, managed care companies have demonstrated only that they can manage costs. Issues such as continuity of care, improved quality of life, and rehabilitation are rarely discussed. Indeed, it is not really accurate to label what is occurring to date as managed *care;* it is merely managed *costs.* And by skimming off easy patients and big profits from the public mental health system, managed care has the definite potential to turn out to be mangled care and to make the mental illness crisis worse than it already is.

For-Profits and Nonprofits

For-profit companies in the mental health care field have given capitalism a bad name. The most highly publicized demonstration of this has been the Psychiatric Institutes of America—National Medical Enterprise (PIA-NME) corporation. Riding the crest of the private, for-profit psychiatric hospital boom of the 1980s, NME purchased PIA as its psychiatric division and rapidly expanded using ethically questionable, and in some cases overtly illegal, treatment practices. Among other acts, PIA-NME was accused of paying kickbacks to psychiatrists and other mental health professionals for referring patients to their hospitals and "taking patients who did not need treatment and keeping them against their will until their insurance coverage ran out."[89]

PIA-NME became highly skilled at inflating hospital costs to obtain every conceivable dollar from insurance companies, CHAMPUS, Medicaid, Medicare, and patients' families. This included practices such as charging patients $40 per day for "relaxation therapy" which consisted of playing taped music in the hall, charging $1,100 per person for three hours of group therapy, and charging a single patient for as many as 15 group therapy sessions, 3 dance therapy sessions, 2 counseling sessions, and 1 individual therapy session in a single day. In the hospital staff lounge, a bulletin board was kept with patients' names "along with the names of their insurance companies and the dates on which their benefits expired."[90] The lengths of patients' hospitalizations coincided remarkably with the length of their insurance coverages, irrespective of diagnoses.

In 1994, PIA-NME pleaded guilty in federal court to paying mental health professionals between $20 million and $40 million in kickbacks and bribes and agreed to pay the government $379 million in fines in the largest health care fraud case ever prosecuted. At last count, the first PhD-licensed counselor had been sentenced to eight years in prison and more than 100 other mental health professionals were under investigation.

For-profit companies in the field of managed health care are also giving capitalism a bad name. A series of articles in the Ft. Lauderdale *Sun-Sentinel* in 1995 about managed care in Florida detailed problems encountered as the state contracted with 24 for-profit managed care companies to provide health care for 1.7 million Medicaid enrollees. Each company is paid a capitated fee per enrollee and then makes more or less profit by delivering more or less medical services. The average Medicaid enrollee in the 24 plans saw a physician 2.3 times in 1994.

The managed care company with the least number of physician visits per enrollee was PacifiCare of Florida, with an average of 0.1 annual physician visits per enrollee (1/23 of the average). One of the physician consultants who advised PacifiCare was Dr. Ismael Hernandez, who was paid $200,000 per year. In 1978, Dr. Hernandez "was convicted of felony tax evasion and spent four months in prison." Enrollees in Physicians Healthcare Plans, another of the managed care companies, had an average of 1.2 annual physician visits. Mike Fernandez, who runs Physicians Healthcare, was paid $200,000 per year in salary plus a leased Mercedes at $13,000 per year plus a leased airplane at $69,000 per year, the last being leased from another company owned by Mr. Fernandez. All of this was charged to the health plan as administrative expenses.

Continental Health Plans of Miami is another of the managed health care companies that has caught the attention of Florida officials. Its original owners, Luis and Zenaida Fonseca, both drive leased Mercedes as does the company's president. Mr. Fonseca subsequently had to relinquish ownership of Continental Health Plans when it was learned that he had previously "pleaded guilty to a felony charge of forgery."

There are, in fact, indications that the managed health care business is not necessarily attracting idealists dedicated to improving health care as their first priority. According to the *Sun-Sentinel*, among 28 companies "that Florida insurance regulators have accepted into the program since 1994," 10 applicants or their key executives "operate health businesses that have drawn fines, poor evaluations, or other sanctions from state medical regulators," and 9 more applicants or company medical directors "are doctors who have been cited by state inspectors for poor patient care practices, sanctioned by medical licensing officials, or are under investigation by federal Medicare fraud auditors."[91]

Psychiatric Institutes of America—National Medical Enterprises has unquestionably demonstrated that for-profit companies in the mental health care field can make big profits while delivering poor quality services. And it has been clearly demonstrated in Florida that for-profit managed care companies in the Medicaid health field can make big profits while delivering poor quality services. What is now taking place is a marriage of the mental health care field with the for-profit managed care of Medicaid enrollees. It might work, but a healthy skepticism and very close monitoring are certainly indicated. In a recent assessment of managed health care, an Ohio legislator commented: "This could be the medical equivalent to selling swampland in Florida."[92]

An example of a for-profit mental health care company that *does* deliver high-quality services to patients with mental illnesses is Northwest Mental Health Services, formed in Seattle in 1984 by Mark Brandow, Stephen Burr, and Maryann Hanson, two psychologists and a social worker who idealistically believed that they could do a better job than public mental health centers of delivering quality psychiatric services. They bid on, and were awarded, the contract for services covering one of the four Regional Support Networks for Washington's King County, which includes Seattle. Subsequently, they opened a 40-bed inpatient unit for patients with an average stay of approximately two weeks and a 60-bed long-stay facility in suburban Auburn.

Northwest Mental Health Services has developed a very good reputation for high-quality services and especially for their willingness to take on some of the most difficult-to-treat patients. For example, a site visit to Chartley House in late 1991 reported that 34 of the facility's 60 residents at that time were receiving the new and highly regarded antipsychotic drug clozapine. At the beginning of 1996, Northwest Mental Health Services had 200 employees and was in the process of turning company ownership over to the employees through a stock option plan.

Although for-profit companies such as Northwest Mental Health Services may make important contributions to solving the mental illness crisis in some areas, it seems likely that nonprofit programs, both private and public, will play the major role. Most of the highly regarded programs in the United States fall into the nonprofit category. The following are some examples:

◇ Monadnock Family Services in Keene, New Hampshire, is a private, nonprofit, community mental health center with an 18-person board. The center provides services for approximately 3,500 people among the 100,000 population in its catchment area. Services for the 350 severely mentally ill recipients of services have been widely praised. Approximately 40 percent of them are employed in programs such as the Wyman Way Co-op, which makes furniture and does carpentry work. The New Hampshire Division of Mental Health and Developmental Services contracts with Monadnock Family Services and with nine other community mental health centers, several of which are also highly regarded, to provide specific services for mentally ill people in their catchment areas. Monadnock Family Services also functions as a mental health managed care company for private firms in the local area and also as part of a statewide managed care company, Behavioral Health Network, which provides mental health managed care for 60,000 participants under Blue Cross-Blue Shield.

◇ Valley Mental Health in Salt Lake City, Utah, is a private, nonprofit, community mental health center that serves a population of

750,000 people. It contracts for acute inpatient care with the University of Utah Medical Center and also utilizes its own Residential Treatment Units for inpatient stays of up to three months. It runs Alliance House, a Fountain House-model clubhouse in a converted fire station, and Valley Storefront, a drop-in center for homeless mentally ill people in a converted transmission repair shop. Its housing network for the mentally ill is highly regarded, as are its psychiatric services in the Salt Lake County Jail. In 1991, Valley Mental Health assumed responsibility for managed care mental health services for all Medicaid recipients in its area. It is a capitated program in which Valley Mental Health receives a monthly, prepaid premium for each Medicaid recipient and in turn assumes full financial risk for all psychiatric services.

◇ San Mateo County Division of Mental Health in California is a public, nonprofit agency providing services for 650,000 people. For many years, it has been regarded as one of the best county mental health programs in the state, utilizing extensive subcontracting with private community agencies. Especially impressive are its two mobile outreach teams to reach those who refuse treatment, a shelter that specifically targets the homeless mentally ill, transition housing for those being discharged from inpatient units, and a program at the College of San Mateo in which approximately 100 mentally ill individuals take courses to learn about symptom management, become peer counselors, or make the transition to regular college courses. In 1995, the Division of Mental Health extended its responsibilities and assumed full risk responsibility for mental health services for Medicaid beneficiaries in the county.

Programs such as Monadnock Family Services, Valley Mental Health, and the San Mateo Division of Mental Health demonstrate the feasibility of delivering high-quality services within a nonprofit system. These three programs are, sadly, not typical of existing psychiatric services and are among the top 20 such programs in the United States. The programs share some common attributes, including stable leadership, an explicit commitment to prioritizing services for the most severely ill users, and the plowing of "profits" back into additional services rather than into a $6 million salary for the chief operating officer.

Other nonprofit organizations could also be used to confront the mental illness crisis. The Mennonites have a 50-year tradition of running a few high-quality psychiatric facilities, including Kings View Hospital in Reedley, California, and Prairie View Mental Health Center in Newton,

Kansas. The Catholic Franciscans have operated St. Francis Residence and other model housing programs for the mentally ill in New York City, and the Volunteers of America have operated some public shelters there. Private, nonprofit psychiatric hospitals might also develop as resources if they can shift their focus from mental health to mental illness. Shephard-Pratt Hospital in Baltimore is an example of a private nonprofit psychiatric hospital that is attempting to do this. All these nonprofit resources should be developed and encouraged to bid on contracts for delivering services to people with mental illnesses.

Accountability and Performance Contracting: How Can Outcomes Be Measured?

Until recent years, the measurement of treatment outcomes for severe psychiatric illnesses was moot because there were no effective treatments. That has changed with the development of a variety of pharmacological and rehabilitative measures that substantially improve the lives of most afflicted people. Treatment outcomes and accountability are becoming major issues in the mental health field just as they are in the health field in general. It has been said, in fact, that "the real revolution that is going to occur in health care reform is accountability."[93]

Accountability and treatment outcome measurements should be important in any healthcare system, either public or private, but they become especially important when public agencies contract for services with private organizations, and thus remove the services from the direct control of elected or appointed officials. The potential for private sector providers to deliver more effective and more efficient health services than those of the public sector providers is matched only by the potential for private sector providers to exploit the system for their personal gain.

Much of the recent interest in measuring treatment outcomes for health care was stimulated by health reform proposals under the Clinton administration. These included a proposal to provide consumers with an annual "report card," which would have listed data on as many as 50 criteria that could be used in choosing competing health plans. A number of states, including New York, Pennsylvania, Florida, Colorado, Oregon, and California, have been actively developing criteria that consumers can use to judge health care systems. In 1995, the National Committee for Quality Assessment published a rating of health plans based on a survey of patients.[94] In addition, Care Data, a New York research firm, published comparative member satisfaction data after surveying 10,272 individuals who belonged to 33 different health plans.[95]

The development of measures for treatment outcomes in psychiatric care is still in its early stages. There has been much discussion about what to measure and how to handle the data, but the consensus appears to be that outcome measures must be both subjective, from the point of view of patients and their families, as well as objective, as rated by outside observers. It is also possible to measure treatment outcomes from different perspectives, for example, from the point of view of individual patients, from the point of view of treatment programs serving multiple patients, and from the point of view of the families and communities that must live with the failure or success of these programs. Many methods for organizing treatment outcome data have been proposed, and the matrix and examples described in the following text and summarized in Table 7.3 are merely illustrative.

Person—Subjective Measures

The subjective measurement of treatment outcomes can be done using measures of quality of life. According to a recent medical review, "since

TABLE 7.3
Measuring Treatment Outcomes for Persons with Serious Mental Illnesses

	Subjective Measures	Objective Measures
Person	Self ratings of quality of life	Interviewer ratings of the person's quality of life and severity of symptoms
Program	Consumer ratings of inpatient, outpatient, rehabilitation, housing, and other services	Patient care indicators; JCAHO,* HCFA,† and other surveys and site visits, preferably unannounced
Family and Community	Family satisfaction surveys; surveys of police and jail personnel, public shelter and soup kitchen managers	Quantitative information from family surveys; number of mentally ill persons using soup kitchens or sleeping in parks; number of police calls for cases related to mental illness

*Joint Commission of Accreditation of Healthcare Organizations.
†Health Care Financing Administration.

the 1970s, the measurement of quality of life has grown from a small cottage industry to a large academic enterprise."[96] Proposed instruments for measuring medical aspects of the quality of life number more than a hundred, the field has its own journal, appropriately named *Quality of Life*, and in 1994 the inaugural meeting of the International Health Related Quality of Life Society took place.[97] For individuals with mental illnesses at least 8 different self-rating quality of life questionnaires have been proposed. Those that have been used most widely in the United States have been the Lehman Quality of Life Interview, developed by Anthony Lehman and colleagues at the University of Maryland, and the Oregon Quality of Life Scale, developed by Douglas Bigelow and colleagues at the University of Oregon.[98]

Quality of life questionnaires for the mentally ill ask them to rate on a scale their relative satisfaction in areas such as housing, food, clothing, income, daily activities, leisure, social relations, family relations, safety, neighborhood, work, religion, health, and tolerance of stress. The questionnaires are of varying lengths, and some have published norms for samples of psychiatric patients in different diagnostic groups.

Person—Objective Measures

Many of the self-rated questionnaires using quality of life measures also have versions that can be filled out by interviewers. The areas to be rated include those previously listed. Inter-rater reliability and validity have been established for some of these instruments. One widely used instrument for objectively assessing persons with serious psychiatric illnesses is the Multnomah Community Ability Scale, which was developed for case managers in Oregon.[99] It is a 17-item scale that can be completed in 5 to 7 minutes and includes an assessment of physical health, intellectual functioning, thought processes, mood abnormality, response to stress, ability to manage money, independence in daily life, acceptance of illness (insight), social acceptability by others, interest in socializing, ability to socialize, extent of social network, meaningful daily activity, medication compliance, cooperation with treatment providers, alcohol or drug abuse, and impulse control.

Objective assessments of treatment outcomes are especially useful for measuring progress; a Canadian study used such an instrument to determine whether the quality of life of patients discharged from psychiatric hospitals continued to improve one and three years after discharge.[100] The Multnomah Community Ability Scale is said to be "highly predictive of inpatient utilization." Other objective scales focusing on treatment outcomes for individual patients have been developed to target specific populations, such as the Sickness Impact Profile used for patients with schizophrenia who are on medication,[101] and a Quality of Life Scale that "is widely used in the evaluation of pharmacologic treatments for schizophrenia."[102]

Program—Subjective Measures

Many of the previously described quality of life scales for patients include questions regarding the person's satisfaction with his or her treatment program. In addition, rating forms have been created to specifically assess this. An example is the Mental Health Consumer Survey and Mental Health Consumer Interview developed by the Department of Psychiatry, University of Washington, under a contract with the Washington State Mental Health Division.[103] Beginning in 1997, the State Mental Health Division is planning to use these surveys to evaluate services for all state contracts for mental health services. The consumer survey includes eight questions that the respondent answers on a 1-to-4 scale:

1. How would you rate the quality of service you have received?
2. Did you get the kind of service you wanted?
3. To what extent has the service met your needs?
4. If a friend were in need of similar help, would you recommend the service to him or her?
5. How satisfied are you with the amount of help you received?
6. Have the services you received helped you deal more effectively with your problems?
7. In an overall, general sense, how satisfied are you with the service you have received?
8. If you were to seek help again, would you come back to the service?

The consumer interview complements the survey by collecting quantitative information on the person's utilization of mental health services. For example, the interview asks how often the person sees his or her therapist, psychiatrist, case manager, and nurse. Such surveys and interviews can be targeted to particular services such as inpatient, outpatient, rehabilitation, or housing. In medicine, such surveys have been found to be useful in predicting future utilization of services. For example, a Canadian study found that homeless adults who were more satisfied with the care they received during an emergency room visit had one-third fewer return visits within one month compared with homeless adults who were less satisfied with their care.[104]

Program—Objective Measures

Objective measures of quality in health and mental health programs have been the mainstay of program evaluation for many years. Most prominent among them have been the accreditation surveys of the Joint Commission on Accreditation of Healthcare Organizations (JCAHO) and the certification surveys of the federal Health Care Financing Administration (HCFA). JCAHO accreditation is required for participation in the Medicare program and, in most states, Medicaid.

JCAHO accreditation and HCFA certification are of limited usefulness for assessing treatment outcomes because their focus is primarily on structure and process. They assess how many psychiatrists are on staff, whether there are regular meetings of specified review committees, whether patient charts contain various notes of specified periodicity, and whether fire doors meet regulations, but they make little attempt to assess what actually happens to patients. The surveys are also voluntary and are usually announced weeks in advance. It is thus possible to get a hospital ready for a survey that occurs once every 3 years but to let it deteriorate for the other 2 years and 11 months. An extreme version of temporary improvements is the midwestern state that allegedly purchased new furniture for one state psychiatric hospital and then moved it from hospital to hospital a few days before the JCAHO accrediting team arrived. Recently JCAHO has begun doing more unannounced surveys; in the first half of 1995 it made 17 unannounced visits for psychiatrically related reasons.[105] JCAHO accreditation surveys are also expensive and are completely paid for by the hospitals; a 1989 estimate of costs for a survey of the UCLA Neuropsychiatric Hospital totaled $326,784, "which represented about 1 percent of the hospital's operating budget for 1989."[106] Finally, JCAHO is a private organization and limits the information that it makes available to the public.

The Accreditation Council on Services for People with Disabilities is another private accrediting agency; it was originally formed by the American Association on Mental Deficiency, the Council for Exceptional Children, and the United Cerebral Palsy Association to set standards and accredit residential facilities for the disabled. In 1993, it took a major step forward by changing the focus of its inspections from process measures to outcome measures. The underlying question regarding eligibility for accreditation was changed from "how were the services or supports provided?" to "what did the service or support do *for* the person?"[107] The outcome-based performance measures utilized by the Accreditation Council include such items as "people choose where and with whom they live," "people have friends," and "people are respected." The limitations of the Accreditation Council are similar to those of JCAHO: Accreditation is voluntary, inspections are usually announced, and most information on deficiencies is not made public.

Another common approach to the objective evaluation of mental health programs is the collection of patient care indicators such as hospital readmission rates, median length of hospitalizations, time spent living in the community between hospitalizations, percentage of persons with severe mental illnesses per total outpatient clinic population, frequency of clinic staff contact with severely mentally ill people, waiting time for initial outpatient appointments, and response time for professionals to return emergency calls. Most states collect some data, although the validity and value vary widely. In New Hampshire, for example, where state officials conduct twice yearly random chart audits in mental health centers to ascertain the validity of data, the quality is much better than in the majority of states that do not perform audits.

These patient care indicators, by themselves, are of limited value in assessing outcome or quality of care. For example, a low hospital readmission rate for psychiatric patients may indicate either that community follow-up care is excellent or that virtually no follow-up care is taking place and the patients are ending up homeless or in jail. Similarly a lower median length of hospitalization may indicate that patients are receiving superior psychopharmacologic, nursing, and social services, or are being discharged before they should be returned to the community. Some of the indicators also say more about process than outcomes. For example, frequency of outpatient staff contact with severely ill patients tells nothing about the quality or appropriateness of the contacts. For these reasons, patient care indicators derive their value primarily from their interpretation in light of the other types of outcome data being collected.

A few states have attempted to compare programs across the state by collecting patient care indicators and outcome measures in a uniform format. California began such a project in 1992 at the same time as it shifted primary responsibility for mental health services from the state to the counties. The state has collected data from 59 publicly funded county programs on 21 outcomes for severely mentally ill adults.[108] These outcomes have included measures such as the following:

- Does not require supervision in living situation.
- Income above poverty level.
- Work-force eligible.
- Working 20 or more hours per week.
- Not arrested in last 6 months.
- Was not a crime victim in last 6 months.
- Received dental care within 2 years.
- Attends enjoyable activities with friends.
- Attends community recreational activity at least once a month.

In 1995, the American Managed Behavioral Healthcare Association (AMBHA), which represents many of the mental health managed care companies, announced the development of a "report card on the performance of managed behavioral health care delivery systems."[109] The "report card" utilizes a combination of patient care indicators, such as "percentage of the enrolled population who received services," and consumer satisfaction questions (e.g., "satisfaction with the intake worker"). AMBHA, like JCAHO, represents the providers of services, and it remains to be seen whether they have the ability to do true comparative ratings and to make the results public.

In three states, patient care indicators have been used by state Alliance for the Mentally Ill (AMI) advocacy groups to compare programs. In 1994, the Alabama AMI published *Survey of the State: Alabama's Mental Illness Services* comparing the state's 22 mental health centers on patient care indicators, such as the percentage of patients seen with severe mental illnesses, as well as on ratings of services satisfaction among families and patients.[110] Previously, the North Carolina AMI had published a survey ranking the state's 41 area mental health programs,[111] and the Michigan AMI compiled data on the state's 55 community mental health boards.[112] These commendable efforts, although preliminary, suggest the great potential of advocacy groups in evaluating public psychiatric services.

New York and Illinois use another approach to objective measurements of public mental health programs. Since 1977 in New York, the Commission on Quality of Care for the Mentally Disabled, an independent state agency, has investigated complaints of abuse or fraud received on its toll-free hotline. It also conducts occasional unannounced site visits of hospitals, group homes, and day programs to assess their effectiveness. The agency publishes its findings, including ratings of state facilities and, when necessary, initiates legal action to correct deficiencies.

The Illinois Office of the Inspector General for the Department of Mental Health and Developmental Disabilities performs many of the same functions as the NYS Commission on Quality of Care. It also investigates abuse and by mandate conducts unannounced site visits to each of the state's 21 facilities for persons who are mentally ill or developmentally disabled, publicly listing the deficiencies. In 1995, Inspector General C. J. Dombrowski set a new standard of performance for such positions when she anonymously signed herself into a state psychiatric hospital for three days to assess the quality of care firsthand.[113]

Family and Community—Subjective Measures

Treatment outcomes can be measured from the point of view of a person or a treatment program, and they can also be measured from the point of view of a person's family or community. An increasing number of treatment programs, both inpatient and outpatient, are using questionnaires to assess the satisfaction of patients' families with the treatment being provided to their family members. The Virginia Department of Mental Health uses a simple, two-page pencil-and-paper survey with ratings of statements such as "My family member was treated with dignity," "I was informed about my family member's progress in treatment," and "I was involved in discharge planning." The Riverside County Department of Mental Health in California has taken subjective family measurement one step further by employing a full-time Family Advocate whose job is to solicit information from families about problems in the county mental health treatment system.

Members of the community can also offer subjective opinions about the efficacy of public psychiatric treatment programs. Managers of public shelters and soup kitchens, police officers, and jail personnel have a unique and important perspective for gauging how well the psychiatric care system is working and whether it is getting better or worse. Investigators could also survey random citizens' perception of how many mentally ill persons in the community are homeless or threatening; in cities with outstanding public psychiatric services, responses to such surveys should differ significantly from those in cities where public psychiatric services are markedly deficient.

Family and Community—Objective Measures

Objective data on the effects of mental illnesses on families can be obtained with random samples. In 1991, the National Alliance for the

Mentally Ill used this approach by engaging researchers at Johns Hopkins University to survey 1,401 randomly selected families. The data included how frequently the person had acted violently toward family members and how much time and money the family was spending on the care and support of the ill person.

At the community level, objective data on treatment outcomes are obtainable from periodic censuses of parks, soup kitchens, jails, and other locations where untreated mentally ill people congregate in large numbers. Another reliable gauge is the number of police calls involving mentally ill persons within a specific time period or reported episodes of violence involving these persons. Objective data obtained from mentally ill persons who respond to surveys may have a direct bearing on the quality of life in the community (e.g., "How often have you slept in parks or other outside public locations in the past year?" "How many times have you been involved in a fight in the past year?" "Have you been arrested within the past year?").

The collection of subjective and objective data on treatment outcomes makes possible performance contracting for services. According to Christopher Jencks: "The idea behind performance contracting is simple: Service providers should be paid more when they do a good job."[114] For performance contracting to work, there must be three things: (1) objectives, (2) means of measuring progress toward those objectives, and (3) contract funds that are payable at an agreed-on rate if objectives are met but at a bonus rate if objectives are exceeded. The last is essentially two-pot funding: one pot is given for doing the job as specified, but a second pot is added for doing an especially good job.

Performance contracting has become prominent in the federal government. Under a proposed program of "Performance Partnership Grants," the federal government and states would agree on specific health objectives, such as increasing the number of children who are fully vaccinated, and then the federal government would pay states for achieving those objectives. Performance contracting is most effective when service providers have as much freedom as possible to use resources to achieve the objectives. The emphasis is on achieving the objectives—the outcome—and not on the steps used to get there—the process. In August 1995, the National Academy of Sciences convened a two-day meeting on performance contracting.

For psychiatric services, a type of performance contracting was developed in Oregon in the 1970s and was included as a recommendation in the 1978 report of President Carter's Commission on Mental Health.[115] It emphasized equal partnership of the local, state, and federal levels of government in establishing performance objectives and the criteria against which they would be evaluated. An important by-product of this attempt to implement performance contracting was guidelines establishing that people with severe mental illnesses should have priority for state-funded services over those with less severe illnesses. The establishment of priorities for services is inherent in performance contracting and will be discussed at greater length in Chapter 9.

Chapter 8

FROM LEGAL FOLLY TO COMMON SENSE: THE RIGHT TO GET WELL

We owe the harmless lunatic a duty to save him from perpetual lunacy if we can. To leave him wholly to himself, even though he hurts no one, is not always kind. Such a course endangers incurable chronicity, and this is cruel to him.[1]

Editorial, *Alienist and Neurologist,* 1883

Patients wander our streets, lost in time, as if in a medieval city. We are protecting their civil liberties much more adequately than we are protecting their minds and their lives.[2]

LLOYD M. SIEGEL, *New York Times,* 1981

The United States, which constitutes only 5 percent of the world's population, has 75 percent of the world's lawyers. According to Philip Howard in *The Death of Common Sense:* "Law, supposedly the backdrop for society, has been transformed into one of its main enterprises. . . . Law itself, not the goals to be advanced by law, is now our focus. Indeed, the main lesson of law without judgment is that law's original goal is lost."[3]

In no area is law without judgment more clearly illustrated than for legal aspects of severe mental illnesses. Psychiatrist Darold Treffert has described a case in which a man, diagnosed with schizophrenia, had been jailed on a misdemeanor charge. The man was known to respond to medication but had no insight into his illness, so he did not take medication voluntarily. At a hearing to determine whether the man was a danger to himself or others and could therefore be treated involuntarily, he was described as refusing to eat or bathe, continuously mute, staring blankly at the ceiling of his jail cell, and "obviously ill to anyone viewing him." Furthermore "a jailor saw him eating feces from the toilet bowl." This last behavior became the focus of the hearing and led to the following exchange between the man's public defender and a psychiatrist who had examined the man:

> *Public defender:* Doctor, would the eating of fecal material on one occasion by an individual pose a serious risk of harm to that person?

> *Doctor:* It is certainly not edible material. . . . It contains elements that are considered harmful or unnecessary.

> *Public defender:* But, doctor, you cannot state whether the consumption of such material on one occasion would invariably harm a person?

> *Doctor:* Certainly not on one occasion.[4]

The public defender then moved to dismiss the action on the grounds that the man was in no imminent danger of physical injury or dying. The judge agreed and dismissed the case. In discussing the case, Treffert derided lawyers' claims that they are protecting a person's liberties in such situations: "The liberty to be naked in a padded cell in a county jail, hallucinating and tormented, without treatment that ought to be given is not liberty; it is another form of imprisonment—imprisonment for the crime of being ill."

Barriers to Treatment

The historical road leading to such legal absurdities has been described by sociologist Rael Jean Isaac and writer Virginia Armat in *Madness in the Streets.* The road began in the civil rights era of the 1960s, when the mentally ill were identified by some lawyers as "a group to be 'liberated' along with blacks, Hispanics, and Third World peoples."[5] In Connecticut, for example, the same lawyers who fought to get mentally ill patients released from psychiatric hospitals also defended the Black Panthers.[6] The goals of the lawyers were to liberate patients who were already hospitalized, to abolish all future involuntary hospitalizations, and ultimately to close the hospitals. A lawyer with the Mental Health Law Project in Washington, DC, summarized his philosophy in 1974: "They're better off outside of a hospital with no care than they are inside with no care. The hospitals are what really do damage to people."[7] Bruce Ennis, a leading lawyer for the American Civil Liberties Union, sounded a similar note: "The goal should be nothing less than the abolition of involuntary hospitalization."[8] Joel Klein, who also worked with the Mental Health Law Project in the 1970s, described the carefully planned legal strategies used by mental health lawyers to close the hospitals because the lawyers believed "that mental hospitals would never be good enough."[9]

The lawyers' first victory in their struggle to liberate hospitalized patients, abolish involuntary commitment, and close state psychiatric hospitals took place in the District of Columbia in 1964, the same year in which the Federal Civil Rights Law was passed. Up until that time, decisions on whether or not to involuntarily commit a psychiatric patient to a hospital were generally left in the hands of psychiatrists. If patients were deemed to be in need of treatment, that was sufficient reason to commit them. In 1964, however, the grounds for commitment in the District of Columbia were changed so that only patients who were a danger to themselves or others could be committed; being in need of treatment was no longer sufficient. In legal terms, the rationale for involuntary commitment was changed from *parens patria*, the responsibility of the state to act as parent and protect disabled persons, to a police power in which the state takes action only if a person is deemed to be dangerous.

In 1966, the United States court in the District of Columbia gave lawyers another important victory when it ruled that patients in St. Elizabeth's Hospital, the District's equivalent of a state psychiatric hospital, were entitled to be treated in a setting that was "the least restrictive alternative." In making the ruling, Judge David Bazelon wrote: "Deprivations of liberty solely because of dangers to the ill persons themselves should not go beyond what is necessary for their protection."[10] Lawyers seized on this ruling to bring suit in almost every state to force psychiatric hospitals to discharge patients to community facilities. As psychiatrists Mark Munetz and Jeffrey L. Geller noted in their analysis of the consequences of this ruling, "Underlying the concept of the least restrictive alternative was a desire to close the public mental hospitals."[11]

The passage of California's Lanterman-Petris-Short (LPS) Act in 1967 was the next legal decision that made rational treatment for the mentally ill increasingly difficult. LPS not only restricted involuntary commitment to persons who were dangerous to self or others or gravely disabled, defined as being unable to feed, clothe, or shelter themselves, but also said that even those who were dangerous could only be involuntarily committed for a maximum of 31 days unless the court appointed a conservator.

The legislative commission that drew up the LPS Act stated explicitly that its intent was to close the state psychiatric hospitals. One of the act's cosponsors described the commission's reasoning this way: "We decided that no law could safely set normative standards for mental health. We remembered that . . . today's madmen can become tomorrow's heroes."[12]

The late 1960s also saw the implementation of Medicaid, Medicare, SSI, SSDI, federal food stamps, and other components of the federal fiscal carrot (see Chapter 7). "Tomorrow's heroes" were therefore discharged from state psychiatric hospitals in increasingly large numbers, driven out by the odd alliance of civil liberties lawyers and conservative state legislators who encouraged deinstitutionalization to save state funds. Either the legal push of changed commitment laws or the fiscal pull of the federal programs would, by itself, have been a powerful engine to drive deinstitutionalization. The synergistic combination caused deinstitutionalization to careen out of control and down a steep embankment, where it remains to this day.

By the early 1970s, lawyers specializing in the civil rights of psychiatric patients had become well organized. Using a variety of legal stratagems, they attacked on several fronts and gained an important victory in a 1971 Alabama court ruling, *Wyatt v. Stickney*. The court ruled that hospitalized psychiatric patients have a right to treatment and that the state must provide adequate staff and resources to provide such treatment. The court even mandated staff-to-patient ratios for psychiatrists, psychologists, social workers, and other professionals. Some of these ratios were patently unattainable, thereby putting pressure on hospitals to discharge patients to improve staff-to-patient ratios. This was what the lawyers intended.[13]

The 1972 *Lessard v. Schmidt* ruling in Wisconsin was equally influential. Until that time, a mentally ill person could be involuntarily hospitalized in Wisconsin if the person required "care and treatment for his own welfare or the welfare of others in the community." In the *Lessard* decision, the judge fundamentally changed the basis of commitment from a civil procedure based on need for treatment to a criminal procedure based on dangerousness. The ruling said that a person could be committed only if "there is an extreme likelihood that if the person is not confined he will do immediate harm to himself or others." Use of words like "extreme" and "immediate" made commitment very difficult. The *Lessard* decision also influenced court rulings in many other states. According to psychiatrist Paul Applebaum, prior to the *Lessard* decision, only nine states used "dangerousness" as the sole criterion for involuntary psychiatric hospitalization, but by the end of the 1970s:

Every state had changed its statute to restrict hospitalization to persons who were dangerous to themselves or others (including dangerousness by virtue of grave disability, defined as an inability to meet one's basic needs) or had interpreted its preexisting statute in this way so as to save it from being found unconstitutional.[14]

In the 1975 case of O'Connor v. Donaldson, mental health lawyers in Florida devised yet another strategy for forcing psychiatric hospitals to discharge patients. Kenneth Donaldson, who had previously been hospitalized and treated for paranoid delusions, was involuntarily admitted to a state psychiatric hospital in 1956. He refused medications and all other treatments but was finally released in 1971. With the assistance of Bruce Ennis and other lawyers, Donaldson then sued the hospital and two of his doctors for confining him for almost 15 years but failing to properly treat him—even though he had refused treatment. Incredibly, the court ruled in Donaldson's favor and assessed compensatory damages of $38,500, later reduced to $20,000, against the doctors. As noted by Isaac and Armat, the major effect of the Donaldson decision was to establish "the principle of the personal liability of psychiatrists in state hospitals. . . . For psychiatrists, it was easier to release patients than to run the risk of damage suits."[15]

The Wyatt, Lessard, and Donaldson decisions were merely the most highly publicized cases among dozens filed by mental health lawyers in the 1970s. These decisions exerted continuing pressure on state hospital physicians and administrators to discharge existing patients and to reject new ones. Still another strategy adopted by the lawyers in the late 1970s was to prevent the treatment of hospitalized psychiatric patients by securing their rights to refuse to take medication; this strategy both encouraged discharges and discouraged admissions.

The most highly publicized cases in the right-to-refuse-medication campaign were Rogers v. Okin, in Massachusetts, and Rennie v. Klein, in New Jersey. In the Rogers case, the judge described medications used to treat psychiatric patients as "mind-altering" and causing "involuntary mind control," virtually ignoring any therapeutic benefit the drugs might have. He therefore ruled that patients had the right to refuse treatment pending a separate judicial hearing for each case. The effect of the ruling was that severely mentally ill patients could be involuntarily committed to a hospital, but the hospital staff could not treat the person without first having a separate court hearing. Alan Stone, President of the American Psychiatric Association at that time, labeled the Rogers decision "the most impossible, ill-considered judicial decision in the field of mental health law."[16]

In creating barriers to the treatment of people with mental illnesses, lawyers have played the leading role. They have had help, however, from a small group of civil libertarian psychiatrists, from Scientologists, and from the federal government through its Legal Services and Protection and Advocacy programs.

Civil libertarian psychiatrists have testified in opposition to involuntary treatment both in individual cases as well as in class action court suits. For example, New York psychiatrist Robert Gould testified that Joyce Brown, the mentally ill street person described in Chapter 5, did not need to be hospitalized and could live successfully on steam grates on the streets. In defending his testimony, Gould later wrote: "We have seen the disastrous results of the abuses of psychiatry in totalitarian regimes and must be on our guard to protect the integrity of the psychiatric profession in this country as well."[17]

Another group that has helped mental health lawyers create barriers to the treatment of psychiatric patients is the Scientologists. An arm of Scientology, the Citizens Commission on Human Rights was established in 1969 "to investigate and expose psychiatric violations of human rights"[18] and has published numerous attacks against involuntary psychiatric hospitalization and the use of psychiatric medications. A 1994 Scientologist publication on involuntary psychiatric hospitalization labeled it as "a truly concrete foundation for totalitarianism" and urged its abolition. The publication also recommended that any psychiatrist who involuntarily hospitalized a psychiatric patient "should be charged with assault and false imprisonment."[19] The publication further claimed that citizens are in danger of being involuntarily psychiatrically hospitalized if "you have a fight with your neighbor who reports you to the police," "you leave a party intoxicated and are walking down the street," or you have neck pain and "a psychiatrist diagnoses this as a 'pain disorder associated with a medical condition.'" Part of the influence of the Scientologists has also come from their support of psychiatrists who oppose involuntary hospitalization and the use of medications. One of these, Dr. Peter Breggin, is married to a former Scientologist and has acknowledged receiving "extensive help from reform-minded allies in the worldwide Church of Scientology."[20]

Perhaps the most important group that has assisted mental health lawyers to erect barriers to psychiatric treatment is, oddly, the U.S. government. The government's support came initially from the Legal Services Corporation, begun as part of President Lyndon Johnson's Great Society programs and intended to provide legal services to poor people. Many civil rights lawyers who wanted to "liberate" psychiatric patients were attracted to the Legal Services Corporation and proceeded to use it for their own purposes. For example, the court suit leading to the *Lessard* decision was filed by the Milwaukee Legal Services[21] and the suit leading to the *Rogers* decision was filed by the Greater Boston Legal Services.[22] As Isaac and Armat noted, in the *Rogers* case one arm of the federal government sued a state government to block psychiatric treatment; taxpayers therefore paid for the lawyers' fees on both sides and also for the settlement of over one million dollars.[23]

Since 1986, the federal government has also helped mental health lawyers create barriers to psychiatric treatment through the Protection and Advocacy for Individuals with Mental Illness Act, usually referred to simply as the "P and A Act." This legislation was intended to enable states to establish services for preventing the abuse and neglect of hospitalized patients with mental illnesses. Like the Legal Services Corporation, however, most state Protection and Advocacy programs were soon taken over by lawyers whose main interests were in "liberating" hospitalized patients and in making it as difficult as possible to involuntarily hospitalize or treat people with psychiatric disorders. Studies of Protection and Advocacy programs show that only 25 percent of their activity has been on cases of patient abuse and neglect. Thirty-nine percent more has been on cases involving "access to services" and 35 percent on "forced treatment" or "inappropriate treatment."[24]

In New York state, for example, the federally funded Protection and Advocacy agency brought suit against a Kingston hospital alleging that psychiatrists at the hospital were involuntarily hospitalizing mentally ill patients who were not "imminently" dangerous to themselves or others. In Kansas, the state Protection and Advocacy agency adopted as a priority the goal of making it easier for hospitalized psychiatric patients to refuse medication. Isaac and Armat summarized the situation:

> In Hawaii, Kentucky, Oregon, Rhode Island, West Virginia, and California, P and A agencies labored to prevent legislative reforms of commitment laws to make it possible to treat severely ill patients before they become actively "dangerous." The right to refuse treatment has become a priority issue for a number of these agencies.[25]

In addition to creating barriers to psychiatric treatment, the federally funded Protection and Advocacy program has also been a major source of funds for people and groups who deny the existence of mental illnesses altogether. Federal Protection and Advocacy funds, along with other federal funds from the National Institute of Mental Health and Center for Mental Health Services, have been the main source of financial support for an annual conference at which these groups attack psychiatry. For example, at the 1995 conference one speaker, Al Siebert, presented a paper entitled "Successful Schizophrenia" in which he called schizophrenia "a healthy, valid, desirable condition—not a disorder" and claimed that "what is called schizophrenia in young people appears to be a healthy transformational process that should be facilitated instead of treated."[26]

Ironically, at the same time as federal funds under Legal Services and the Protection and Advocacy programs have been used to deny the existence of mental illnesses and to help lawyers erect barriers to treatment, other federal funds have been used to conduct research on the causes of mental illnesses and to find better treatments. Frequently, a single agency, the National Institute of Mental Health, has simultaneously funded research to find better treatments *and efforts by lawyers to ensure that the treatments cannot be used.* This would be analogous to having the National Cancer Institute, which funds research on the causes and treatment of cancer, also fund legal services to protect the rights of smokers to smoke. Many severe mental illnesses are marked by disorders of thinking that impair logical thought. In this case, the federal government appears to have implemented disordered thinking as its official policy.

The federal Protection and Advocacy program, funded at over $20 million per year, was created in 1986 to be part of the solution to the mental illness crisis. Instead, the program has become part of the problem, and it should therefore be abolished.

The Consequences of Legal Folly

Michael Perry, diagnosed with schizophrenia at age 16, was hospitalized twice at Central State Hospital in Louisiana.[27] Following discharge from the hospital, he was referred to a mental health center for follow-up care, but the follow-up never took place. Mr. Perry had no insight into his illness and refused to take medication when not hospitalized. Louisiana has an outpatient commitment statute under which outpatients must take medication, but it is rarely used and was not used in this case.

In July 1983, Mr. Perry, unmedicated, murdered his father and mother, two cousins, and a 2-year-old nephew. Initial psychiatric examinations confirmed that he had chronic schizophrenia and was incompetent to stand trial. He was therefore given antipsychotic medications involuntarily, which produced significant clinical improvement. A psychiatrist then said that Mr. Perry was competent to stand trial and Mr. Perry, appearing to be rational in court, insisted on withdrawing his insanity plea. He therefore had to stand trial for the murders. He was convicted and sentenced to death.

When his medication was stopped again, Mr. Perry relapsed into chronic schizophrenia; his lawyers argued that he therefore could not be executed. A judge ruled that Mr. Perry could be involuntarily medicated so that he could be made sane enough to be executed. The judge's decision was appealed to the United States Supreme Court, and finally in 1992, the Louisiana Supreme Court ruled that Mr. Perry could not be involuntarily medicated just to get him sane enough to execute.

The state of Louisiana was unwilling to use outpatient commitment to involuntarily medicate Mr. Perry to control the symptoms of his illness. But once he committed the crimes, the state was willing to involuntarily medicate him so that he could stand trial for the crimes he committed while unmedicated. Once convicted and sentenced, medication was stopped and he relapsed into psychosis. One court ruled that Mr. Perry could again be involuntarily medicated so that he could be made sane enough to be executed, but the higher courts overruled it. Mr. Perry continues to sit in prison, largely unmedicated and insane, where he will spend the rest of his life. He cannot take medication regularly because if he does he might become sane and could then be executed.

Although this case represents an extreme example of the consequences of mental health law, thousands of less extreme, although equally absurd, cases could be cited. Some people who are involuntarily hospitalized cannot be treated for their mental illness for weeks or months, pending a court hearing. Patients with both tuberculosis and a severe mental illness who refuse medication for both conditions are often involuntarily medicated for their tuberculosis but not for their mental illness. Persons with brain disorders such as schizophrenia and manic-depressive illness are often allowed to live on steam grates and eat from dumpsters, whereas those with other brain disorders such as Alzheimer's disease and multiple sclerosis are not allowed to live that way. And some people with severe mental illnesses are discharged from psychiatric hospitals and allowed to live in roach-infested rooms, jails, public shelters, or cardboard boxes on the street and we call the latter the "least restrictive setting." As psychiatrist Loren Roth succinctly summarized the legal situation: "A large number of patients have been kidnapped by a small number of lawyers in order to make a philosophical point on their behalf."[28]

The most visible consequences of mental health law are homelessness, incarceration, and episodes of violence by the mentally ill. Homelessness is a frequent outcome of a failure to hospitalize. Consider the following:

◇ Judy, diagnosed with paranoid schizophrenia, lives on the streets of New York. "Sometimes she screams for hours at a time, hurling obscenities into the air. . . . She said that she owned all the land in the neighborhood and that she has been on that corner for centuries. . . . Although there have been at least four attempts to institutionalize Judy in several states, she has never been committed to a psychiatric hospital. . . . In 1976, Judy said she was ready to be committed. However, according to her mother, a lawyer visited her in the mental health center where she was awaiting the psychiatric hearing and convinced Judy that she should not be hospitalized. The lawyer then represented Judy at the hearing and the case was dismissed."[29]

◇ A graduate of Harvard University and Columbia Law School, Gary became severely mentally ill and homeless in New York. He was observed eating from garbage cans and had lost much weight. "Gary's friends and family are trying to help him. But apparently because of legal ambiguities involved in committing a person to a psychiatric hospital without his consent, along with a shortage of beds in these hospitals, they have not succeeded. . . . [A former Harvard classmate said] "I told the police 'I know where he is. Why can't I just have his mother come and pick him up?' They told me I could've gone to jail for violating his civil liberties."[30]

◇ She was a college graduate who had been married to a lawyer before she became sick. "The mentally ill woman was on the floor of her Dupont Circle apartment with cockroaches crawling all over her when the Rev. John Steinbruck and his wife Erna found her. She wouldn't talk and she wouldn't eat. The Steinbrucks called in the police to have her committed to St. Elizabeth's mental hospital, where she had been treated before for paranoia. But when the police arrived, the officers said they could not have her committed because she did not pose an immediate life-threatening danger to herself or others, the District's standard for involuntary commitment." She became homeless shortly thereafter.[31]

Police officers and jail officials also experience the consequences of mental health law on a daily basis:

◇ A jail official in Louisiana said, "Once mental cases have been ordered to the state mental hospital, we have a hard time getting the hospitals to take these people."[32]

◇ According to a jail official in Wisconsin, mentally ill individuals in jail "who attempt suicide or whatever, enough to qualify for commitment, are taken to [mental health] professionals for help, but almost beat the transport officer back to the jail because they don't qualify as mentally ill."[33]

◇ In Los Angeles, Michael Love, severely mentally ill, was picked up for a misdemeanor offense and taken to a mental health center for possible hospitalization. "The counselors began a futile, four-hour search for a hospital bed. There were no psychiatric beds available anywhere in Los Angeles County," nor would there be "in the foreseeable future." Love was therefore taken to jail and charged with trespassing.[34]

Such scenarios are common. In an Oregon study that examined cases in which a mentally ill person had been arrested, the researchers found that "in about half the cases a failed attempt at commitment [to a psychiatric hospital] had preceded the arrest."[35]

I have pointed out the relationship between failure to treat and episodes of violence. Failure to take medication is one of three major predictors of violent behavior, yet mental health lawyers have continuously expanded the rights of the mentally ill to refuse medication. The results of a Canadian study indicate that mentally ill people who take medication regularly have a low incidence of violent behavior.[36] Past history of violence is another major predictor of violent behavior, yet in many states mental health lawyers have restricted testimony regarding past episodes of violence in determining the present need for involuntary hospitalization and treatment.

Given the success of mental health law in emptying public psychiatric hospitals and in making it increasingly difficult to hospitalize and treat people with mental illnesses, why are things not even worse than they are? Psychiatrist Paul Applebaum provides a partial answer to this question in his book *Almost a Revolution*. He contends that when "confronted with psychotic persons who might well benefit from treatment, and who would certainly suffer without it, mental health professionals and judges alike were reluctant to comply with the law...."[37] In what Applebaum labels "the dominance of the commonsense model," the laws are sometimes simply disregarded.

Applebaum also contends that mental health professionals regularly use "their discretion to expand the scope of commitment statutes by admitting patients who might not qualify under strict criteria but are thought to be in need of care."[38] It would probably be difficult to find any American psychiatrist working with the mentally ill who has not, at a minimum, exaggerated the dangerousness of a mentally ill person's behavior to obtain a judicial order for commitment of someone in need of care.

Families also exaggerate their family member's symptoms to get the person committed to a hospital. In a 1989 study of 83 families in Philadelphia, 18 percent "said they had lied or exaggerated to officials in order to get a relative committed. Experience, they said, taught them that they had no choice. In fact a number of local officials with the Alliance for the Mentally Ill (AMI), a nationwide support group for families, say they privately counsel families to lie, if necessary, to get acutely ill relatives hospitalized. . . . They say they were attacked when they weren't; they say their children tried to kill themselves when they didn't. . . . 'How else are you going to get them any help?' asked Joy McCoy, president of the Delaware County AMI."[39] Thus, ignoring the law, exaggerating symptoms, and outright lying by families to get care for those who need it are important reasons the mental illness system is not even worse than it is.

A tragic consequence of the efforts of mental health lawyers to make it difficult to hospitalize and treat the mentally ill is that the person's symptoms may irreversibly worsen. It has been suspected for many years that a failure to treat people with medication may cause permanent damage, but data to support this suspicion have only recently become available. In 1991, for example, the psychiatrist Richard Wyatt published an analysis of 22 studies in which persons with schizophrenia were maintained off medication for varying periods. Wyatt concluded "that some patients are left with a damaging residual if a psychosis is allowed to proceed unmitigated [without medication] . . . it may be biologically toxic."[40] Since 1991, studies by McEvoy et al.,[41] Lieberman et al.,[42] and Waddington et al.[43] have demonstrated that people with schizophrenia who have gone for an extended period without medication take longer to respond to medication, do not respond as well, and are more likely to have residual symptoms such as muteness and cognitive dysfunction. It has also been shown that discontinuing lithium medication for manic-depressive patients may produce an irreversible worsening of symptoms; the person does not respond as well to lithium when it is restarted.[44] The situation with severe mental illnesses thus appears analogous to that for insulin-dependent diabetes, in which failure to medicate produces irreversible damage to the kidney, eye, and circulatory system.

These findings have profound implications for mental health law. Since failure to treat appears to produce irreversible clinical deterioration in some cases, lawyers who urge mentally ill clients to not take medication, and who work to change laws so that it becomes extremely difficult to medicate those who are mentally ill, might theoretically be liable for damages if sued later by these people. Since knowledge of the damaging long-term effects of the failure to medicate is recent, lawyers could not be sued retrospectively for actions impeding treatment prior to approximately 1991, but actions after that date may be potentially litigable. Suits could be brought either on behalf of a person against a specific lawyer or by class action against an organization such as the Bazelon Center for Mental Health Law (formerly the Mental Health Law Project) in Washington, the New York Civil Liberties Union, or specific Protection and Advocacy agencies.

Another consequence of mental health law is a significant increase in treatment costs. For example, a Massachusetts study compiled data on the estimated number of staff hours required to process patients' refusals to take medication during the 18 months following the *Rogers* court decision.[45] Approximately 7,000 hours of staff time were required for psychiatrists and other mental health professionals to prepare documents, meet with attorneys, travel to hearings, and testify. An additional 10,500 hours of Department of Mental Health lawyers' time and 3,000 hours of paralegal time were spent handling the petitions and working on the cases. This time estimate did not include the hours invested by the attorneys for the patients, independent evaluators, court personnel, or judges.

Such expenses also do not include the costs of the mentally ill people occupying hospital beds while they await court hearings. In Massachusetts, this averaged between 60 and 120 days per person. In New York State, it averaged 38 days, and a study estimated the bed costs as $3.4 million for one year.[46] In Minnesota, it averaged 80 days, and for one hospital alone "researchers estimated that the costs incurred in processing sixteen refusing patients over two years totaled $150,000."[47]

In addition to costs associated with the rights of the mentally ill to refuse treatment, there are also costs associated with the relapse and rehospitalization of ill people who discontinue their medication. Mental health lawyers have played a major role in encouraging discontinuance of medication by exaggerating long-term side effects and by impeding the use of conditional release, outpatient commitment, guardianship, and other legal mechanisms designed to improve medication compliance. Psychiatrists Peter Weiden and Mark Olfson published an extensive analysis of the direct cost of rehospitalization for persons with schizophrenia who discontinue their medication; the cost for a two-year period in the United States was $740 million.[48]

The Issue of Insight

The problem of insight is fundamental to thinking about legal aspects of treatment for the mentally ill. It is the problem of the self-measuring ruler and what to do when the ruler is broken. The noted psychiatrist Emil Kraepelin recognized early in this century that "understanding of the disease [schizophrenia] disappears fairly rapidly as the malady progresses in an overwhelming majority of cases,"[49] but until recently, surprisingly little research had been carried out on this phenomenon.

An extensive study of insight in 412 people with various psychoses and depression was published by Xavier Amador and his colleagues in New York.[50] Using a scale to assess insight "across a variety of manifestations of illness," they found that among 221 persons with schizophrenia, 57 percent were markedly (32 percent) or moderately (25 percent) unaware that they were psychiatrically impaired. Among 40 persons with manic-depressive illness, awareness was slightly better, although the "severely manic BP [manic-depressive] group scored as poorly as the SZ [schizophrenic] group on the majority of items."

These findings are similar to another study of insight carried out in "91 mixed psychotic patients" by Anthony David and his colleagues at London's Institute for Psychiatry.[51] They reported that 47 percent of the patients scored 8 points or less on an 18-point scale of insight and thus had markedly or moderately impaired insight. Both studies, therefore, suggest that approximately half of all people with severe mental illnesses have limited insight that they have a brain disorder, need hospitalization, or need medication.

Another psychiatric study supports this conclusion. In assessing insight on 75 recently hospitalized patients diagnosed with schizophrenia, researchers found that only 48 percent "manifested adequate performance across all three measures" of insight, with the sicker patients doing more poorly.[52] The results would have shown even greater loss of insight if the sickest patients had not been excluded from the study because they were unable to participate. Thus, the issue of insight and mental illness appears to be as English writer H. G. Woodley described it in 1947: "Madness is as death, in that one is transferred to another life and, like death, one passes over to it without knowing that one has crossed the border."[53]

That insight is impaired in many who are mentally ill should not be surprising. The brain—the organ we use to think about ourselves—is the same organ that is affected in psychiatric disorders. A preliminary study that attempted to link impaired insight to impaired function of specific brain regions concluded that the frontal lobes are probably affected,[54] but more research needs to be done on this question. It has also become clear that insight is not a unitary phenomenon—people may have insight into one aspect of their illness but not another; for example, they may understand that the voices they hear are coming from inside their head and are not real and yet have no understanding that they need medications to control the voices. Logic, like insight, is sometimes impaired.

Common sense suggests, and research studies confirm, that the mentally ill with greater insight into their condition are more likely to seek psychiatric help when they become sick and also to comply with treatment regimens. A study carried out by researchers in Pittsburgh, found that, among 52 patients with schizophrenia, those with insight were more likely to be admitted to the hospital as voluntary patients, whereas those with little or no insight were more likely to be admitted involuntarily.[55] Another study found that persons with schizophrenia who had impaired insight were less likely to comply with the demands of a work rehabilitation program.[56]

Insight is critical in determining whether or not mentally ill people take the necessary medications to control their symptoms. Obviously, people who do not believe they are sick see little need for medication compliance. Yet, for most people with severe mental illnesses, medications are the single most important component of their treatment plans. The effectiveness of medications for disorders such as schizophrenia and manic-depressive illness has been exhaustively documented (see Chapter 1), and patients who take medications regularly have a much lower rehospitalization rate and a much higher rate of successful rehabilitation.

According to a review of studies on the relationship of insight and medication compliance in schizophrenia, "The bulk of the evidence reviewed supports the general notion that displaying an awareness of illness in schizophrenia is associated with better medication compliance and clinical outcome"[57] One study, for example, reported 45 percent compliance by persons with insight, but only 17 percent among those with impaired insight.[58]

Impaired insight is the single most important reason why the mentally ill do not take medications regularly and is thus the most important cause of relapse. It is, however, not the only cause of medication noncompliance. Medication side effects such as sedation, restlessness, tremors, or sexual impotence also contribute to noncompliance. A poor doctor-patient relationship, concurrent alcohol or drug abuse, confusion about the dosage and timing of the medication, inability to pay for the medication, and fears of becoming addicted are also causes of noncompliance. People with manic-depressive illness may also be noncompliant because they enjoy the highs of their manic state and the self-importance that accompanies grandiose delusions.

Medication noncompliance is not a problem that is unique to mental disorders. Patients have compliance problems with every disease for which long-term medication is necessary—hypertension, rheumatoid arthritis, diabetes, epilepsy, and tuberculosis, to name a few. It is only in severe mental disorders, however, that the *major* cause of noncompliance is impaired insight because critical areas of the brain are affected. And since impaired insight is the most important cause of medication noncompliance and relapse, treatment programs must recognize this fact if they hope to be successful.

The Need for Involuntary Treatment

Except in emergency situations, voluntary persuasion should always first be attempted before involuntarily hospitalizing or medicating a person who is mentally ill. Such attempts should include educating the person about his or her brain disorder, the potential benefits and risks of the proposed treatment, and the risks of nontreatment. It should also include listening carefully to the person's complaints about side effects of previous medication so alternate medications can be considered. Finally, those advocating involuntary treatment must ensure that the treatment facility is physically attractive, competently staffed, and respectful of the person's dignity and privacy. Patients who refuse voluntary hospitalization or medication in a run-down facility staffed by sadistic nursing assistants, an uncaring social worker, and an incompetent psychiatrist may not be refusing treatment because their insight and judgment are impaired but rather because their insight and judgment are perfectly intact.

Ultimately, however, because approximately half of all people with severe mental disorders have impaired insight, involuntary hospitalization and treatment will be necessary to treat some of them. Since they do not believe that anything is wrong with them, they see no reason to accept hospitalization or medication. They *know* the CIA implanted electrodes in their brain that are producing the voices. They *know* they own the White House. They *know* they are loved by a famous movie star. They *know* they are being followed and watched 24 hours a day. And no amount of education or persuasion is going to change their minds.

The voluntary outreach services for the homeless mentally ill who live on streets, in parks, under bridges, and in abandoned buildings illustrate the frequent failure of persuasion. Several cities have implemented such programs, usually run by religious organizations and staffed by humane, patient, and caring outreach workers. In New York City one such organization is Project Reachout, which began services in 1979. Over the years, it has handed out thousands of blankets and tens of thousands of sandwiches in efforts to persuade the homeless mentally ill to accept help. According to one longtime staff member, however, Project Reachout has had only a "handful of successes," but "hundreds of our failures are already dead."[59] Project Reachout, like most similar voluntary outreach programs, does not publish any data on its success rate. With what is now known about impaired insight in most of the homeless mentally ill, it is not surprising that efforts to persuade them should have had such limited success.

Many of those who are seriously ill must therefore be hospitalized and medicated involuntarily, and laws in most states should be changed to accommodate their needs. Because the laws in virtually every state were changed in the 1970s and 1980s to deter involuntary hospitalizations, in most states the person must be a danger to self or others to be committed. In some states and among some judges, this is interpreted very strictly so that, as one exasperated observer noted, "You either have to be trying to kill yourself in front of the judge or trying to kill the judge." Being "gravely disabled" is also a criterion for commitment in some states but, like dangerousness to self or others, it is often interpreted very strictly.

To solve the mental illness crisis, it will be necessary to reinstitute need-for-treatment criteria for commitment. Prior to the rise of the mental health bar, these criteria were included in almost all state commitment statutes, but were subsequently deleted. Studies have shown that among all individuals who can be involuntarily committed for psychiatric treatment under the need-for-treatment criteria, only half of them can also be committed under danger-to-self-or-others criteria.[60] This suggests that a large number of severely ill people cannot be involuntarily treated under present laws because they do not have enough insight to realize that they are sick and need treatment. They constitute the vast majority of the mentally ill who are homeless, in jails and prisons, or involved in acts of violence. It has become clear that dangerousness alone is not a sufficient standard for involuntary treatment. As columnist Charles Krauthammer noted: "That standard is not just unfeeling, it is uncivilized. The standard should not be dangerousness but helplessness. Society has an obligation to save people from degradation, not just death."[61]

In recent years, several states have made efforts to broaden the criteria for commitment, but these efforts have been strongly contested by mental health lawyers. In 1979, Washington became one of the first states to reverse the decade-long trend toward restricting commitment criteria to dangerousness. The impetus to the change was a highly publicized murder of a wealthy Seattle couple by their 23-year-old mentally ill neighbor.[62] The revised Washington commitment criteria included provision for those who were in need of treatment but not necessarily dangerous.

Since 1979, several other states, including Alaska, Arizona, Colorado, Hawaii, Kansas, North Carolina, Rhode Island, and Texas, have also broadened their criteria for involuntary commitment. For example, Hawaii revised its statutes to allow for the commitment of persons who were "obviously ill," which was defined as a "condition in which a person's current behavior and previous history of mental illness, if known, indicate a disabling mental illness, and the person is incapable of understanding that there are serious and highly probably risks to health and safety involved in refusing treatment."[63] Inclusion of the clause "incapable of understanding" introduced the concept of impaired insight into the commitment criteria, something few other states have done.

In 1983, the American Psychiatric Association proposed a model law for the involuntary commitment of mentally ill persons; the law included commitment for persons whose behavior indicates "significant deterioration" of their psychiatric condition and who are thus in need of treatment. The proposed law was sharply criticized by mental health lawyers. Leonard Rubenstein of the Bazelon Center for Mental Health Law labeled it as "a guild product, written simply to reduce society's control over psychiatric decisions"[64] and was quoted as saying: "Outpatient treatment is almost always preferable to institutionalization, and if none is available, many people are better off left in the streets than committed."[65] One defender of involuntary commitment publicly called the opponents of such laws "anti-treatment advocates" and characterized them as follows: "They seem content to sacrifice a few lives here and there to uphold an abstract doctrine. Their intent, if noble, has a chilly, Stalinist justification—the odd tragedy along the way is warranted to ensure the greater good."[66]

In addition to changing standards for the involuntary commitment, it is also necessary to modify the standard of proof required by courts for commitment. To make involuntary commitment more difficult, mental health lawyers successfully persuaded some state legislatures to change the standard of proof from the traditional "clear and convincing evidence" to the much more stringent "beyond a reasonable doubt"—the standard of proof required in criminal cases. In 1979, the United States Supreme Court affirmed that "clear and convincing evidence" was an acceptable level of proof under the Constitution for commitment of mentally disabled persons, although some states still use "beyond a reasonable doubt."

Laws must also be changed in some states so that relevant information for consideration of possible involuntary hospitalization can be entered as evidence. As Richard Lamb and Mark Mills have noted, in such hearings it is more sensible to use informal rules of evidence than to apply strict courtroom procedures: "For example, testimony could be heard from all parties with relevant information without rigorous adherence to such doctrines as the hearsay rule. . . ."[67] This is especially true for information regarding potential dangerousness and need-for-treatment. Past episodes of violence, concurrent abuse of drugs or alcohol, and a history of medication noncompliance are known to be major predictors of potential dangerousness in the mentally ill, yet in some states the person's past history is specifically excluded from consideration.

A provision for interstate reciprocity of commitment should also be developed. Since commitment laws are state, not federal, in origin, a person committed for treatment in one state is not committed when he or she goes to another state. Many of the mentally ill are peripatetic and move continuously from state to state either for delusional reasons or otherwise. Without reciprocity, it will continue to be virtually impossible to get most such persons into treatment. It is also necessary to have interstate reciprocity of medical records and other information relevant for determining a person's possible need for involuntary hospitalization or outpatient treatment.

The issue of involuntary treatment arises most often for those who need to be committed to a psychiatric hospital as inpatients. However, involuntary treatment also may be necessary for mentally ill outpatients. Involuntary treatment of outpatients can take place under three possible conditions: conditional release, guardianship, and outpatient commitment.

Conditional release occurs when a person has been involuntarily committed as an inpatient to a psychiatric hospital and is released a few days or weeks later conditional on taking medication or otherwise following a treatment plan. If such persons do not comply, they can be involuntarily returned to the hospital. The hospital superintendent, not the court, makes the decision. Technically, patients on conditional release remain on the hospital rolls, which makes the hospital legally liable for the persons' actions. For this reason, many states have markedly reduced issuing conditional releases, although they are still widely used in New Hampshire, and also in most states specifically for mentally ill persons who have committed crimes.

Guardianships, also known as conservatorships, occur when the court appoints someone to make treatment decisions for a mentally disabled person. Guardianships are widely used for mentally retarded people and for those who are mentally incapacitated because of Alzheimer's disease or other brain disorders. Only in the state of California and in specific counties such as Dane County, Wisconsin, are guardianships common for people with mental illnesses. A person's guardian can insist that he or she take prescribed medication and can order the person to be involuntarily hospitalized if necessary.

A variant of guardianships that has been used in Oregon and a few other states is an advanced directive document in which mentally ill persons, not the courts, appoint someone they trust to make treatment decisions for them in the event that they become incompetent to do so.[68] These documents are often referred to as "health care proxies" or "Ulysses contracts" after the Greek mythical hero who, to avoid destruction by the seductive sea-nymph Sirens, had his crew bind him to the mast "and his people to be strictly enjoined, whatever he might say or do, by no means to release him until they should have passed the Sirens' island."[69] The problem with such directives is that there is no guarantee the mentally ill person was competent when executing the contract. There is also no provision for ensuring that the person appointed to make treatment decisions has any competency to do so.

A third type of involuntary treatment of psychiatric outpatients is outpatient commitment. This is a court order saying that the mentally ill persons must take medication and comply with other aspects of their treatment plan or that person can be involuntarily hospitalized. Although outpatient statutes exist in 35 states and the District of Columbia, they are only used with any frequency in Arizona, the District of Columbia, Iowa, Kansas, Michigan, Nebraska, North Carolina, North Dakota, Rhode Island, Utah, Vermont, Washington, and Wisconsin.[70]

Conditional releases, guardianships, and outpatient commitments are all effective methods for improving patients' compliance with medication, reducing hospital readmissions, and decreasing violence. Studies in North Carolina[71,72] and Arizona[73] demonstrated that mentally ill persons on outpatient commitment were much more likely to take their medication and follow their treatment plan. Outpatient commitment also reduced rehospitalization by 50 percent in the District of Columbia[74] and by 80 percent in North Carolina.[75] Most importantly, violent behavior was substantially reduced by the use of conditional release in New Hampshire[76] and Oregon[77] and by outpatient commitment in Arizona.[78]

Even with the use of conditional releases, guardianships, and outpatient commitments, compliance with medication is sometimes a problem for those who have limited insight into their need for medication. A variety of mechanisms are available to ensure that such patients get their medication as prescribed; these include direct observation, long-acting injections, blood levels, and urine markers.

In inpatient settings, direct observation is common for persons taking antipsychotic and antimanic medication, as well as for other patients with conditions in which medication compliance is important but problematic (e.g., persons taking antituberculous drugs, Antabuse, or methadone). For those who refuse to take medication and are skilled in appearing to swallow pills but later spit them out, liquid preparations are often used. Intramuscular injections of long-acting depot preparations are also widely used for two commonly used antipsychotics, fluphenazine and haloperidol, but are not available for other antipsychotic or antimanic medications. Such injections are necessary only every two to four weeks.

Measuring blood levels of lithium, widely used to treat manic-depressive illness and sometimes schizophrenia, is an effective means of measuring the lithium taken the previous day but not in the days preceding. For this reason, collecting blood for lithium testing must be done on a random, unannounced basis to measure true compliance. Blood levels of carbamezepine and some other medications used for manic-depressive illness are also reliable, but blood levels of most antipsychotic drugs have not yet become reliable enough to use as indicators of medication compliance.

Measuring medication compliance by testing the urine has been little used but can be done by including small amounts of riboflavin, a water-soluble vitamin, in a capsule with the medication. The riboflavin can then be detected in the urine for up to 24 hours by putting the urine under ultraviolet light. The riboflavin detection test has been used in studies of mentally ill people taking antipsychotic drugs[79,80] as well as in studies of medication compliance in tuberculosis.[81] The riboflavin is tasteless and has no side effects. Its limitation is that the test is qualitative rather than quantitative—it tells you that the person took some medication but not how much. Like blood levels for lithium, the urine riboflavin test only measures medication taken recently so it also would have to be used on a random, unannounced basis to be effective. Isoniazid and its metabolites have also been used as urinary markers of medication compliance.[82,83] Presumably, if pharmaceutical companies perceived a market for such urinary markers, they could develop compounds capable of indicating quantitative as well as qualitative levels of the medication.

Involuntary hospitalization and medication for the mentally ill with impaired insight must include legal safeguards against abuse, including prompt judicial hearings, representation by counsel, and the right to appeal. It may also be appropriate to have laypersons, including mentally ill persons who themselves are in remission, on the mental illness hearings and appeals boards. The average citizen is more willing to commit the disabled for involuntary treatment than is the average judge. In a national survey, 87 percent of people "said that mentally ill homeless [persons] should be sent to mental hospitals even if they don't want to go."[84]

Despite legal safeguards, there will continue to be formidable resistance by mental health lawyers and civil libertarians to involuntary hospitalization and medication. They will claim that individual liberty is more important and that having some untreated mentally ill persons who are homeless, incarcerated, or dead is the price we must pay for such liberty. From a medical point of view, however, defending the right of a person with a severe mental illness to remain psychotic is analogous to defending the right of a person with diabetes to remain in a coma. In a civilized society, liberty and cruelty should not be confused.

Perhaps the best response to the civil libertarian argument against involuntary treatment was offered by Herschel Hardin, who for nine years was Director of the British Columbia Civil Liberties Association. After one of his children developed schizophrenia, he wrote:

> Here is the Kafkaesque irony: Far from respecting civil liberties, legal obstacles to treatment limit or destroy the liberty of the person. . . . Such victims are prisoners of their illness. Their personalities are subsumed by their distorted thoughts. They cannot think for themselves and cannot exercise any meaningful liberty. . . . Medication can free victims from their illness—free them from the Bastille of their psychoses—restore their dignity, their free will and the meaningful exercise of their liberties.[85]

Addressing this problem, the journalist Charles Krauthammer sounded a similar theme:

> In fact, the homeless mentally ill are abandoned, not free. Nor is their degraded condition at all inevitable. It is the result not of mysterious determining forces, but of a failed, though well-intended social policy. And social policy can be changed. In this case, it will not be easy. There will

be a lot of thundering from civil libertarians. But it certainly can be done.[86]

Benefits That Are Not Beneficial

People with severe mental illnesses receive three kinds of income benefits: Supplemental Security Income (SSI), Social Security Disability Income (SSDI), and Veterans Administration (VA) disability payments. SSI is available to anyone who is disabled, has few assets and almost no income; in 1995 the payment was $458 per month for a single adult living alone. SSDI is available only to those who have worked long enough to qualify for Social Security; in 1995, the payment was up to $661 per month for adults. VA disability payments are made to veterans "whose disabilities resulted from injury or disease incurred while in or aggravated by active military duty, whether in wartime or peacetime."[87] Although such benefits are referred to as "service connected," that does not mean that the disease was caused by military service but merely that it began while on military service. Benefits vary depending on the degree of disability, number of dependents, rank, and whether special medical services are needed; in 1995 the basic payment was $1,823 per month regardless of other assets.

The arbitrariness of these programs is striking. Consider three hypothetical men who graduate from high school together. The first man goes to work in a factory, works for two years, then develops schizophrenia and is approved for SSI. The second man goes to work in a factory and works for six years before developing schizophrenia, by which time he qualifies for SSDI. The third man joins the army, but after three years, he too develops schizophrenia and is approved for 100 percent service connected disability. In 1995, the first man would have received $458 per month, the second man $661 per month, and the third man $1,823 per month, all tax free, even though they all have the same disorder and the same degree of disability.

A second noteworthy fact about the SSI, SSDI, and VA benefits programs is that the payments are almost entirely unrelated to the person's treatment and rehabilitation programs. Since the payments all come from federal funds (with the exception of state SSI supplements in 27 states), the incentive at the state and local level is to get as many persons as possible approved for these programs so they will not use welfare benefits or other state or local funds. For example, when a young man with untreated manic-depressive illness applies for SSI, there is no incentive to ascertain whether he would still need SSI if he was being adequately treated. Once the mentally ill person has been approved for federal benefits, there is a disincentive to get well since that would mean possible loss of SSI or SSDI income or of eligibility for Medicaid (for SSI) or Medicare (for SSDI), or the possibility of VA benefits being reduced to a lower level of disability. Professionals who work with the mentally ill often have clients who could hold part-time jobs or work intermittently but who refuse to do so because of their fear of losing their benefits.

The most singular fact about SSI, SSDI, and VA benefits is the degree to which they are being misused to support alcohol and drug abuse. The total amount of money involved is impressive; in 1994 federal benefits paid to the mentally ill included $5.6 billion in SSI, $9.6 billion in SSDI, and $2.2 billion in VA benefits, or $17.4 billion total. The proportion of those funds going to support alcohol and drug abuse is unknown, but there are suggestions that it is substantial.

Andrew Shaner and other researchers at the UCLA School of Medicine studied 105 men who were diagnosed with both schizophrenia and cocaine addiction.[88] They had had an average of 10 psychiatric admissions, and one-third of them were homeless. All the men were receiving SSI, SSDI, or VA disability benefits with an average payment of $650 per month. Over a 15-week period, their expenditures and cocaine use were carefully monitored. The researchers found that "cocaine use, psychiatric symptoms, and hospital admissions all peaked during the first week of the month, shortly after the arrival of the disability payment." Furthermore, "the average patient spent nearly half his total income on illegal drugs," specifically 47 percent on cocaine and 2 percent more on alcohol. Most disturbing was that "many subjects reported spending more—sometimes considerably more—than their total legal income on drugs," suggesting that they were also involved in criminal activities. Sally Satel, a psychiatrist who has studied the problem of the misuse of benefits by psychiatrically ill individuals, labels it "a process of social iatrogenesis: the inadvertent exacerbation of disease by an economic policy intended to promote well-being."[89]

Is there any way to estimate what percentage of the total $17.4 billion in SSI, SSDI, and VA income benefits are being misused for alcohol and drug abuse? A recent study of 253 mentally ill persons in Wisconsin reported that 35 percent of them met diagnostic criteria for alcohol or drug abuse or dependence within the previous year.[90] This finding is consistent with the Epidemiologic Catchment Area (ECA) study and other studies except in urban areas, where the percentage of persons dually diagnosed with mental illness and a drug or alcohol problem may be even higher. If we estimate that 35 percent of the mentally ill have dual diagnoses, and if that subgroup is spending between 25 and 50 percent of their income on alcohol and drugs, then the total amount of SSI, SSDI, and VA income benefits being misused for alcohol and drug abuse is between $1.2 and $2.5 billion. That constitutes a significant contribution to the liquor industry and the illegal drug trade.

The most publicized case of such benefits abuse is Larry Hogue, diagnosed with manic-depressive illness and drug addiction (see Chapter 5). Mr. Hogue received $36,000 per year in VA and other disability benefits, most of which he apparently spent on crack cocaine and other illegal drugs. For 10 years, he terrorized a Westside neighborhood until he became a cause célèbre and was eventually removed from the streets.

For a substantial number of SSI, SSDI, and VA beneficiaries, therefore, the benefits they are receiving are not beneficial. As Sally Satel succinctly notes: "Society's responsibility to the disabled poor involves helping them meet their basic needs, not subsidizing their self-destruction."[91] What are the solutions?

First, suggestions have been made but not implemented that all mentally ill persons with dual diagnoses of alcohol or drug addiction should automatically have responsible representative payees. For many, the most appropriate payee would be their treatment program so that the misuse of funds could be monitored and improvement in their substance abuse problem could be tied tightly to their overall treatment plan. A good model for such a program was set up by Richard Ries at the University of Washington for people with schizophrenia and alcohol or drug abuse. According to a description of it:

> Dr. Ries's program serves as an institutional payee, setting up bank accounts for the patients, managing SSI checks, and paying their bills. It also gives patients an incentive to comply with treatment by allowing them to earn back money remaining after their basics are covered, provided they keep clinic appointments and pass urine tests.[92]

The program has reduced hospital readmissions.

Second, consideration should be given to standardizing SSI, SSDI, and VA monetary benefits. The present disparities, based purely on chance, are both illogical and unfair. Standardization could be done by a commission consisting of officials from the Social Security Administration and the Veterans Administration and by introducing the necessary legislation. Consideration should also be given to setting payments for two levels of disability—partial and total. A person receiving partial disability would be allowed to work up to, for example, 30 hours a week without losing benefits. This would take into account the reality that many mentally ill are capable of part-time work although few are able to work full time. Under the current system, people who could hold part-time jobs are discouraged from doing so because they would lose their benefits if they worked more than a few hours a week. This, then, is another example of benefits that are not beneficial.

Chapter 9

FROM THE WOODY ALLEN
SYNDROME TO BRAIN DISEASE

*The most important achievement which the advance of scientific research
has brought to psychiatry in our century is the firm foundation of the notion of the somatic basis of mental disorders.*[1]
EMIL KRAEPELIN, 1877, German psychiatrist

T he third major cause of the mental illness crisis is ideological. The
nineteenth-century concept of mental illnesses as brain disorders was replaced early in this century by a spectrum concept that subsumed mental
illnesses under the broad heading of mental health. Mental health in turn
was linked to social reform and liberal causes and therefore mental health
and mental illnesses have both been highly politicized.

The spectrum concept of mental illness and mental health has also led
to the idea that almost everyone is, more or less, mentally ill. In addition,
progress on research and treatment for mental illnesses has been significantly retarded because research funding, treatment resources, and professional expertise have been diverted from mental illnesses to a vast array of
nonmedical problems and social issues.

The Merging of Mental Illness with
Mental Health and Social Reform

Prior to 1909, there was no confusion about mental illness and mental
health. According to one historian, "The late 19th century was an era of

extreme somaticism in psychiatric thought . . . psychiatrists and neurologists agreed that insanity was a disease of the brain or a symptom of such disorder."[2] Representative of such thinking was John P. Gray, president of what would become the American Psychiatric Association, editor of the *American Journal of Insanity*, and for 32 years superintendent of the largest psychiatric hospital in the nation. Gray was the first hospital superintendent to employ a pathologist to look for abnormalities in the brains of the mentally ill after death and was firmly convinced that biological events caused mental illnesses. Like most of his colleagues, Gray was politically and socially conservative and he staunchly opposed efforts to attribute immoral or criminal behavior to brain disorders.[3] If the concept of mental health was used at all in the late nineteenth century, it was merely to signify the absence of any disorders of the brain.

This all changed in 1909 with the founding of the National Committee for Mental Hygiene in February of that year and Sigmund Freud's visit to America in September. The National Committee for Mental Hygiene was part of a national movement toward the prevention of disease and followed the creation of the National Association for the Study and Prevention of Tuberculosis in 1904 and the American Association for the Study and Prevention of Infant Mortality in 1909. The National Committee for Mental Hygiene was intended by its originator, Clifford W. Beers, to be a reform movement for public psychiatric hospitals, but it was almost immediately usurped by Alfred Meyer and other psychiatrists to become a movement to promote mental hygiene.

At the time, Dr. Meyer was an enthusiastic promoter of Sigmund Freud's ideas and was prominently in attendance when Freud lectured at Clark University later that year. Freud believed that all mental disorders were on a continuum and caused by early childhood experiences, especially experiences that were sexual in nature. Meyer and other American psychiatrists enthusiastically embraced the continuum theory and used it to promote the concept of prevention. Mental hygiene thus became the call to arms for those who wished to prevent mental illnesses.

Mental hygiene also became linked, from its earliest days, to social reform and liberal political thought. Social reform efforts were prominent at the time, stimulated by publication of journalistic exposés such as Lincoln Steffens' *Shame of the Cities* and Upton Sinclair's *The Jungle*. Movements were under way to abolish city slums, child labor, corruption in government, the sale of alcohol, and unsanitary working conditions, among other iniquities. The mental hygiene movement adopted many of these causes as its own because of its belief that "mental disorders tend to thrive on the soil of faulty habits and unsatisfactory environments,"[4] in the words of C. Macfie Campbell, a psychiatrist and close associate of Dr. Meyer.

Within 10 years of its founding, the National Committee for Mental Hygiene had been completely taken over by psychiatrists who were followers of Freud as well as social reformers. Dr. Campbell "urged employers to improve the moral atmosphere as well as lighting and ventilation" in workplaces.[5] William A. White, who edited the first American journal of psychoanalysis, claimed that mental hygiene included "all forms of social maladjustment and even of unhappiness." White promoted reform movements for "sanitary factory conditions, wholesome foods, tenement inspection, child labor laws, juvenile courts, and special provisions to enable pregnant and nursing women to remain at home."[6] Thomas Salmon, medical director of the National Committee for Mental Hygiene and later president of the American Psychiatric Association, was also a devout Freudian who spoke of early family relationships as a "psychic infection." Salmon urged that "the frontiers of psychiatry" be extended to school and prison reform efforts so that psychiatrists could "devise some practical methods of utilizing this knowledge for dealing with concrete social problems."[7]

In the 1920s, the mental hygiene movement incorporated the nascent child guidance movement, which had arisen from concerns about juvenile delinquency. The National Committee for Mental Hygiene, with private foundation support, opened demonstration child guidance clinics in five cities to educate mothers about Freudian child-rearing principles and thus, it was said, prevent mental disorders and juvenile delinquency. Social workers constituted the core staff of these clinics and have remained a mainstay of the mental hygiene movement ever since that time.

In the 1930s, mental hygiene and Freudian psychoanalysis became even more closely associated with social reform and liberal political thought. As Hitler's tentacles spread across central and eastern Europe, large numbers of psychoanalysts fled to the United States. Many of them had strong socialist leanings, including Siegfried Bernfeld, Bruno Bettelheim, Otto Fenichel, Erich Fromm, and Wilhelm Reich. The fusion of psychoanalysis and socialism found its fullest expression among New York's intelligentsia, whose leaders, such as Philip Rahv, William Phillips, Dwight Macdonald, Mary McCarthy, Edmund Wilson, and Lionel Trilling, were all followers of Freud as well as of either Marx or Trotsky.[8]

I should add, parenthetically, that Freud himself never understood how his ideas had became associated with social reform and liberal politics among his American supporters. Freud personally supported politically conservative regimes in Austria, opposed the Russian Revolution, and praised Benito Mussolini as "a cultural hero." The use of Freud's ideas to support political beliefs to which he was personally opposed was almost certainly a major reason Freud made so many derogatory comments about America in his later years.[9]

By the time of Freud's death in 1939, then, the continuum concept of mental disorders had largely replaced the older idea that some people have brain disorders and others do not. Mental health was a relative concept, with disorders like schizophrenia and manic-depressive illness being merely one end of the spectrum. Elvin Semrad, a prominent psychoanalyst, often told his trainees that "psychotic patients are no different than we are, just a little crazier."[10] The causes of most mental disorders were thought to reside in the person's childhood experiences and social circumstances. Prevention, therefore, logically dictated intervention at the level of childhood experiences and social circumstances leading to the linkage of mental health and social reform.

Siberia, USA: The Politicalization of Mental Health

The increasing prominence of mental health in the United States following World War II made conservatives uneasy. The National Association for Mental Health, which evolved from the National Committee for Mental Hygiene in 1950, launched a massive publicity campaign with slogans such as "Mental Health Is Everybody's Business" and "Build Mental Health— Our Children's Birthright—The Nation's Strength." Conservatives were even more alarmed by public pronouncements from psychiatrists suggesting a prominent role for themselves in the affairs of the nation. In 1941, for example, George Stevenson, medical director of the National Committee for Mental Hygiene and president of the American Psychiatric Association, had asserted that wars were "mental health problems" because they had their roots in "psychological and psychopathological problems."[11] Five years later, G. Brock Chisholm, president of the World Federation for Mental Health, outlined a less than modest role for his colleagues: "If the race is to be freed from its crippling burden of good and evil, it must be psychiatrists who take the original responsibility. . . . With the other human sciences, psychiatry must now decide what is to be the immediate future of the human race. No one else can. And this is the prime responsibility of psychiatry."[12]

In listening to such pronouncements, conservative Americans suspected that the psychiatrists and other mental health advocates were talking about values, not scientific facts. Such suspicions had been raised as early as 1938, when sociologist Kingsley Davis published an analysis of the mental hygiene movement. Mental hygiene, Davis announced bluntly, had nothing whatsoever to do with mental illness but rather was a system of values. Davis argued, "Mental hygiene hides its adherence behind a scientific facade. . . . [Mental hygiene is a] social movement and a source of advice concerning personal conduct."[13] In essence, Davis was accusing the mental hygiene movement of promoting its own values under the guise of science. Conservatives suspected that the values being promoted by mental hygiene and mental health were liberal values.

Conservative Americans selected an unlikely place to take a stand against the mental health movement. In 1955, legislation was introduced into Congress to permit Alaska, which had not yet become a state, to build a psychiatric hospital for its residents. Up until then, there had been no psychiatric hospital in Alaska and its ill citizens had been sent to a private psychiatric hospital in Portland, Oregon.

Conservative groups, led by the Minute Women, USA, circulated thousands of letters and petitions claiming that the proposed hospital would be used by liberal psychiatrists to involuntarily hospitalize conservatives and other political dissidents. Mrs. Gene Birkeland, a housewife in California, wrote an article claiming that the hospital would become "Siberia, USA . . . a concentration camp for political prisoners under the guise of care and treatment of mental cases,"[14] similar to those in use in the Soviet Union. The legislation, said Mrs. Birkeland, "will place every resident of the United States at the mercy of the whims and fancies of any person with whom they might have a disagreement, causing a charge of 'mental illness' to be placed against them." "Siberia, USA" became the battle cry for the opposition movement.

Senate hearings on the proposed Alaskan hospital legislation took place on February 20 and 21, 1956, before the Subcommittee on Territories and Insular Affairs. The House Un-American Activities Committee was simultaneously holding highly publicized hearings on Communist subversives in government; on February 21 two ex-government officials invoked the Fifth Amendment 83 times, refusing to tell the Committee whether they had been members of the Communist Party while working for the government. The Communist menace was at its peak, and no conspiratorial scheme appeared to be, at first glance, too fantastic.

Mrs. Birkeland and several other witnesses testified against the proposed hospital in particular and against mental heath in general. Mental illness was too broadly defined, she said, and susceptible to subjective interpretation by psychiatrists. Other witnesses attacked the World Health

Organization and the World Federation for Mental Health as Communist-front organizations and claimed that the Alaskan hospital bill was merely an opening wedge to "provide machinery under which, when the time comes, the state (that is the Federal Government) will have omnipotent power over all the people." Many of the senators found such testimony perplexing. Senator Henry Jackson, chairman of the Subcommittee, noted, "We have been deluged with wires [opposing this legislation]. Some of them made sense, and I must say some of them I do not understand at all." Senator George Malone expressed puzzlement at the strength of the opposition to the legislation: "We have been going along here for 180 years in our Republic and taking care of the insane. . . . When did it become so complex and controversial?"

Despite opposition, the legislation passed and the psychiatric hospital was built in Alaska. However, conservative opposition to mental health had been established. Over the next several years, initiatives to open mental health clinics ran the risk of encountering fierce opposition. In Delaware, 35 young men in black leather jackets disrupted an organizing meeting of a local mental health organization, shouting that mental health was a Communist plot. In Utah in 1961, anti-mental-health lobbyists packed a meeting of the state legislature that was considering setting up mental health services. In Wisconsin, opponents "caused the defeat of some twenty mental health measures that seemed certain of passage." The magazine of the Daughters of the American Revolution published a two-part series on mental health, describing it as "a Marxist weapon" and alleging that 80 percent of American psychiatrists were foreigners and that "most of them [were] educated in Russia."[15] The executive director of the Dallas Association of Mental Health received threatening telephone calls, and an academic symposium on mental health in Lubbock, Texas, was picketed. In New Hampshire, the *Manchester Union Leader* carried the following editorial in 1957 under the title "Mental Health Mania":

> Although we have been extremely interested in mental health problems over the years and impressed by the many scientific advances toward improved treatment and care of the mentally ill, we have been even more appalled at the almighty gall of those psychiatrists who are seeking to expand psychiatry from help for abnormal minds to the control and regulation of the normal. There are those who would incorporate the evil techniques of brainwashing into the science of psychiatry toward the goal of making YOU a well-regulated little citizen of the world. This small, but influential, group of men and women is not really interested in helping the mentally ill, but rather in modifying human nature to bring about a new world order.[16]

The heartland of the anti-mental-health movement was southern California. There the movement was adopted by some members of the John Birch Society and was well financed. Literature was widely distributed with allegations such as: "Mental health programs are part of a Communist plot to control the people's minds." "Mental hygiene is a subtle and diabolical plan of the enemy to transform a free and intelligent people into a cringing horde of zombies." "Do we want to become a regimented nation, brainwashed and brain-fed through a powerful army of psychiatrists?" In the suburbs of Los Angeles a large billboard was erected in July 1958 with the following message:

> It is amazing and appalling how many supposedly intelligent people have been duped by such COMMUNIST SCHEMES AS FLUORIDATION and 'Mental Health,' especially since both the AMERICAN LEGION and the D.A.R. have publicly branded 'Mental Health' as a COMMUNIST PLOT to take over our country.

When the Los Angeles City Council was asked to vote on a proposal to allow an unoccupied health center to be used as a mental health clinic, the measure was defeated 11 to 0.[17] One of the senators from California at the time was Richard Nixon, who had been elected in 1950 and would play an important role in opposing the mental health movement when he became President.

In the end, however, the opposition of the 1950s did not appreciably slow the mental health movement, primarily because Siberia, USA, was also adopted by groups with other agendas, such as opposition to the fluoridation of water or the promotion of anti-Semitism. At the 1956 Senate hearing, one of those testifying against the Alaskan psychiatric hospital was John Kasper, a virulent anti-Semite, segregationist, and disciple of Ezra Pound. Kasper testified:

> The whole concept of mental health is quite curious to me. . . . Psychiatry is a foreign ideology; it is alien to any kind of American thinking. . . . Its history began with Sigmund Freud who is [sic] a Jew. . . . I think it is important to realize that almost 100 percent of all psychiatric therapy is Jewish and that about 80 percent of the psychiatrists are Jewish. . . . I am opposed to any nation who attempts to usurp American nationality and the Jews are nationalists of another country. Some of them have tried to do this and are trying to do this.[18]

Such testimony allowed mental health professionals and the media to deride "Siberia, USA" as a fringe phenomenon of little consequence. The legacy of the movement, however, was the clear suggestion that many conservative Americans had a fundamental distrust of mental health practitioners and programs, and that the "mental health" concept carried with it heavy political baggage.

Why Conservatives Mistrust Mental Health

In 1967, as the first federally funded Community Mental Health Centers were opening and deinstitutionalization of patients from state psychiatric hospitals was accelerating, Richard Schmuck and Mark Chesler, both social scientists, published a thoughtful analysis of why many conservative Americans opposed mental health programs. Even as their paper was being circulated, events of the 1960s and 1970s were providing support for many of their conclusions. Opponents of the mental health movement felt increasingly vindicated in their mistrust.

One of the reasons conservatives opposed mental health, maintained Schmuck and Chesler, was that "mental health practitioners encourage immorality, sin, and social disorganization."[19] This was at a time of major campus unrest and the rise of the counterculture, with its emphasis on free love. The intellectual leaders of that generation were Herbert Marcuse, Norman O. Brown, Paul Goodman, Margaret Mead, and Benjamin Spock; all of them had been deeply influenced by Freud's ideas in general and by the destructive consequences of sexual repression in particular.

Herbert Marcuse, who had a doctorate in philosophy, published his influential *Eros and Civilization: A Philosophical Inquiry into Freud* in 1955 and *One-Dimensional Man* nine years later. A leader of the Students for a Democratic Society (SDS) called these books "the most exciting works available,"[20] and the New York chapter of the SDS held a conference on Marcuse's work. Sexual repression, argued Marcuse, was the source of most of society's problems. Such repression had been necessary in the earlier stages of civilization but was necessary no longer; its abolition would allow humankind to return to a type of infantile sexuality that Marcuse labeled "polymorphous perversity." Mark Rudd and other leaders of the student uprisings at Columbia University acknowledged their inspiration by Marcuse, and their slogan, "the riot is the social extension of the orgasm," was Marcusean in origin. Marcuse was a Marxist, and he openly supported Angela Davis, who had been one of his students, when she was accused of smuggling arms into San Quentin prison.[21]

Norman O. Brown, a professor of classics, was also convinced that sexual repression was the Rosetta Stone for understanding civilization. His *Life Against Death: The Psychoanalytical Meaning of History* was widely read by students and depicted a nonrepressive utopia in which there would be "a little more Eros and less strife."[22] Theodore Roszak called the work of Brown and Marcuse "one of the defining features of the counterculture."[23]

Paul Goodman's *Growing Up Absurd* [24] was also widely read on campuses and linked sexual with political repression. A devout follower of both Freud and Reich, Goodman was openly bisexual and an anarchist and was called "the chief spokesman for the non-Marxist tradition of western radicalism."[25] Goodman was an active participant in campus uprisings at Berkeley and elsewhere, and a 1965 survey of SDS campus leaders found that far more of them had read Marcuse and Goodman than had read Marx, Lenin, or Trotsky.[26]

Margaret Mead was one of the most sought-after campus speakers in the 1960s, widely known for her *Coming of Age in Samoa*, [27] in which she depicted an idyllic, and in retrospect largely fictional, society in which sexual repression virtually did not exist. Mead had been strongly influenced by both Freudian and Marxist thought in her early years, and her liberal agenda, which she promoted on campuses, included premarital sex, nudism, and the legalization of LSD and mescaline.[28]

Benjamin Spock, a pediatrician and author, was also a devout Freudian who undertook personal psychoanalysis three times and utilized Freudian principles in his classic book, *Baby and Child Care*. He was also very popular on college campuses for his liberal views and outspoken opposition to the war in Vietnam. In 1967, he was arrested at an antiwar demonstration for the first of many times.

Marcuse, Brown, Goodman, Mead, and Spock—all were identified with mental health, liberal views, and campus activism. During these same years the Esalen Institute at Big Sur, California, became popular, combining various psychotherapies with nude encounters in hot baths. From the viewpoint of an outsider who had no special interest in Freud or liberal political views, it must have seemed that achieving better mental health consisted primarily of either taking off one's clothes or leading a campus riot. Indeed, from that point of view, mental health *did* appear to encourage immorality and social disorganization.

Another reason conservatives mistrusted mental health, according to the analysis of Schmuck and Chesler, was that it "de-emphasizes personal responsibility." One year after Schmuck and Chesler wrote this, Karl Menninger published *The Crime of Punishment*, which argued that criminals should not be held fully responsible for their behavior because it was the product of their early childhood experiences. Menninger, in fact, contended that "all the crimes committed by all the jailed criminals do not equal in total social damage that of the crimes committed *against* them,"[29] primarily by their mothers through bad child-rearing practices. To punish criminals, said Menninger, is therefore unfair because what they really need is treatment. Menninger recommended that prisons be changed to therapeutic institutions under the supervision of psychiatrists and social workers: "This would no doubt lead to a transformation of prisons, if not to their total disappearance in their present form and function."[30]

Menninger's views circulated widely because he was one of the best known psychiatrists in the United States. As much as any single person, Menninger was probably responsible for the widespread belief that mental health professionals are soft on crime. Some would argue, moreover, that mental health professionals are not merely soft on criminals being responsible, but are soft on *anyone* being responsible. They point, for example, to John Bradshaw, a leader of the "recovery movement," who has claimed that 96 percent of people come from dysfunctional families. Wendy Kaminer in *I'm Dysfunctional, You're Dysfunctional*, [31] Charles Sykes in *A Nation of Victims*, [32] and others have effectively derided this don't-blame-me-I'm-not-responsible national ethos and placed much of the responsibility for it at the door of mental health professionals. Sykes has written:

> Our victim culture is fueled in large measure by the desire to redefine inappropriate conduct as diseases or "addiction." If our philandering, gambling, shopping or even our criminal conduct is the result of "illness" rather than a result of poor character, or immoral decisions, we are off the hook. We have abolished sin by medicalizing it.[33]

Still another reason conservatives opposed mental health programs, according to Schmuck and Chesler's 1967 analysis, was that "mental health programs are politically and ideologically biased" and are "extensions of the federal bureaucracy . . . with increasing federal control of health and welfare programs." At the time this was written in 1967, federally funded Community Mental Health Centers (CMHCs) were opening, representing the first time federal funds had been used for building local mental health clinics. The purpose of the CMHCs was not merely to treat mental illnesses, according to Stanley Yolles, who was director of the National Institute of Mental Health, but also "to improve the lives of the people by bettering their physical environment, their educational and cultural opportunities, and other social and environmental conditions."[34]

The National Institute of Mental Health (NIMH) encouraged the newly opened CMHCs to pursue social action programs in promoting mental health. Leonard Duhl of NIMH claimed that "the totality of urban life is the only rational focus for concern with mental illness . . .

our problem now embraces all of society and we must examine every aspect of it to determine what is conducive to mental health."[35] Matthew Dumont, another NIMH staff member, argued that poverty was a major cause of mental illness and that it was therefore "the responsibility of mental health professions to devote at least some of their attention to these issues, or the battle against mental illness will be lost."[36]

With NIMH's encouragement, some of the CMHCs did attempt to become social change agents in their communities. In Chicago, a CMHC hired veteran community activist Saul Alinsky to help plan its approach to mental health. In Philadelphia, a CMHC community board proposed that its mission should include "underlying causes of mental health problems such as unequal distribution of opportunity, income, and benefits of technical progress."[37] In Los Angeles, a CMHC organized local citizens to get a stoplight installed on a busy street near a school. And in New York City, a CMHC opened a series of Neighborhood Service Centers that became involved with problems such as garbage collection services, rat control, housing code enforcement, and the organization of tenant councils. As mental health professionals, they were merely carrying out the charge of leaders of their profession, such as Leon Eisenberg, who had said: "As citizens, we bear a moral responsibility, because of our specialized knowledge, for political action to prevent socially induced psychiatric illness."[38] From the point of view of mental health professionals, such social actions were logical and consistent with their mandate. From the point of view of some conservatives, these activities appeared politically biased, an extension of federal control and indistinguishable from existing social services.

The Presidential Politics of Mental Health: From Kennedy and Nixon to Reagan and Clinton

Probably the single most important event that linked mental health to liberal politics was the poll conducted by *Fact* magazine in 1964, during the presidential race between Republican Barry Goldwater and Democrat Lyndon Johnson. *Fact* sent a questionnaire to members of the American Psychiatric Association asking them to give an opinion about Goldwater's mental health and fitness to be President. Over two thousand psychiatrists responded to the poll, with most of them questioning Goldwater's mental health and fitness and the results were widely publicized. Since none of the psychiatrists had examined Goldwater, it was both inappropriate and unprofessional for them to publicly offer an opinion.

People familiar with presidential politics were not surprised at the *Fact* poll because mental health professionals, as a group, were known to vote strongly liberal. In fact, it is doubtful if there is any professional group in the United States that has voted more consistently liberal for the past half century. Psychoanalysts, for example, gave Henry Wallace and the Progressive Party 22 percent of their votes in 1948; Truman (Democrat) got 62 percent, and Dewey (Republican) only 12 percent. The Republicans received only 21 percent of psychoanalysts' votes in 1952 (Eisenhower), 15 percent in 1956 (Eisenhower), 6 percent in 1960 (Nixon), and 3 percent in 1964 (Goldwater).[39] Because of the association of mental health and social reform, it is not surprising that mental health professionals were attracted to the party of Franklin Roosevelt's New Deal and Harry Truman's civil rights initiatives.

But it was President John Kennedy who permanently bonded the mental health professions to the Democratic Party. Kennedy had a sister who had been born mildly mentally retarded and then, as a young adult, had become mentally ill as well; she was therefore given a lobotomy which, rather than improving her condition, caused her to become much more disabled.[40] Kennedy was very interested in issues of mental illness and mental retardation and appointed a committee to make recommendations regarding possible legislation. In January 1963, Kennedy spoke of "the abandonment of the mentally ill and the mentally retarded to the grim mercies of custodial institutions" in his State of the Union address. One month later, he delivered his historic special message to Congress entitled "Mental Illness and Mental Retardation," in which he proposed federally funded Community Mental Health Centers (CMHCs) as "a bold new approach." The legislation passed Congress easily and was signed by Kennedy on October 31, 1963; it would be the last piece of major legislation he would sign before being assassinated three weeks later.

Because of the association of mental health and CMHCs with the Democratic Party, nobody was very surprised when Republican President Richard Nixon targeted the CMHC program for cutbacks shortly after taking office in 1968. Nixon had been a California senator during the 1956 "Siberia USA" hearings, and his home political base in southern California was the center of anti-mental-health sentiment. Nixon was also acutely aware of the role psychiatrists had played in attempting to discredit Barry Goldwater in 1964. The CMHC Act was due to expire, and Nixon recommended to Congress that the program be phased out. Hearings were held in July 1968, but the Democratic Congress ignored Nixon's wishes and voted to not only continue the program but to expand it.

This skirmish was the first fight in what was to become a six-year mental health war between the Nixon, and later Ford, Republican White House and the Democratic Congress. Each year, the White House recommended reducing or discontinuing the CMHC program, and each year Congress continued it. A major fight erupted in 1973, when President Nixon impounded and refused to spend funds that had been appropriated by Congress for the CMHCs; the National Council of Community Mental Health Centers went to federal court and obtained an injunction ordering the Nixon administration to release the impounded funds. Nixon's attention from such fights was increasingly diverted by the war in Vietnam and later by the Watergate scandal. Finally in August 1974, President Nixon resigned. Congress reauthorized the CMHC legislation the following year, whereupon President Gerald Ford immediately vetoed it. Congress, however, overrode the veto and the CMHCs survived.

The election of Democrat Jimmy Carter to the White House in 1976 promised to produce a friendlier political climate for mental health. Carter's wife, Rosalynn, had actively promoted CMHCs in Georgia, and Carter's deputy campaign director, Peter Bourne, was a psychiatrist. One of Carter's first acts was to create a President's Commission on Mental Health, with his wife as Honorary Chairperson. Thirty-five panels were assembled and the Commission held public hearings to carry out the Commission's mandate "to review the mental health needs of the nation and make recommendations to the President as to how the nation might best meet these needs."

The product of the Commission was a 2,139-page report, which was submitted to President Carter in April 1978. At no point did the report define "mental health" but rather focused on a wide variety of issues that it labeled as "mental health problems":

> America's mental health *problems* cannot be defined only in terms of disabling mental illnesses and identified psychiatric disorders. They must also include the damage to mental health associated with unrelenting poverty and unemployment and the institutionalized discrimination that occurs on the basis of race, sex, class, age, and mental or physical handicaps. They must also include conditions that involve emotional and psychological distress which do not fit conventional categories of classification or service.[41]

The Carter Commission on Mental Health, then, was a logical extension of the spectrum concept of mental health that had grown steadily in the United States for half a century. People with brain disorders played a small role in the Commission's deliberations; the section on schizophrenia was just three pages long, and affective disorders such as manic-depressive illness and severe depression were discussed in six pages. The report also contained 117 recommendations to the President, but by 1980, when the recommendations had been formulated as a legislative plan, President Carter had been defeated for reelection and they were therefore moot. Since 1980, Ms. Carter has continued to actively fight for mental health issues and to argue publicly that "health care reform must not provide care based on a hierarchy of pain but embrace all those who suffer from mental health problems. . . . It should promote mental health practices as well as provide for prevention."[42]

Like Nixon following Kennedy, the election of President Ronald Reagan following Carter in 1980 promised hard times for the mental health community. Reagan was also a product of the southern California milieu in which the concept of "mental health" was politically suspect, and during his two terms he showed no interest in it. With his conservative domestic agenda, Reagan made an inviting target for the mental health community, and he was increasingly blamed for the problems of deinstitutionalization and for trying to cut disabled persons from the SSI and SSDI rolls. In retrospect, it appears that Reagan should only legitimately be blamed for the second of these.

Although it has been common practice to blame Ronald Reagan for the problems of deinstitutionalization in California during his governorship, the discharge of patients from California's state hospitals began in 1955 under Republican Governor Goodwin Knight. It continued at the same pace from 1959 to 1967 under Democratic Governor Edmund Brown, and by the time Reagan took over as governor in 1967 more than two-thirds of the patients who were destined to be deinstitutionalized had already been discharged. Under Reagan, deinstitutionalization continued at the same rate until 1972, when it leveled off.[43]

The indiscriminant attempt to purge people who were not truly disabled from the SSI and SSDI roles between 1981 and 1983 is the mental health issue for which President Reagan and his staff can legitimately be blamed. The previous Congress had mandated the Social Security Administration to review the eligibility of disabled recipients "to insure that only the truly disabled receive disability benefits."[44] Immediately after taking office, officials under President Reagan ordered an acceleration of these reviews and a stricter interpretation of qualifications for disability. Many of these reviews were said to be "scandalously perfunctory,"[45] and approximately 300,000 people, including a disproportionate number who were severely mentally ill, were cut off from SSI and SSDI benefits over the following two years. Court suits challenging the review process were instituted in 1982 and continued until mid-1983, when the Reagan Administration ceased its efforts to purge the SSI and SSDI rolls amidst a torrent of public criticism. Mental health had already been highly politicized before President Reagan took office, but the SSI-SSDI debacle further solidified the association of mental health with Democrats and anti-mental-health sentiment with Republicans.

With the return of the Democratic Party to the White House in 1992, the hopes of the mental health community again soared. Tipper Gore, the Vice President's wife, held a master's degree in psychology, had been co-chairperson of the Child Mental Health Interest Group of the National Mental Health Association, and acknowledged that she herself had sought counseling when her son had been seriously injured.[46] Moreover, Ms. Gore subscribed to the traditional but erroneous mental health maxim which alleges that severe mental illnesses arise from a failure to treat problems in childhood:

> It is long past time that we begin putting the needs of the children first. We delay at our peril, for at least half of the children who go unserved will grow up with full-blown disabilities as adults, requiring extensive and expensive care.[47]

Within this context it was understandable that Ms. Gore pushed for full mental health coverage under President Clinton's proposed health care reform. As chairperson of the Mental Health Work Group of the Health Reform Task Force, Ms. Gore argued that mental illnesses should be treated at full parity with physical illnesses and that everyone should be eligible for treatment who had a diagnosed mental disorder that "poses a serious risk for functional impairment in family, work, school or community activities."[48] A large coalition of mental health providers, including the American Association for Marriage and Family Therapy and the American Counseling Association, lobbied aggressively for full mental health coverage under health care reform with as few restrictions as possible. However, the economists who were looking at the costs of the proposals for full mental health parity labeled them as a "black hole" and "a bottomless pit."[49]

The arguments about parity for mental health services became moot when President Clinton's proposed health care reform went up in electoral flames with the election of a Republican Congress in 1994. In retrospect, Tipper Gore's efforts represented one more skirmish in the ongoing mental health war between liberals and conservatives, Democrats and Republicans. Mental health had been tied to a political cause, and insofar as mental illnesses were part of mental health they, too, had been politicized by association.

When looked at objectively, however, the politicalization of mental illnesses makes no logical sense. Schizophrenia, manic-depressive illness, and other severe disorders are no more inherently political than Parkinson's disease or Alzheimer's disease. But as long as mental illnesses are linked to a continuum of mental health, they will continue to be politicized.

When Everybody Is Mentally Ill, Nobody Is Mentally Ill

An important corollary of the spectrum concept of mental disorders is that almost any undesirable behavior or constellation of traits can be labeled as a disorder. Since there is no scientific division between brain disorder and non-brain disorder, the concept of mental disorder becomes infinitely and arbitrarily expandable. This is precisely what has happened in the half century since Freud's death.

A useful way to measure the expansion of mental disorders in the United States is to examine successive editions of the American Psychiatric Association's *Diagnostic and Statistical Manual of Mental Disorders,* [50] usually abbreviated as *DSM.* Between 1952 and 1994, there have been five editions of this manual: *DSM-I* (1952), *DSM-II* (1968), *DSM-III* (1980), *DSM-III-revised* (1987), and *DSM-IV* (1994). *DSM-I* listed 106 mental disorders and was only 126 pages long. *DSM-IV* includes over 300 mental disorders and is 886 pages long. Included in *DSM-IV* are behaviors as varied as disorder of written expression (315.2), childhood conduct disorder (312.8), breathing-related sleep disorder (780.59), pathological gambling (312.31), adjustment disorder with anxiety (309.24), and avoidant personality disorder (301.82).

The boundaries of many of these designated mental disorders are vague. For example, a child can be diagnosed with oppositional defiant disorder (313.81) if he/she often exhibits any four of the following traits during a six-month period and "the behavior causes clinically significant impairment in social, academic or occupational functioning": loses temper, argues with adults, refuses to follow requests or rules, deliberately annoys people, blames others for mistakes, is touchy, is angry, or is spiteful. Because of such vagueness *DSM-IV* has been criticized for its "mingling of science and social values," its "medicalizing so many social problems," and for having "no coherent standard of what constitutes a mental disorder."[51]

With these broad designations of mental disorders, it is not surprising that prevalence surveys have found a very high prevalence of mental disorders in the general population. The most recent such study, the National Comorbidity Study, reported on diagnostic interviews with 8,098 adults who were selected to be representative of the adult American population. It found that "nearly 50 percent of respondents reported at least one lifetime disorder, and close to 30 percent reported at least one 12-month disorder."[52] This overall prevalence was consistent with the results of the Epidemiologic Catchment Area survey done a decade earlier and suggested to its authors that "the prevalence of psychiatric disorders is greater than previously thought to be the case." Newspapers reported the results as "1 in 2 Found to Suffer Mental Disorder."[53] Such reports, which imply that half the population is mentally disabled, are a logical outgrowth of the spectrum concept of mental disorders. They also suggest that psychiatry has expanded its purview to include an ever-increasing number of behaviors and people. For citizens who do not trust psychiatrists or other mental health practitioners, such reports can be a source of concern.

When the results of the National Comorbidity Survey and similar studies are translated into costs, the unreality of full parity coverage for mental disorders becomes apparent. In 1995, there were approximately 209 million Americans ages 14 and over. According to the National Comorbidity Survey 30 percent of them, or 62.7 million, suffer from a diagnosable mental disorder in any given year. Under the health care reform plan proposed by President Clinton, each person would have been eligible for up to 30 outpatient visits each year. Outpatient psychotherapy visits in the United States average at least $80 per visit, or $2,400 for 30 visits. If only half of the 62.7 million eligible Americans chose to use their outpatient benefits, the total annual cost would be over $75 billion dollars. Even allowing for some reduction of costs by having the patients pay part of the fee, it is clear that no nation will ever be wealthy enough to afford coverage for the treatment of all mental disorders as defined under the spectrum concept.

UFO Abduction Therapy and the Diversion of Mental Illness Resources

Another important corollary of the spectrum concept of mental disorders is that resources originally intended for research on, and treatment for, severe mental illnesses have instead been diverted to the broad, and some would say infinite, needs of mental health. As a result, research and treatment for mental illnesses such as schizophrenia and manic-depressive illness are far behind most of American medicine.

The diversion of research resources is illustrative. In 1945, when legislation was introduced in Congress to create a National Neuropsychiatric Institute as it was then to be known, the intent was explicitly said to be "conducting researches, investigations, experiments, and demonstrations relating to the cause, diagnosis, and treatment of neuropsychiatric disorders." Testimony of officials from the U.S. Department of Health, Education and Welfare and comments by congressmen at the hearings indicated that "neuropsychiatric disorders" referred to the disorders that during World War II caused almost 500,000 people to be hospitalized in state psychiatric hospitals and that caused 856,000 men to be rejected for military service.

Fifty years later, an examination of the research portfolio of the National Institute of Mental Health, which was the name eventually given to the proposed National Neuropsychiatric Institute, reveals an extraordinary array of research being supported under the rubric of mental health. Included among grants funded in fiscal year 1994 were research on childhood development, marriage, divorce, self-esteem, work experience, delinquency, and teen pregnancy. Mental health appeared to encompass almost everything from "Mechanisms of Perception by Sonar" in bats to "Mechanisms of Creativity" in humans, and from "Correlates of Uncertain Parentage in a Monogamous Bird" to "Well Being at Midlife" in humans. Research on mental health covers just about everything, but at the expense of less research on severe mental illnesses.

Another example of the diversion of resources from mental illnesses to mental health was the federally funded Community Mental Health Centers (CMHCs) program. At the congressional hearings that established the program in 1963, the target population for CMHC services was clearly established to be persons with severe mental illnesses, especially those diagnosed with schizophrenia, manic-depressive illness, and severe depression, who constituted the majority of patients in state psychiatric hospitals. At the hearings, a spokesperson for the Kennedy administration specifically noted that "the basic purpose of the president's program is to redirect the focus of treatment of the mentally ill from state mental hospitals into community mental health centers."[54] Representative Oren Harris, the chairman of the committee holding the hearings, similarly noted: "What you ultimately hope to accomplish by this [CMHC] program is to reduce the number of patients in the big state hospitals to a minimum, and ultimately down the line to more adequately take care of the patients in the local center. . . ."

The census of the state psychiatric hospitals *did* in fact decrease sharply following the opening of CMHCs, but as described in Chapter 7, the decrease had virtually nothing to do with the CMHCs. Most CMHCs, originally intended to target the state hospital population, instead focused on a broad spectrum of mental health problems. By the mid-1970s, a clear trend had developed for CMHCs to treat a *decreasing* percentage of severely mentally ill people and an *increasing* percentage of people with diagnoses of "social maladjustment" and "no mental disorder."[55] A small number of exemplary CMHCs did a commendable job in assuming responsibility for state psychiatric hospital patients but for the vast majority of CMHCs such patients constituted no more than 20 percent, and often less than 10 percent, of their patients. Once again, a resource that had been originally created to serve the mentally ill had been usurped to serve mental health.

The most flagrant example of this diversion of resources has been the diversion of mental health professionals. Federal and state governments have spent literally billions of public dollars to train psychiatrists, psychologists, psychiatric social workers, and other professionals so that there would be enough to provide care for the mentally ill. Once trained, however, the vast majority of these professionals decided to provide psychotherapy and counseling for people with mental health problems rather than to treat people who were mentally ill. In effect, for the past 40 years, we have trained mental *health* professionals when we should have been training mental *illness* professionals.

The spectrum concept of mental disorders, in which virtually anyone can qualify for an official psychiatric diagnosis, further facilitates the diversion of professionals from mental illnesses to mental health. A study based on 1987 data reported that during that year Americans made 79.5 million outpatient visits for psychotherapy.[56] The total cost of these visits was $4.2 billion, which constituted 8 percent of all medical outpatient expenditures and 19 percent of Medicaid outpatient expenditures in the United States.

The study also suggested that the vast majority of people undertaking outpatient psychotherapy did not have severe mental illnesses but rather had problems of mental health. Less than 8 percent of them were diagnosed with schizophrenia or manic-depressive illness and only 2.4 percent required psychiatric hospitalization. Depression, anxiety, and adjustment disorders were the most common diagnoses.

A widely publicized example of the diversion of professional resources from mental illnesses to mental health is UFO Abduction Therapy, promoted by John E. Mack, a Professor of Psychiatry at Harvard Medical School.[57] Dr. Mack does psychotherapy on people who believe they have been abducted by space aliens from unidentified flying objects (UFOs). He claims to have treated over 100 such persons, some as young as four years of age, and bills their medical insurance companies for the therapy in at least some cases.[58] It is unclear what DSM-IV diagnostic label Dr. Mack uses for his billing, but posttraumatic stress disorder (309.81) would appear to be suitable. Being abducted by aliens certainly qualifies one as being "exposed to a traumatic event" and the claimed invasive sexual procedures performed on most of the abductees by the space aliens qualifies as "a threat to the physical integrity of self."

Perhaps the best-known symbol of psychotherapy, and the diversion of professionals from mental illnesses to mental health, is Woody Allen. During his highly publicized legal battles in 1993, it was revealed that Allen had been in psychotherapy for 33 *years*, 21 of them with one psychoanalyst, and during some periods he was seeing two different therapists. His long-term companion, Mia Farrow, was also in psychotherapy, as was a daughter, who had started therapy at age 5, and a son, who had started at age 3. Even the family dog was seeing an "animal behaviorist" at $150 an hour. The media dubbed this endless psychotherapy "the Woody Allen syndrome," and New York City Mayor Edward Koch added: "If I were building a statue to Dr. Freud, and I were going to put it in New York, and the statue was going to be Freud in his office, it would be Woody Allen on the couch."[59]

Woody Allen is obviously an extreme example of mental health run amok, but he illustrates the concentration of professional resources that can occur. Elsewhere in New York, thousands of the mentally ill, including those living on the streets, were receiving little or no help because no professionals were available to treat them. The training of most mental health professionals is paid for, at least in part, by public tax dollars. In addition, medical insurance and public funds, especially Medicaid, pay for more than half the cost of all psychotherapy.[60] Since psychotherapy is highly concentrated among more highly educated and affluent people, the use of public funds to pay for psychotherapy and the training of psychotherapists is really a public subsidy for this segment of society. It is therefore not unlike subsidies given to farmers as price supports or to industries for depreciation of their capital goods, although psychotherapy is not usually considered in those terms.

Divorcing Mental Illness from Mental Health

The merging of mental illness and mental health early in this century has led to a politicalization of mental illness and to diversion of its resources. This politicalization and diversion have been major contributors to the mental illness crisis. The logical solution to the problem is to permanently divorce mental illness from mental health and then to prioritize research and services so that the most severely ill go to the head of the line.

Divorcing mental illness from mental health is easier said than done. For most of this century, we have thought in terms of mental *health* professionals, mental *health* centers, and mental *health* programs. What is needed is to change these concepts to mental *illness* professionals, mental *illness* centers, and mental *illness* programs. One way to do this is to merge the brain disorders that we presently refer to as psychiatric illnesses with the brain disorders we call neurological illnesses. Thus schizophrenia, schizoaffective disorder, manic-depressive disorder, autism, and severe forms of depression, panic disorder, and obsessive-compulsive disorder—the conditions defined as severe mental illnesses by the National Advisory Mental Health Council—would be merged with neurological illnesses such as multiple sclerosis, Parkinson's disease, and Alzheimer's disease.

In practice, this would mean that there would be no National Institute of Mental Health. Research on mental illnesses would be carried out by a National Brain Research Institute that would merge some of the research presently being carried out by the National Institute of Mental Health with that being carried out by the National Institute of Neurological Disorders and Stroke. It makes no sense to have two separate research institutes both carrying out research on brain disorders, as is presently the case. It is like having two research institutes for disorders of the heart or two institutes for disorders of the liver.

Merging the two research institutes whose primary responsibility is brain disorders would promote collaborative research efforts, lead to a more efficient utilization of neuroimaging and other expensive research resources, and decrease administrative costs. It would also clearly differentiate mental illnesses from mental health and thus effectively divorce them. Merging the two research institutes would also significantly decrease the discrimination and stigma that presently accrues to mental illnesses; having schizophrenia would ultimately be viewed in the same light as having Parkinson's disease.

What would happen to research presently being carried out at the National Institute of Mental Health that does not concern mental illnesses? The basic neuroscience research could be merged with similar neuroscience research being carried out by the National Institute of Neurological Disorders and Stroke and incorporated into the new National Brain Research Institute. Research that logically belongs in other research institutes could be so assigned: Research on child development could be given to the National Institute on Child Health and Human Development. Research on human behavior and social problems that does not fit into any of the existing institutes of the National Institutes of Health could be assigned to the National Science Foundation, which has traditionally supported behavioral research.

The divorce of mental illness and mental health would also lead to the abolition of state departments of mental health. Medical care for all brain disorders, both psychiatric and neurological, would be the responsibility of state departments of health and the same clinics, professionals, and reimbursement schemes would be utilized for severe depression and obsessive-compulsive disorder as are used for epilepsy and head injuries. Brain disorders such as multiple sclerosis and Parkinson's disease require extensive rehabilitation and social services just as do brain disorders such as schizophrenia and manic-depressive illness, and these services would also be integrated. At the training level, academic departments of psychiatry and neurology would also be combined to produce neuropsychiatrists who would be specialists in all nonsurgical brain disorders.

How to Prioritize Services

Divorcing mental illness from mental health is the first step toward improving research and services on these brain disorders and solving ideological aspects of the mental illness crisis. The second step is to establish a coherent system for prioritizing research and services. In the United States, the rapid increase in health care costs demands that prioritization must take place. Rationing is the allocation of scarce resources, and it is not a question of *whether* rationing will take place but rather *how* it will be determined.

In fact, the rationing of medical resources, including research and services for mental illnesses, is already taking place. When research funds of the National Institute of Mental Health are allocated for social problems, fewer funds are available for research on mental illnesses. The allocation of mental health center professionals for marital counseling means that fewer professionals are available for following up the mentally ill who fail to come in for medication. The allocation of multiple psychiatrists and psychologists to provide literally thousands of hours of psychotherapy for Woody Allen and his family means that those hours are not available for the mentally ill streetpeople who live in Central Park directly in front of Mr. Allen's apartment. The present rationing system is largely supply-driven with the professionals themselves, including those in the National Institute of Mental Health, deciding how to allocate the research and services resources. Until recently, the only constraints on the supply-side rationing of services has been what insurance companies would pay for and, in a few counties and states, diagnostic priorities that had been mandated by public officials.

A variety of criteria may be used to prioritize medical services, including services for brain disorders. These include:

1. *Structural and functional abnormalities.* It is possible to define brain disorders using anatomical, chemical, and neurological criteria, as is done, for example, for multiple sclerosis. For psychiatric disorders such as schizophrenia and manic-depressive illness, these structural and functional abnormalities are rapidly being defined.

2. *Functional impairment.* In 1993, the National Center for Mental Health Services proposed criteria for severe mental illnesses that were based primarily on functional considerations. It suggested that severe mental illnesses should include any diagnosable mental disorder in adults "that has resulted in functional impairment which substantially interferes with or limits one or more major life activities" and in children "which substantially interferes with or limits the child's role or functioning in family, school or community activities." These criteria were widely criticized as being too broad and amorphous. However it is possible to develop functional criteria that would be more useful.

3. *Likelihood of benefit from treatment.* In 1994, Oregon implemented a medical care rationing system for Medicaid recipients in which medical and psychiatric conditions were rank ordered primarily on likelihood of benefit from treatment. The ranking was done following an elaborate and extended gathering of information from professionals and advocacy groups and a series of public hearings.[61] Using these criteria, psychiatric conditions that respond to treatment, such as major depression and obsessive-compulsive disorder, were ranked high but conditions unlikely to respond to treatment, such as hypochondriasis and antisocial personality disorder, were ranked low.

4. *Economic cost-benefit.* Various proposals have been made to ration medical care based on cost-effectiveness. For example, one study estimated that if every woman aged 20 to 75 were given a Pap smear every three years to detect cervical cancer, it would cost $13,300 for every year of life saved.[62] Similar analyses can be utilized for rationing services for mental illnesses.

5. *Social cost-benefit.* Social cost-benefit considerations enter into medical rationing decisions on a regular basis although they are not often publicly discussed. For example, in determining the priority of people awaiting a heart or liver transplant, level of education and potential productivity to society are usually included. Social considerations for prioritizing mental

illnesses might include such things as homelessness, episodes of violence, and the effects on families and communities of large numbers of mentally ill people who are not being treated.

6. *Fairness.* Fairness and moral considerations include factors such as the personal responsibility of the individual for his or her medical or psychiatric condition. It suggests that individuals should be held at least partially fiscally responsible for the medical and psychiatric complications of volitional acts. This issue arises frequently among substance abusers whose condition has been caused by volitional acts of alcohol or drug use. It also arises in conditions caused by smoking, obesity, medication noncompliance, or other factors thought to be under the person's control. In terms of prioritization of services, the principle of fairness suggests that conditions for which the person bears no personal responsibility should have some priority over conditions for which the person bears some responsibility.

Any combination of these criteria could be utilized to prioritize services for people with brain disorders. Developing such priorities will become increasingly important as stricter economic limits are placed on medical care.

Prioritization of mental illnesses is already taking place in a few states such as New Hampshire and Oregon. In New Hampshire, the state legislature in 1981 mandated that persons with severe and chronic mental illnesses should receive priority for services in state-funded mental health centers. The legislation specifically stated:

> Priority emphasis shall be placed on treatment and rehabilitative services for severely mentally disabled persons who are former patients of New Hampshire hospital and other such psychiatric institutions, and other such severely mentally disabled persons at risk of being so institutionalized. Such priority emphasis shall mean that no funds shall be allocated or expended for any other purpose unless minimum program standards for the severely mentally disabled have been fulfilled.[63]

An active state Alliance for the Mentally Ill advocacy group, strong leadership in the state Division of Mental Health, and support from the governor's office were all important in translating this prioritization into operational criteria. Currently, all mental health agencies in New Hampshire are required to assess every person being seen on four criteria: diagnosis, degree of functional impairment, duration of functional impairment, and amount of service utilization. The severity of illness of patients on the mental health agency's caseload determines the agency's allocation of state funds and access to beds in the state psychiatric hospital. To check on the validity of the information received from each mental health agency, Division of Mental Health staff twice each year conduct audits of random samples of patients with the sample size being determined by the previous audit's error rate. This prioritization of public psychiatric services for the more severely ill, combined with a state-of-the-art state psychiatric hospital and several excellent community mental health centers, is why New Hampshire is currently regarded as having the best public psychiatric services in the United States.

Oregon is another state that developed criteria for prioritizing services for mental illness. In 1981 the state legislature established three levels of priority:[64]

Priority 1. A person at immediate risk of hospitalization, or "a hazard to the health and safety of themselves or others," or "at risk of removal from their home."

Priority 2. "A person who because of the nature of his or her illness, family income, or geographic location is unlikely to obtain services from other providers."

Priority 3. "A person experiencing mental emotional disturbances but who is not likely to require hospitalization in the foreseeable future."

These priorities were defined in detail by the State Mental Health Division. Counties and other private contractors have been required to adhere to the state priorities for use of state funds. The extensive work that Oregon did in prioritizing services for people with mental illnesses made possible the development of performance contracting, as described in Chapter 7.

The marriage of mental illness and mental health has been doomed from its inception, since the two are fundamentally incompatible. Mental illness is concerned with brain disorders and pathology, whereas mental health is concerned with behaviors and values. Mental illness is a legitimate responsibility of medicine, which seeks to cure the individual sufferer, whereas mental health belongs to social services, and seeks to promote personal growth and improve human kind. Mental illness is inherently apolitical, but mental health has become strongly political. Now that the children are grown, it is time for a divorce.

Chapter 10

LOOKING FORWARD: WHERE WE SHOULD BE GOING

Deinstitutionalization has run its course. It has left in its aftermath a legacy of many positive changes that are probably permanent, but it has also left a legacy of problems that it spawned and that it is unlikely to solve. It is time, therefore, for a fresh look at the present and future of mental health long-term care policy.[1]

WILLIAM R. SHADISH, ARTHUR J. LURIGIN,
AND DAN A. LEWIS, 1989*

T he mental illness crisis is not unique to the United States. Canada, Australia, New Zealand, and virtually every country in Europe have seen increasing numbers of mentally ill persons who are homeless, in jails and prisons, and committing acts of violence as a consequence of not receiving treatment. The United States is the leader, but several other countries appear to be working hard to catch up.

In England, on December 31, 1992, Ben Silcock climbed into the lion's den at the London Zoo. Silcock had suffered from schizophrenia for 10 years and had received little treatment since being discharged from the hospital. He was floridly delusional and convinced that he could talk to the lions. A photographer who happened to be nearby took pictures of a

---

*William Shadish is a psychologist at Memphis State University; Arthur Lurigin is a psychologist at Loyola University; and Dan Lewis is a sociologist and is director of the Center for Urban Affairs and Policy Research at Northwestern University.

lion attacking and mauling Silcock; although critically injured, Silcock survived. The pictures were widely shown in newspapers and on television and, as Silcock's lack of psychiatric care became widely publicized, there was a public outcry. The *Daily Mail* noted, "The mutilation he [Silcock] endured by the lion, however, is no more savage or shocking than the damage inflicted on him both by the illness itself and by the incompetence, confusion, and downright neglect with which he and his family have been treated over the past years."[2]

Two weeks before Silcock's tragedy, Jonathan Zito, a young man waiting for a train at a London station, had been selected at random and was stabbed to death by Christopher Clunis. Clunis had a six-year history of paranoid schizophrenia, multiple hospital admissions with grossly inadequate follow-up, and eight previous known episodes of violence. In the week before the killing, "He had threatened members of the public with a screwdriver and a bread knife."[3] The murder was highly publicized and a subsequent government inquiry described a "wretched catalogue of administrative failure"[4] in Clunis's psychiatric care.

Coincidentally, both of these episodes took place during an ongoing governmental "confidential inquiry into homicides and suicides by mentally ill people" that had been initiated in 1991 because of similar episodes. The results of the inquiry, made public in 1994, identified more than 100 suicides and 34 homicides by mentally ill persons over an 18-month period. At least 13 of the homicides "followed a period of non-compliance with recommended treatment."[5] In the six weeks following the release of the results of the inquiry, there were seven more publicized episodes involving severely mentally ill persons, including "a second person climbing into the lion's den in London Zoo"[6] and being badly mauled. In England and many other countries, as in the United States, the crisis appears to be growing progressively greater.

Research: The Ultimate Solution

The ultimate solution to the mental illness crisis is to discover the specific causes of, and better treatments for these disorders. If, for example, researchers identified a specific gene, virus, developmental defect, reversible chemical abnormality, or other cause, better treatments would almost certainly follow and it might even be possible to prevent many cases. The resultant savings in both human and economic terms would be immense.

Until recent years, however, research on severe mental illnesses had been seriously neglected. Leadership for such research was vested in the

National Institute of Mental Health (NIMH) at the time of its creation in 1946, with a specific mandate for "conducting researches, investigations, experiments, and demonstrations relating to the cause, diagnosis, and treatment of neuropsychiatric disorders." The NIMH had comparatively little interest in such research, however, and for almost 40 years, research in this area lagged markedly behind research in other areas of medicine. As late as 1984, NIMH was spending only $16.7 million out of its total budget of $250 million for research on schizophrenia, the most devastating and costly of all mental illnesses. At that time, it was calculated that just $14 per year was being spent on research for every person with schizophrenia; whereas research funds for every person with cancer amounted to $300, for every person with muscular dystrophy $1,000, and for every person with AIDS $10,000. From an economic viewpoint alone, the failure to research the causes and treatment of severe mental illnesses was a foolish misallocation of fiscal resources.

Resources for such research began improving in the late 1980s. Much of the credit was attributable to Senator Pete Domenici of New Mexico and other members of Congress, many of whom had family members suffering from mental illnesses, who demanded that NIMH allocate more resources to research on these illnesses. At the same time, several private foundations began supporting research on neuroscience in general and severe mental illnesses in particular. Foremost among these was the Howard Hughes Medical Institute, which designated neuroscience as one of its priority research areas; the National Alliance for Research on Schizophrenia and Depression (NARSAD); the Theodore and Vada Stanley Foundation; and the continuing support of the Scottish Rite of Freemasonry. By 1994, NIMH research funds for schizophrenia had increased to approximately $106 million, a sixfold increase since 1984, with $10 million more available from the Veterans Administration and the private foundations. Research allotments for manic-depressive illness were approximately $22 million from NIMH and $8 million from the Veterans Administration and the foundations. Basic neuroscience research, which may potentially benefit all psychiatric and neurological disorders, was being supported with approximately $622 million in 1994 from programs in the National Institutes of Health, the National Science Foundation, the Veterans Administration, and the Howard Hughes Medical Institute.

There is considerable debate about the optimal level of research funding for severe mental illnesses and what percentage of the funds should be targeted toward specific diseases versus toward basic neuroscience research. As I mentioned in Chapter 1, the annual cost of these illnesses is approximately $27 billion for direct treatment costs alone and $74 billion if indirect costs are included. The latter figure includes most of the $38 billion in federal Medicaid, Medicare, SSI, SSDI, and other federal programs discussed in Chapter 7. To put $74 billion into perspective, it is more than the total 1994 state budgets for all states except California and it is also more than the 1994 budget for the federal departments of Commerce, Energy, Housing and Urban Development, Interior, Justice, and State combined. If research produced a cure for even one-quarter of existing cases of severe mental illnesses, the savings in federal costs alone would be $9.5 billion per year.

The importance of research for people suffering from these disorders was eloquently expressed by psychiatrist John Nemiah when he wrote:

The *Narrenschiff* [Ship of Fools] of old is still afloat in spirit, and whether drifting rudderless on inner-city streets or confined in the dry dock of asylum, it is destined to remain in service until psychiatric research provides us with a more profound and useful knowledge of the etiology of insanity.[7]

Improved Services: An Interim Solution and Summary of Recommendations

Until research provides more definitive answers regarding causes and treatments, we will continue to be faced with providing psychiatric services for an estimated 5.6 million people who are mentally ill. As I have emphasized in earlier chapters, we know how to provide services that are high quality, humane, and cost-effective, but for a variety of reasons we do not do so. The following summary highlights my major recommendations from preceding chapters for achieving such services.

1. *The economic solution: Single responsibility funding.* Cost-shifting between federal and state, and state and local governments is the single largest cause of the mental illness crisis.

   a. Single responsibility funding is the proposed solution. The states would be given authority for planning and for financing services, although the funds may be derived from federal and local as well as state taxes. The states would also be held accountable for treatment outcomes, and this would continue to be true even if the states subcontract for the services with county or city governments or with private sector providers.

b. Block grants of federal funds to the states are consistent with single responsibility funding as long as the states are required to spend those funds on the target population and treatment outcomes are being measured.

c. The measurement of treatment outcomes is mandatory for solving the present crisis. If treatment outcomes are being measured, then performance contracting becomes possible.

d. We do not yet know the optimal system of financial incentives for ensuring quality services for people who are mentally ill. Therefore, it is appropriate to encourage state and local governments to try different arrangements, using public, private, nonprofit, and for-profit resources, as long as treatment outcomes are being measured and the outcomes of the various financial arrangements are being assessed. At the same time, the dismal record to date of the for-profit sector in providing services for individuals with severe mental illnesses should be acknowledged and makes it more likely that definitive solutions will come from the nonprofit sector.

2. *The legal solution: Recognition of the need for involuntary treatment.* Since approximately half of all persons with severe mental illnesses have impaired insight because of their illnesses and therefore do not recognize their need for treatment, a substantial number of the mentally ill will have to be treated involuntarily if they are going to be treated at all. The failure to do so is a major contributor to this crisis.

a. Involuntary commitment laws for hospitalization and treatment should be based not only on dangerousness to self or others, but also on the need for treatment. As measures of insight improve and scales with good inter-rater reliability are developed, a measure of insight should also be included in commitment criteria.

b. In assessing a mentally ill person's need for involuntary treatment, the person's past history should always be considered. Special attention should be directed to the person's history of violent behavior, alcohol and drug abuse, and noncompliance with medication since these are known to be the major predictors of future violent behavior.

c. Conditional release, guardianships, and outpatient commitment should be available and used for mentally ill persons who are in need of involuntary treatment and who can live successfully in the community as long as they take their medication.

d. Interstate reciprocity should be established and enforced for mentally ill persons who are involuntarily committed to treatment in one state.

e. The federally funded Protection and Advocacy program should be abolished.

f. For mentally ill persons who also abuse alcohol or drugs, SSI, SSDI, and VA benefits should be paid directly to a representative payee who is directly connected to the person's treatment program. The person's benefits should become part of the treatment plan to reduce the person's alcohol or drug abuse. The benefits would therefore change from being part of the problem to being part of the solution.

g. SSI, SSDI, and VA benefits for mentally ill persons should be standardized. Consideration should also be given to establishing two levels of disability—partial and total—to encourage people to work who are capable of doing so.

h. A small percentage of the mentally ill are not capable of living in the community because of the severity of their symptoms, their propensity toward violent behavior, their concurrent alcohol or drug abuse, or their nonresponsiveness to all available medication. It should be acknowledged that long-term hospitalization is both appropriate and necessary for these patients.

3. *The ideological solution: Divorce mental illness from mental health.* The continuum concept, which has dominated twentieth-century thinking about mental disorders, is an important cause of the mental illness crisis. Severe mental illnesses are *not* merely one end of a mental health continuum. It is therefore necessary to return to the nineteenth-century idea that these illnesses are in a different category from problems of mental health. A divorce of mental illness from mental health could be accomplished by the following:

a. A National Brain Research Institute should be formed by a merger of the National Institute of Mental Health and the National Institute of Neurological Disorders and Stroke.

b. State departments of mental health should be abolished. People with severe mental illnesses should be the responsibility of the state department of health and should receive services in the same clinics as do patients with other neurological disorders.

c. In medical schools, the departments of psychiatry and neurology should merge. The joint department would train neuropsychiatrists who would be specialists in neurological disorders, mental illnesses, and other nonsurgical disorders of the brain.

d. Since medical resources are finite, a system of prioritization should be established in which severe mental illnesses are prioritized along with other medical disorders. A combination of criteria could be used, including structural and functional brain abnormalities, functional impairment, likelihood of benefit from treatment, economic cost-benefit, social cost-benefit, and fairness.

e. Since severe mental illnesses would no longer be part of a mental health spectrum, they should no longer be politicized.

What Should Be the Role of the Federal Government?

Single responsibility funding, with responsibility fixed at the state level, would not eliminate the federal government's role. In fact, many of the current functions of the federal government should be continued. Federal functions that would be necessary to achieve optimal care for the mentally ill include the following:

1. *Research on causes and treatment.* Health research under federal institutions such as the National Institutes of Health and the Centers for Disease Control is one of the most effective functions of the federal government. Research on severe mental illnesses should be continued under a National Brain Research Institute (see Chapter 9).

2. *Data collection.* The federal government should continue to carry out surveys and research projects that provide information on the number of people who have severe mental illnesses. Some of this data, such as the Epidemiologic Catchment Area (ECA) study, are useful to establish national norms. Other data should be collected in a standardized fashion by each state to use for purposes of comparison. Such data should include measures of treatment outcomes (see Chapter 7). For example, data could be collected on the incidence of alcohol and drug abuse among people with severe mental illnesses, the percentage of jail inmates who are mentally ill, and the number of mentally ill who have part-time or full-time employment. A federal agency could then use this

information to periodically publish a "report card" comparing data from each state. Random audits would establish the validity of the data.

3. *Demonstration projects.* Although some states may decide to fund services demonstration programs, this is also a reasonable function for the federal government. For example, a federal agency might fund a project in selected rural states to assess the effectiveness of physician assistants and nurse practitioners in diagnosing and treating persons with severe mental illnesses using a psychiatrist-consultant by means of interactive video telemedicine. Federal demonstration projects should be rigidly time-limited; in the past, states have converted some federal "demonstration" projects into ongoing federal subsidies.

4. *Standards and enforcement.* The federal government should have standards for the care of the mentally ill. It may wish to set its own standards, such as is presently done by the Health Care Financing Administration (HCFA), or it may wish to adopt standards created by private organizations such as the Joint Commission on Accreditation of Healthcare Organizations (JCAHO). For example, the federal government may specify that all nursing professionals and paraprofessionals working in residential care facilities for people with severe mental disorders should know how to recognize the early signs of tardive dyskinesia, a side effect of commonly used antipsychotic medications, and the symptoms of alcohol use in patients who are taking disulfiram (Antabuse), a drug used to discourage drinking in alcohol abusers. The federal government would not specify the minimum hours of training the nursing personnel should be given, nor how the training should be given, but rather would set a standard for the outcome of such training.

Enforcement of standards would come through federal inspections coordinated by the Inspector General of the Department of Health and Human Services. Although states would be expected to also do inspections to enforce state standards, a federal role is necessary to ensure that individual states do not significantly fail to meet minimum federal standards. In the event that they did, such states would be referred to the federal courts and the Department of Justice for appropriate action. Possible outcomes might resemble the following decision by a judge in a 1995 court case:

> *State Official Ordered To Live at Troubled Home (Memphis)*—A federal judge has ordered Tennessee's mental health commissioner to spend weekends at a state institution for the retarded where he says patients are dying of neglect.

"I'm terribly frustrated and terribly tired of this pass-the-buck job that you've done," U.S. District Judge Jon McCalla told Marjorie Nelle Cardwell in ordering her to spend every fourth weekend at the center. McCalla also imposed a $5,000-a-day fine until the state solves problems at Arlington Developmental Center.

As of July, 11 residents of the 400-bed institution had died in the previous 10 months, about twice the expected rate. Witnesses blamed some deaths on a lack of supervision, saying residents, unable to feed themselves, may have choked to death or gotten pneumonia after sucking food into their lungs.[8]

The Year 2001: What Should Services Look Like?

Providing humane, high-quality care for people who are unable to care for themselves is one of the fundamental functions of government and is part of the social contract. If we begin today to address the problems that are causing the mental illness crisis, within five years we should have largely solved it.

If we do this, what should services for the mentally ill look like in the year 2001? The services can, perhaps, be best described by revisiting some of the cases cited previously:

◇ Thomas McGuire will not hang himself. When he comes to an emergency room in acute mania and refuses treatment, he will be treated involuntarily. He will be kept in the hospital long enough to stabilize him on medication and to begin educating him and his family about his illness. Following discharge, he will remain on conditional release status for at least a year to ensure that he continues to take medication. He will also be taught how to reduce stress, which can be a precipitating factor in the recurrence of his illness. In short, he will be treated in the same manner as when he presented at the emergency room with a heart attack.

◇ Phyllis Iannotta will not be brutally murdered. She will be placed on outpatient commitment following her initial psychiatric hospitalization to ensure that she takes medication. If she becomes lost to follow-up, she will be returned to the mental illness treatment system by the nuns who run the women's shelter where she sometimes stays or by police officers who patrol Pennsylvania Station where she also lives; both shelter operators and police officers will have been trained to recognize the symptoms of severe mental illness and to call the mobile psychiatric treatment unit, which can initiate hospitalization. Following her stabilization on medication, Ms. Iannotta will be referred to a small group home patterned after the Fairweather Lodges in which all the residents work part-time. Ms. Iannotta will have a job in a factory for 20 hours a week doing work similar to that which she did for 22 years before becoming sick. Her income will consist of her factory wages plus a monthly government check for partial disability.

◇ George Wooten will not be jailed 100 times. Instead he will enter a jail diversion program during one of his initial incarcerations because jail officials will have been trained to recognize the symptoms of severe mental illness. He will then be assigned to a special Program for Assertive Community Treatment (PACT) team that specializes in treating mentally ill persons who also abuse drugs. His government disability check will be sent directly to a member of the treatment team, who will be the representative payee and who will help Mr. Wooten learn how to manage his funds. As he demonstrates his ability to avoid street drugs, ascertained by random urine testing, Mr. Wooten will be given increasing responsibility for his own funds.

◇ Sylvia Seegrist will not shoot 10 people in a shopping mall. During one of her initial hospitalizations she will be tested for insight, and it will be clear that her insight is severely impaired. She will therefore be placed on outpatient commitment status and will be required to take the medication she needs to prevent recurrence of her schizophrenia. She will join a clubhouse rehabilitation program, be trained as a medical technician, work 30 hours a week and live on her own. She will eventually live with, and later marry, another medical technician with whom she is working.

◇ Larry Hogue will not terrorize New York's West 96th Street. His pattern of cocaine abuse, psychiatric hospitalizations, and repeated encounters with law enforcement officials will become apparent very quickly because hospital officials will have a computerized capacity to access summary data on Mr. Hogue's police records. He will be tried in a variety of structured outpatient programs, including having a representative payee. However, he will continue to abuse cocaine and engage in antisocial behavior and therefore will be involuntarily committed to one of New York State's four remaining long-term hospitals, where he will remain for several years.

◇ Malcoum Tate will not terrorize his family and will not be killed by his sister. In the early stages of his illness, his need for involuntary outpatient commitment will become clear and he will be put on injectable antipsychotic medication once a month. On this medication he will be virtually symptom-free. He will be enrolled in a vocational training program in auto mechanics and will eventually be able to work full-time and be self-supporting.

These are not fanciful scenarios. They are the alternatives to similar tragedies that will occur if mentally ill men and women continue to commit suicide, be murdered, live on the streets and in shelters, be incarcerated in jails and prisons, and terrorize families and communities. They are the alternatives to having hundreds of thousands of severely ill people continue to live in the shadows of life.

What will it take to turn things around? How many more tragedies must occur before we say, Enough! At what point will public outrage penetrate the consciousness of federal officials, governors, mental health commissioners, county executives, mayors, and state and local legislators? They, ultimately, must be held responsible for these tragedies. They, ultimately, must implement the economic, legal, and ideological reforms necessary to reverse the present situation.

One measure of a civilized society is the care it provides for its disabled members. The care being provided for people with severe mental illnesses in America today is a disgrace. We have the knowledge that is needed to do much better. Whether or not we have the will is the question.

A p p e n d i x

THE MAGNITUDE OF DEINSTITUTIONALIZATION

The following table shows the magnitude of deinstitutionalization for 48 states and the District of Columbia. Alaska and Hawaii became states after deinstitutionalization was under way and are therefore not included. Since the total population of the United States increased from 164 million in 1955 to 260 million in 1994 and since the rate of population change varied markedly for different states, 1994 state population figures can be used to calculate the number of patients who theoretically would have been in public mental hospitals in 1994 if the hospitalization rate had been the same as that which existed in 1955. The effective deinstitutionalization rate, then, is the actual number of patients in public mental hospitals in 1994 subtracted from the theoretical number with the difference expressed as a percentage of the theoretical number (for a discussion of this table, see Chapter 1). The importance of looking at population change when assessing the magnitude of deinstitutionalization can be illustrated by looking at Nevada, which is especially anomalous because it actually had more patients in public psychiatric hospitals in 1994 (760) than it had in 1955 (440). It's *actual* deinstitutionalization rate is therefore plus 72.7 percent. However, because Nevada's total population increased more than sevenfold during the 40-year period, its *effective* deinstitutionalization rate, based on the population, was minus 71.4 percent.

State	Patients in Public Mental Hospitals Dec. 31, 1955*	Patients in Public Mental Hospitals Dec. 31, 1994†	Actual Deinstitution- alization Rate (percent)	Theoretical Number of Patients in Public Mental Hospitals in 1994, Based on Population Change since 1955‡	Effective Deinstitutionalization Rate (percent)
Rhode Island	3,442	63	98.2	4,156	98.5
New Hampshire	2,733	137	95.0	5,514	97.5
Arkansas	5,086	183	96.4	7,203	97.5
Vermont	1,294	63	95.1	1,975	96.8
Massachusetts	23,178	793	96.6	23,889	96.7
West Virginia	5,619	224	96.0	5,410	95.9
California	37,211	3,814	89.8	91,641	95.8
Wisconsin	14,981	891	94.1	20,680	95.7
Ohio	28,663	1,849	93.5	35,273	94.8
Colorado	5,720	775	86.5	13,470	94.2
Oklahoma	8,014	675	91.6	11,575	94.2
Illinois	37,883	2,845	92.5	47,153	94.0
Idaho	1,221	138	88.7	2,225	93.8
Kentucky	7,700	645	91.6	10,108	93.6
Arizona	1,690	462	72.7	6,947	93.3
Missouri	12,021	1,109	90.8	15,339	92.8
Montana	1,919	196	89.8	2,579	92.4
Connecticut	8,668	958	88.9	12,324	92.2
South Carolina	6,042	830	86.3	10,052	91.7
Texas	16,445	2,930	82.2	34,883	91.6
Washington	7,631	1,330	82.6	15,060	91.2
Indiana	11,151	1,320	88.2	14,706	91.0
Louisiana	8,271	1,091	86.8	12,084	91.0
Florida	8,026	2,766	65.5	29,857	90.7
Oregon	4,886	855	82.5	9,066	90.6
Minnesota	11,449	1,593	86.1	16,469	90.3
Tennessee	7,693	1,142	85.2	11,629	90.2
Iowa	5,336	513	90.4	5,217	90.2
Utah	1,337	326	75.6	3,257	90.0
New York	96,664	11,286	88.3	109,980	89.7
North Dakota	1,993	213	89.3	2,057	89.6
New Mexico	950	209	78.0	1,984	89.5
Nebraska	4,788	599	87.5	5,662	89.4
New Jersey	22,262	3,405	84.7	31,976	89.4
Pennsylvania	40,920	4,787	88.3	45,072	89.4
Maryland	9,273	1,820	80.4	17,236	89.4
Maine	2,996	440	85.3	3,995	89.0
Virginia	11,303	2,540	77.5	20,796	87.8

(Continued)

State	Patients in Public Mental Hospitals Dec. 31, 1955*	Patients in Public Mental Hospitals Dec. 31, 1994[†]	Actual Deinstitution- alization Rate (percent)	Theoretical Number of Patients in Public Mental Hospitals in 1994, Based on Population Change since 1955[‡]	Effective Deinstitutionalization Rate (percent)
Michigan	21,798	3,711	83.0	28,415	86.9
North Carolina	9,960	2,203	77.9	16,608	86.7
Georgia	11,701	3,239	72.3	22,663	85.7
Wyoming	655	147	77.6	1,014	85.5
Kansas	4,420	883	80.0	5,393	83.6
Alabama	7,197	1,649	77.1	9,934	83.4
Mississippi	5,295	1,208	77.2	6,837	82.3
South Dakota	1,603	317	80.2	1,749	81.9
Delaware	1,393	539	61.3	2,536	78.7
Washington, DC	7,318	1,148	84.3	5,280	78.3
Nevada	440	760	+72.7	2,658	71.4
Totals	558,239	71,619	82.0	821,586	91.3

*Patients in public prolonged-care hospitals for mental disease, December 31, 1955. Does not include patients on extended leave or outpatients. Statistics based on reports from 216 of 217 state and 47 of the 48 county hospitals. From *Patients in Mental Institutions 1955, Part II Public Hospitals for the Mentally Ill*. Public Health Service Publication no. 574. Washington, DC: U.S. Department of Health, Education, and Welfare, 1956.

[†]Resident patients in state and county mental hospitals, 1994 survey. Survey and Analysis Branch, Center for Mental Health Services, SAMSHA, U.S. Department of Health and Human Services.

[‡]Calculated by taking the ratio of patients to total population for each state in 1955 and assuming that the same ratio would have existed in 1994 based on the 1994 population.

References

CHAPTER 1:   PEOPLE IN THE SHADOWS: THE MANY FACES OF
MENTAL ILLNESS

1. Rewald, J. (1962). *Post-impressionism: From van Gogh to Gauguin.* New York: Museum of Modern Art, p. 321.
2. Torrey, E. F., Erdman, K., Wolfe, S. M., & Flynn, L. M. (1990). *Care of the seriously mentally ill: A rating of state programs* (3rd ed.). Washington, DC: Public Citizen Health Research Group and National Alliance for the Mentally Ill, pp. 175–176.
3. Health care reform for Americans with severe mental illnesses: Report of the National Advisory Mental Health Council. (1993). *American Journal of Psychiatry, 150,* 1447–1465.
4. Ibid.
5. Ibid.
6. Ibid.
7. Von Korff, M., Nestadt, G., Romanoski, A., Anthony, J., Eaton, W., Merchant, A., Chahal, R., Kramer, M., Folstein, M., & Gruenberg, E. (1985). Prevalence of treated and untreated *DSM-III* schizophrenia. *Journal of Nervous and Mental Disease, 173,* 577–581.
8. Munetz, M. R., & Geller, J. L. (1993). The least restrictive alternative in the postinstitutional era. *Hospital and Community Psychiatry, 44,* 967–973.

CHAPTER 2:   NOWHERE TO GO: HOMELESSNESS AND
MENTAL ILLNESS

1. Domenici, P. V. (1987, March 26). Street people who are mentally ill. *Washington Post,* p. A27.
2. Baker, F., Isaacs, C. D., & Schulberg, H. C. (1972). *Study of the relationship between Community Mental Health Centers and state mental hospitals* (NIMH contract no. HSM-42-70-107, p. iii). Boston: Socio-Technical Systems Associates.
3. A service delivery assessment on Community Mental Health Centers. (1979). *Inspector General Report of the Department of Health, Education and Welfare.*
4. Kates, B. (1985). *The murder of a shopping bag lady.* New York: Harcourt Brace Jovanovich. (All information on Ms. Iannotta is taken from this book.)
5. Ibid., p. 21.
6. Ibid., p. 13.
7. Holloway, L. (1995, February 3). Airport homeless: A long pleasant layover. *New York Times,* pp. A1, B5.
8. Jencks, C. (1994). *The homeless.* Cambridge: Harvard University Press, p. 16.

9. Ibid., p. 17.

10. Arce, A. A., Tadlock, M., Vergare, M. J., & Shapiro, S. H. (1983). A psychiatric profile of street people admitted to an emergency shelter. *Hospital and Community Psychiatry, 34*, 812–817.

11. Bassuk, E. L., Rubin, L., & Lauriat, A. (1984). Is homelessness a mental health problem? *American Journal of Psychiatry, 141*, 1546–1550.

12. Breakey, W. R., Fischer, P. J., Kramer, M., Nestadt, G., Romanoski, A. J., Ross, A., Royall, R. M., & Stine, O. C. (1989). Health and mental health problems of homeless men and women in Baltimore. *Journal of the American Medical Association, 262*, 1352–1357.

13. Koegel, P., Burnam, A., & Farr, R. K. (1988). The prevalence of specific psychiatric disorders among homeless individuals in the inner city of Los Angeles. *Archives of General Psychiatry, 45*, 1085–1092.

14. Vernez, G., Burnam, M. A., McGlynn, E. A., Trude, S., & Mittman, B. S. (1988). *Review of California's program for the homeless mentally disabled.* Santa Monica, CA: RAND Corporation.

15. *Psychiatry and homeless mentally ill persons. Report of the Task Force on the Homeless Mentally Ill.* (1990). Washington, DC: American Psychiatric Association.

16. Gelberg, L., Linn, L. S., & Leake, B. D. (1988). Mental health, alcohol and drug use, and criminal history among homeless adults. *American Journal of Psychiatry, 145*, 191–196.

17. *Mentally ill and homeless: A 22-city survey.* (1991). Washington, DC: The United States Conference of Mayors.

18. Broder, D. S., & Rich, S. (1991, November 9). Mayors discern growth in mentally ill homeless. *Washington Post*, p. A2.

19. Mundy, P., Robertson, M., Robertson, J., & Greenblatt, M. (1990). The prevalence of psychotic symptoms in homeless adolescents. *Journal of the American Academy of Child and Adolescent Psychiatry, 29*, 724–731.

20. Gelberg, L., & Linn, L. S. (1988). Social and physical health of homeless adults previously treated for mental health problems. *Hospital and Community Psychiatry, 39*, 510–516.

21. Breakey et al., op. cit.

22. Gelberg & Linn, op. cit.

23. Hibbs, J. R., Benner, L., Klugman, L., Spencer, R., Macchia, I., Mellinger, A. K., & Fife, D. (1994). Mortality in a cohort of homeless adults in Philadelphia. *New England Journal of Medicine, 331*, 304–309.

24. Berren, M. R., Hill, K. R., Merikle, E., Gonzalez, N., & Santiago, J. (1994). Serious mental illness and mortality rates. *Hospital and Community Psychiatry, 45*, 604–605.

25. Marshall, M., & Gath, D. (1992). What happens to homeless mentally ill people? Follow up of residents of Oxford hostels for the homeless. *British Medical Journal, 304*, 79–80.

26. Cisneros, H. G. (1993, December 5). The lonely death on my doorstep. *Washington Post*, p. C1.

27. Lamb, H. R., & Lamb, D. M. (1990). Factors contributing to homelessness among the chronically and severely mentally ill. *Hospital and Community Psychiatry, 41*, 301–305.

28. Krueger, C. (1990, October/November). Shooting of mentally ill man rocks mental health community. *Minnesota Mental Health Advocate*, p. 1.
29. Thomas-Lester, A., & Duggan, P. (1995, March 7). Victim in lion mauling had psychiatric problems. *Washington Post*, p. A1.
30. Dugger, C. W. (1992, January 12). Big shelters hold terrors for the mentally ill. *New York Times*, pp. 1, 22.
31. Darves-Bornoz, J. M., Lempérière, T., Degiovanni, A., & Gaillard, P. (1995). Sexual victimization in women with schizophrenia and bipolar disease. *Social Psychiatry and Psychiatric Epidemiology*, 30, 78–84.
32. Breakey et al., op. cit.
33. Cooper, C. J. (1988, December 18). Brutal lives of homeless S.F. women. *San Francisco Examiner*, pp. A1, A18.
34. Susser, E., Valencia, E., & Conover, S. (1993). Prevalence of HIV infection among psychiatric patients in a New York City men's shelter. *American Journal of Public Health*, 83, 568–570.
35. Alex, T. (1989, August 3). Drifter beaten, dies. *Des Moines Register*, p. 1A.
36. Lembede, M. (1988, August 30). Man charged in homeless woman's death. *Washington Post*, p. A14.
37. Mossman, D., & Perlin, M. I. (1992). Psychiatry and the homeless mentally ill: A reply to Dr. Lamb. *American Journal of Psychiatry*, 149, 951–957.
38. Ibid.
39. Ibid.
40. Cohen, C., & Thompson, K. S. (1993). Letter to the editor. *American Journal of Psychiatry*, 150, 990.
41. Cohen, C., & Thompson, K. S. (1992). Homeless mentally ill or mentally ill homeless? *American Journal of Psychiatry*, 149, 816–823.
42. Kozol, J. (1988). *Rachel and her children*. New York: Crown.
43. Rossi, P. (1989). *Down and out in America*. Chicago: University of Chicago Press.
44. Baum, A. S., & Burnes, D. W. (1993). *A nation in denial*. Boulder: Westview Press.
45. White, R. (1992). *Rude awakenings*. San Francisco: ICS Press.
46. Jencks, op. cit.
47. Koegel, Burnam, & Farr, op. cit.
48. Breakey et al., op. cit.
49. Gelberg, Linn, & Leake, op. cit.
50. Jencks, op. cit., p. 43.
51. Ibid., p. 22.
52. Goleman, D. (1987, September 11). New York: Mentally ill plagued by poor supervision, experts say. *New York Times*, pp. A1, B6.
53. Lamb & Lamb, op. cit.
54. Drake, R. E., Wallach, M. A., & Hoffman, J. S. (1989). Housing instability and homelessness among aftercare patients of an urban state hospital. *Hospital and Community Psychiatry*, 40, 46–51.
55. Belcher, J. R. (1988). Rights versus needs of homeless mentally ill persons. *Social Work*, 33, 398–402; Belcher, J. R. (1988). Defining the service needs of homeless mentally ill persons. *Hospital and Community Psychiatry*, 39, 1203–1205.
56. Gladwell, M. (1995, January 22). Backlash of the benevolent. *Washington Post*, pp. A1, A18.

57. Baxter, E., & Hopper, K. (1982). The new mendicancy: Homeless in New York City. *American Journal of Orthopsychiatry, 52*, 393–408.

CHAPTER 3: JAILS AND PRISONS

1. Torrey, E. F., Stieber, J., Ezekiel, J., Wolfe, S. M., Sharfstein, J., Noble, J. H., & Flynn, L. M. (1992). *Criminalizing the seriously mentally ill.* Washington, DC: National Alliance for the Mentally Ill and Public Citizen Health Research Group, p. 43. All other quotations in this chapter unless otherwise noted are from this report.
2. Kilzer, L. (1984, June 3). Jail as a "halfway house" . . . or long-term commitment? *Denver Post*, p. 3.
3. Grob, G. N. (1973). *Mental institutions in America.* New York: Free Press, p. 97.
4. Grob, G. N. (1966). *The state and the mentally ill.* Chapel Hill: University of North Carolina Press, p. 22.
5. Ibid., p. 24.
6. Grob, *Mental institutions in America,* op. cit., p. 116.
7. Deutsch, A. (1937). *The mentally ill in America.* New York: Doubleday, Doran and Co., p. 159.
8. Ibid., p. 165.
9. Wine, F. H. (1888). *Report on the defective, dependent and delinquent classes of the population of the United States.* Washington, DC: U.S. Government Printing Office.
10. Swank, G., & Winer, D. (1976). Occurrence of psychiatric disorder in a county jail population. *American Journal of Psychiatry, 133*, 1331–1333.
11. Bolton, A. (1976). *A study of the need for and availability of mental health services for mentally disordered jail inmates and juveniles in detention facilities.* Boston: Arthur Bolton Associates.
12. Whitmer, G. (1980). From hospitals to jails—The fate of California's deinstitutionalized mentally ill. *American Journal of Orthopsychiatry, 50*, 65–75.
13. Teplin, L. A. (1990). The prevalence of severe mental disorder among male urban jail detainees: Comparison with Epidemiologic Catchment Area program. *American Journal of Public Health, 80*, 663–669.
14. Guy, E., Platt, J. J., Zwerling, I., & Bullock, S. (1985). Mental health status of prisoners in an urban jail. *Criminal Justice and Behavior, 12*, 29–53.
15. Torrey et al., op. cit.
16. Jemelka, R., Trupin, E., & Chiles, J. A. (1989). The mentally ill in prisons: A review. *Hospital and Community Psychiatry, 40*, 481–485.
17. James, J. F., Gregory, D., Jones, R. K., & Rundell, O. H. (1980). Psychiatric morbidity in prisons. *Hospital and Community Psychiatry, 11*, 674–677.
18. Steadman, H. J., Fabisiak, S., Dvoskin, J., & Holohean, E. J. (1987). A survey of mental disability among state prison inmates. *Hospital and Community Psychiatry, 38*, 1086–1090.
19. Jemelka et al., op. cit.
20. Ibid.
21. Ibid.
22. Steinwachs, D., Kasper, J., & Skinner, E. (1992). *Final report: NAMI family survey.* Supported by the MacArthur Foundation, Arlington, VA: National Alliance for the Mentally Ill.

23. Gelberg, L., Linn, L. S., & Leake, B. D. (1988). Mental health, alcohol and drug use, and criminal history among homeless adults. *American Journal of Psychiatry*, *145*, 191–196.

24. Lamb, H. R., & Lamb, D. M. (1990). Factors contributing to homelessness among the chronically and severely mentally ill. *Hospital and Community Psychiatry*, *41*, 301–305.

25. *State and federal prisons report record growth during last 12 months.* (1995, December 3). Washington, DC: U. S. Department of Justice, Bureau of Justice Statistics.

26. Tobar, H. (1992, June 9) County OKs payment in jail beating. *Los Angeles Times.*

27. Torrey et al., op. cit. p. 59.

28. Collet, M. (1981, December 15). The crime of mental health. *Valley Times* (Pleasanton, CA).

29. Torrey et al., op. cit. p. 60.

30. Simmons, G. (1994, October 11). Inmate under suicide watch beaten to death. *Jackson Clarion-Ledger*, p 3

31. *Insane and in jail: The need for treatment options for the mentally ill in New York's county jails* [mimeo]. (1989). Correctional Association of New York.

32. Tobar, H. (1991, August 25–26). When jail is a mental institution. *Los Angeles Times.*

33. Jemelka, R. (1991). The mentally ill in local jails: Issues in admissions and booking. In H. J. Steadman (Ed.), *Jail diversion for the mentally ill* (pp. 35–63). Washington, DC: U.S. Department of Justice National Institute of Corrections, citing a study by L. Le Brun.

34. Tobar, 1991, op. cit.

35. King, M. (1983, December 27). Who cares for Kentucky's mentally ill? *Louisville Courier-Journal.*

36. Rogers, P. (1993, August 1). Plan aims to help mentally ill inmates. *Miami Herald*, p. 3B; also review of jail case record of Josue Mesidor, the inmate who died.

37. Moore, M. (1991, May 8). Jailers off the hook for prisoner's death. *Missoulian.*

38. Ciotta, R. (1987, February). For some mentally ill, road to treatment begins in jail. Newspaper account included in the *Erie AMI Newsletter* (Buffalo, NY).

39. Torrey et al., op. cit.

40. Sloat, B. (1994, September 8). Prison horrors for mentally ill, report reveals. *Cleveland Plain Dealer*, pp. 1–A, 10–A.

41. Grinfeld, M. J. (1995, April). Treatment of mentally ill in California's Pelican Bay Prison ruled unconstitutional. *Psychiatric Times*, p. 3.

42. Hurst, J. (1993, August 12). Suit assails no-medication policy at state prison. *Los Angeles Times*, pp. B1, B4.

43. *State and federal prisons*, op. cit.

44. Penrose, L. (1939). Mental disease and crime: Outline of a comparative study of European statistics. *British Journal of Medical Psychology*, *18*, 1–15.

45. Palermo, G. B., Smith, M. B., & Liska, F. J. (1991). Jails versus mental hospitals: A social dilemma. *International Journal of Offender Therapy and Comparative Criminology*, *35*, 97.

46. Abramson, M. (1972) The criminalization of mentally disordered behavior. *Journal of Hospital and Community Psychiatry*, *23*, 101–105.

47. Teplin, L. A. (1983). The criminalization of the mentally ill: Speculation in search of data. *Psychological Bulletin*, *94*, 54–67, quoting a 1973 study by Blair.

48. Bolton, op. cit.

49. Abramson, op. cit.

50. Valdisseri, E. V., Carroll, K. R., & Hartl, A. J. (1986). A study of offenses committed by psychotic inmates in a county jail. *Hospital and Community Psychiatry, 37,*
163–165.

51. *Diversion and treatment services for mentally ill detainees in the KCCF. Final report of contract for
the State of Washington Department of Corrections.* (1991, December 31). Delmar, NY:
Policy Research Associates.

52. Mulhern, B. (1990, December 15–18). Everyone's problem, no one's priority. *Capital Times* (Madison, WI).

53. Ibid.

54. Tobar, 1991, op. cit.

55. Ibid.

56. Fine, M. J., & Acker, C. (1989, September 13). Hoping that the law will find an
answer. *Philadelphia Inquirer.*

57. Rabkin, J. (1979). Criminal behavior of discharged mental patients: A critical appraisal of the research. *Psychological Bulletin, 86,* 1–27.

58. Sosowsky, L. (1980). Explaining the increased arrest rate among mental patients:
A cautionary note. *American Journal of Psychiatry, 137,* 1602–1605.

59. Belcher, J. R. (1988). Are jails replacing the mental health system for the homeless mentally ill? *Community Mental Health Journal, 24,* 185–195.

60. Foderaro, L. W. (1994, October 6). For mentally ill inmates, punishment is treatment. *New York Times,* p. A1.

61. Gamino, D. (1993, April 17). Jail rivals state hospital in mentally ill population.
Austin American-Statesman.

62. Seib, P. (1995, November 13). Jail is the wrong place for mentally impaired people. *Dallas Morning News,* p. 9.

63. Keene, L. (1993, July 6). A helping hand keeps mentally ill out of jail. *Seattle Times,*
pp. A1, A7.

64. Rother, C. (1995, March 30). For jails and the mentally ill, a sentence of growing
stress. *San Diego Union-Tribune.*

65. Grinfeld, M. J. (1993, July). Report focuses on jailed mentally ill. *Psychiatric Times,*
pp. 1–3.

CHAPTER 4: WALKING TIME BOMBS: VIOLENCE AND THE MENTALLY ILL

1. Lamb, H. R. (1987). Incompetency to stand trial. *Archives of General Psychiatry, 44,*
754–758.

2. Seegrist, R. S. (1986, August 24). What happened to Sylvia? *Philadelphia Inquirer
Magazine,* pp. 12–34.

3. Gray, J. P. (1857). Homicide in insanity. *American Journal of Insanity, 14,* 119–143.

4. Brown, P. (1985). *The transfer of care: Psychiatric deinsitutionalization and its aftermath.*
London: Routledge & Kegan Paul.

5. Rabkin, J. (1979). Criminal behavior of discharged mental patients: A critical appraisal of the research. *Psychological Bulletin, 86,* 1–27.

6. Sosowsky, L. (1980). Explaining the increased arrest rate among mental patients:
A cautionary note. *American Journal of Psychiatry, 137,* 1602–1605.

7. Klassen, D., & O'Connor, W. (1990). Assessing the risk of violence in released mental patients: A cross-validation study. *Psychological Assessment: A Journal of Consulting and Clinical Psychology, 1,* 75–81.

8. Lindqvist, P., & Allebeck, P. (1990). Schizophrenia and crime: A longitudinal follow-up of 644 schizophrenics in Stockholm. *British Journal of Psychiatry, 157,* 345–350.

9. Monahan, J. (1992). Mental disorder and violent behavior. *American Psychologist, 47,* 511–521.

10. Link, B. G., Andrews, H., & Cullen, F. T. (1992). The violent and illegal behavior of mental patients reconsidered. *American Sociological Review, 57,* 275–292.

11. Wesseley, S. C., Castle, D., Douglas, A. J., & Taylor, P. J. (1994). The criminal careers of incident cases of schizophrenia. *Psychological Medicine, 24,* 483–502.

12. Shore, D., Filson, C. R., & Rae, D. S. (1990). Violent crime arrest rates of White House case subjects and matched control subjects. *American Journal of Psychiatry, 147,* 746–750.

13. Martell, D. A., & Dietz, P. E. (1992). Mentally disordered offenders who push or attempt to push victims onto subway tracks in New York City. *Archives of General Psychiatry, 49,* 472–475.

14. Steinwachs, D. M., Kasper, J. D., & Skinner, E. A. (1992). *Family perspectives on meeting the needs for care of severely mentally ill relatives: A national survey.* Arlington, VA: National Alliance for the Mentally Ill.

15. Hatfield, A. B. (1990). *Family education in mental illness.* New York: Guilford, p. 33, citing a study by Swan, R. W., & Lavitt, M. R. (1986). *Patterns of adjustment to violence in families of the mentally ill.* New Orleans: Tulane University School of Social Work, Elizabeth Wisna Research Center.

16. Straznickas, K. A., McNeil, D. E., & Binder, R. L. (1993). Violence toward family caregivers by mentally ill relatives. *Hospital and Community Psychiatry, 44,* 385–387.

17. Tardiff, K. (1984). Characteristics of assaultive patients in private hospitals. *American Journal of Psychiatry, 141,* 1232–1235.

18. Runions, J., & Prudo, R. (1983). Problem behaviors encountered by families living with a schizophrenic member. *Canadian Journal of Psychiatry, 28,* 383–386.

19. Doe, J. (1987, May 6). My brother might kill me. *New York Times,* p. A13.

20. Swanson, J. W., Holzer, C. E., Ganju, V. K., & Jono, R. T. (1990). Violence and psychiatric disorder in the community: Evidence from the Epidemiologic Catchment Area surveys. *Hospital and Community Psychiatry, 41,* 761–770.

21. Hodgins, S. (1992). Mental disorder, intellectual deficiency, and crime. *Archives of General Psychiatry, 49,* 476–483.

22. Monahan, op. cit.

23. Torrey, E. F. (1994). Violent behavior by individuals with serious mental illness. *Hospital and Community Psychiatry, 45,* 653–662.

24. Petersson, H., & Gudjonsson, G. H. (1981). Psychiatric apsects of homicide. *Acta Psychiatrica Scandinavica, 64,* 363–372.

25. Smith, J., & Hucker, S. (1994). Schizophrenia and substance abuse. *British Journal of Psychiatry, 165,* 13–21.

26. Lindqvist & Allebeck, op. cit

27. Smith & Hucker, op. cit.

28. Weiden, P. J., Dixon, L., Frances, A., Appelbaum, P., Haas, G., & Rapkin, B. (1991). Neuroleptic compliance in schizophrenia. In C. Tamminga & C. Schulz (Eds.),

Advances in neuropsychiatry and psychopharmacology: Vol. 1. Schizophrenia research. New York: Raven.

29. Bartels, J., Drake, R. E., Wallach, M. A., & Freeman, D. H. (1991). Characteristic hostility in schizophrenic outpatients. *Schizophrenia Bulletin, 17,* 163–171.

30. Smith, L. D. (1989). Medication refusal and the rehospitalized mentally ill inmate. *Hospital and Community Psychiatry, 40,* 491–496.

31. Link et al., 1992, op. cit.

32. Taylor, P. (1985). Motives for offending amongst violent and psychotic men. *British Journal of Psychiatry, 147,* 491–498.

33. Yesavage, J. A. (1982). Inpatient violence and the schizophrenic patient: An inverse correlation between danger-related events and neuroleptic levels. *Biological Psychiatry, 17,* 1331–1337.

34. Weaver, K. E. (1983). Increasing the dose of antipsychotic medication to control violence [Letter]. *American Journal of Psychiatry, 140,* 1274.

35. Torrey, E. F., Stieber, J., Ezekiel, J., Wolfe, S. M., Sharfstein, J., Noble, J. H., & Flynn, L. M. (1992). *Criminalizing the seriously mentally ill.* Washington, DC: National Alliance for the Mentally Ill and Public Citizen Health Research Group, p. 48.

36. *Insane and in jail: The need for treatment options for the mentally ill in New York's county jails* [Mimeo]. (1989). Correctional Association of New York.

37. Krakowski, M. I., Convit, A., Jaeger, J., Lin, S., & Volavka, J. (1989). Neurological impairment in violent schizophrenic inpatients. *American Journal of Psychiatry, 146,* 849–853.

38. Whitmer, G. (1980). From hospitals to jails—The fate of California's deinstitutionalized mentally ill. *American Journal of Orthopsychiatry, 50,* 65–75.

39. Taylor, P. J., Mullen, P., & Wessely, S. (1993). Psychosis, violence, and crime. In J. Gunn & P. J. Taylor (Eds.), *Forensic psychiatry: Clinical, legal, and ethical issues* (pp. 330–372). London: Butterworth & Heinemann.

40. Link, B. G., & Strueve, A. (1994). Psychotic symptoms and the violent/illegal behavior of mental patients compared to community controls. In J. Monahan & H. J. Steadman (Eds.), *Violence and mental disorder: Developments in risk assessment.* Chicago: University of Chicago Press.

41. Taylor et al., op. cit.

42. Apperson, L. J., Mulvey, E. P., & Lidz, C. W. (1993). Short-term clinical prediction of assaultive behavior: Artifacts of research methods. *American Journal of Psychiatry, 150,* 1374–1379.

43. Lidz, C. W., Mulvey, E. P., & Gardner, W. (1993). The accuracy of predictions of violence to others. *Journal of the American Medical Association, 269,* 1007–1011.

44. Violence among mentally ill found to be concentrated among those with comorbid substance abuse disorders. (1995, December 2). *Psychiatric News,* p. 8.

45. Lamb, op. cit.

46. Michigan takes steps to improve procedures for dealing with criminally insane. (1994, January 21). *Psychiatric News,* p. 8.

47. Barbanel, J. (1988, March 2). Brooklyn double murder: Mental patient and a flawed system. *New York Times,* pp. B1, B4.

48. Ablow, K. R. (1991, February 12). Murder with no apparent motive. *Washington Post Health,* p. 9; Grinfeld, M. J. (1995, March). Suit threatens to expand malpractice liability. *Psychiatric Times,* pp. 1–5.

49. Guthrie, D., & Hogan, J. (1991, April 18). Murder suspect had been hospitalized here. *Kalamazoo Gazette*, p. A1; Mental health system's flaws lead to tragedy [Editorial]. (1991, April 19). *Kalamazoo Gazette*, p. A10.

50. Miller, B. (1993, July 10). Woman freed on insanity plea held in new slaying. *Washington Post*, p. B1; Davis, P., & Miller, B. (1993, July 13). Police had warning of violence. *Washington Post*, p. B1; Twomey, S. (1993, July 15). When insanity collides with humanity. *Washington Post*, p. B1.

51. Bavley, A. (1993, June 26). Killing points up concern over care for mentally ill. *Kansas City Star*, p. A-18.

52. Wahl, O. F. (1987). Public vs. professional conceptions of schizophrenia. *Journal of Community Psychology, 15,* 285–291.

53. Link, B. G., Cullen, F. T., Frank, J., & Wozniak, J. F. (1987). The social rejection of former mental patients: Understanding why labels matter. *American Journal of Sociology, 92,* 1461–1500.

54. Day, D. M. (1986). Portrayal of mental illness in Canadian newspapers. *Canadian Journal of Psychiatry, 31,* 813–816.

55. Wahl, O. F. (1992). Mass media images of mental illness: A review of the literature. *Journal of Community Psychology, 20,* 343–352.

56. Wahl, O. F., & Roth, R. (1982). Television images of mental illness: Results of a metropolitan Washington media watch. *Journal of Broadcasting, 28,* 599–605.

57. Signorelli, N. (1989). The stigma of mental illness on television. *Journal of Broadcasting and Electronic Media, 33,* 325–331.

58. Margolick, D. (1992, November 1). Lowenstein killer moves toward freedom. *New York Times*, pp. B49, B54.

59. Anderson, J. W. (1986, October 11). Man smashes Constitution case. *Washington Post*, pp. B1–B2.

60. Castaneda, R. (1989, October 26). Sen. Glenn assaulted. *Washington Post*, p. B1.

61. Drifter indicted in church fires. (1992, February 14). *Washington Post*, p. A19.

62. Fan obsessed with skater sentenced to mental hospital. (1992, June 2). *Los Angeles Times*, p. A22.

63. Locy, T. (1995, March 21). Clinton not the target, defense says. *Washington Post*, p. C1.

64. Smothers, R. (1990, April 25). Man shoots 5, killing one, in a Georgia shopping mall. *New York Times*, p. A16.

65. Prochnau, B. (1986, May 13). The twisted tale of human slaughter. *Washington Post*, pp. C1–C2.

66. Peterson, B. (1988, May 22). Tainted food tied to school rampage. *Washington Post*, p. A3.

67. Smothers, R. (1989, September 16). Disturbed past of killer of 7 is unraveled. *New York Times*, p. A10.

68. San Francisco office gunman carried letter detailing woes. (1993, July 4). *Washington Post*, A20.

69. Boodman, S. G. (1994, October 4). Predicting violence among the mentally ill. *Washington Post Health*, p. 7.

70. Man charged in clinic killings is called "delusional" by doctor. (1995, July 25). *New York Times*, p. A9.

71. Tavris, C. (1987, September 9). Acts of violence by mentally ill raise questions. *Los Angeles Times*, p. 3.

72. Driscoll, K. (1992, June 21). Accused killer's parents struggle to mend system and themselves. *Rochester Democrat and Chronicle*, pp. 1A, 6A.
73. Lawes, C. (1991, June 20). Jackson soup kitchen director gunned down. *Jackson Clarion-Ledger*, pp. A1, A13.
74. Lichtblau, E., & Drummond, T. (1990, October 20). Did mental care system fail Betty Madeira? *Los Angeles Times*, pp. B1, B5.
75. Cohn, R. (1988, April 1). Man who killed stepfather with bow gets 10-year term. *Lexington Herald-Leader*, p. C1.
76. Suspect's ills are described. (1987, November 29). *Washington Post*, p. A20.
77. Terwilliger, C. (1993, December 5). Tragic slide into private horror. *St. Paul Press-Enterprise*, pp. A3, A8.
78. Lore, D. (1990, July 24). Mind medicine. *Columbia State*, p. 3.
79. Gutterman, R. S. (1994, November 9). School shooting suspect known as troubled, odd. *Cleveland Plain Dealer*, p. 3A.
80. Baltimore man charged in mother's slaying. (1990, December 27). *Washington Post*, p. D3.
81. Kuhlman, T. L. (1992). Unavoidable tragedies in Madison, Wisconsin: A third view. *Hospital and Community Psychiatry, 43*, 72–73.
82. Butterfield, F. (1996, January 31). Killing of 2 nuns prompts questioning of mental care. *New York Times*, p. A10.
83. Sarra, G. (1996, January 28). Reports of DuPont's eccentricity were rife. *Washington Post*, p. A4.
84. Lagos, J. M., Perlmintter, K., & Saexinger, H. (1977). Fear of the mentally ill: Empirical support for the common man's response. *American Journal of Psychiatry, 134*, 1134–1137.
85. Steadman, H. J. (1981). Critically reassessing the accuracy of public perceptions of the dangerousness of the mentally ill. *Journal of Health and Social Behavior, 22*, 310–316.
86. Monahan, op. cit.

Chapter 5:   Psychiatric Ghettos: Communities and Families

1. Denying the mentally ill [Editorial]. (1981, June 5). *New York Times*, p. A26.
2. The discharged chronic mental patient. (1974, April 12). *Medical World News*, pp. 47–58.
3. Hilts, P. J. (1980, October 27). Mental health revolution: Clearing "warehouses." *Washington Post*, pp. A1–A3.
4. The discharged chronic mental patient, op. cit.
5. Fentress, C. (1981, May). Emptying the madhouse: The mentally ill have become our cities' lost souls. *Life*, pp. 56–62.
6. Phillips, B. J. (1991, July 23). No one to ease his demon grip. *Philadelphia Inquirer*, p. 9.
7. The Ocean Grover, a brochure published by the Ocean Grove Camp Meeting Association, summer 1995 issue.
8. New Jersey now. (1933, May). *National Geographic*, p. 543.
9. Nordheimer, J. (1992, July 12). Shore towns dread release of mentally ill. *New York Times*, p. A25.

10. Vignettes of Ocean Grove are taken from material submitted to the Monmouth County Mental Health Board, May 1992, and from interviews with residents, November 1995.

11. Craig, W. (1987, March). Asylum by the sea. *New Jersey Reporter*, pp. 8–26.

12. The discharged chronic mental patient, op. cit.

13. Kihss, P. (1980, November 23). Influx of former mental patients burdening city, Albany is told. *New York Times*.

14. The danger of dumping the mentally ill [Editorial]. (1979, December 26). *New York Times*, p. A26.

15. Barbanel, J. (1985, November 15). On the streets, tough test for new homeless policy. *New York Times*, pp. A1, B1, B5.

16. Barbanel, J. (1987, October 30). 10 homeless people held at Bellevue Mental Unit. *New York Times*, p. B3.

17. The mental health sieve [Editorial]. (1988, October 2). *New York Times*, p. A24.

18. I'm sick, I'm sick, and I have no one [Editorial]. (1985, October 25). *New York Times*, p. A18.

19. Dugger, C. W. (1995, January 7). State called patient violent, then let him roam. *New York Times*, pp. A1, A26.

20. James, G. (1995, December 15). Hospitals never knew past of patient in stabbing case. *New York Times*, p. B3.

21. McFadden, R. D. (1993, December 12). A long slide from privilege ends in chaos on the L.I.R.R. *New York Times*, pp. A1, A56.

22. Sullivan, R. (1986, July 12). City inquiry in ferry slashing criticizes hospital for release. *New York Times*, p. A1.

23. Hays, C. L. (1989, April 12). Man was held in earlier knife incident. *New York Times*, p. B3.

24. Man is sought in attack on 2 in Central Park. (1990, August 1). *New York Times*, p. B4.

25. Baquet, D. (1991, January 21). Drifter sought Bellevue help before murder. *New York Times*, p. B1.

26. Patron stabbed by berserk man at film theater. (1990, November 15). *New York Times*, p. B13.

27. Isaac, R. J., & Jaffee, D. J. (1995, December 23). Mental illness, public safety. *New York Times*, p. A27.

28. Rangel, J. (1986, August 15). Student seized in shootout got care in Georgia. *New York Times*, p. B3.

29. Hornblower, M. (1985, November 19). Deak-Perera chairman fatally shot in office. *Washington Post*, p. A3.

30. McFadden, R. D. (1994, September 2). Suspect in stagehand's killing is termed driven by paranoia. *New York Times*, pp. B1–B2.

31. Sullivan, R. (1989, October 17). Killer of pregnant Bellevue doctor says at trial that he was insane. *New York Times*, p. A1.

32. Gonzalez, D. (1993, January 21). Homeless man was treated before slaying. *New York Times*, pp. B1, B5.

33. Barbanel, J. (1988, September 26). Slaying in cathedral spurs scrutiny of mental health care. *New York Times*, p. B1.

34. Tabor, M. B. W. (1991, October 2). Mental hospital escapee is held in stabbing death of father. *New York Times*, pp. B1, B6.

35. Hays, C. L. (1989, January 9). Queens woman charged with killing mother. *New York Times*, p. B1.

36. Myers, S. L. (1993, January 23). Queens man kills wife and 2 girls, police say. *New York Times*, p. 25.

37. Herbert, B. (1995, January 7). Double-trouble killers. *New York Times*, p. A23.

38. Amateur hour at mental health. (1995, January 7). *New York Times*, p. A22.

39. Isaac & Jaffee, op. cit.

40. Information about Joyce Brown is taken from Isaac, R. J., & Armat, V. C. (1990). *Madness in the streets*. New York: Free Press, pp. 256–260; Will, G. F. (1987, November 19). A right to live on a sidewalk? *Washington Post*, p. A23; Rezendes, M. (1988, February 20). The cry from the street. *Washington Post*, pp. B1, B7; and Cournos, F. (1989). Involuntary medication and the case of Joyce Brown. *Hospital and Community Psychiatry*, 40, 736–740.

41. Stengel, R. (1987, September 14). At issue: Freedom for the irrational. *Time*, p. 88.

42. Gold, P. (1987, October 19). Revolving doors trap mentally ill. *Insight*, pp. 22–23.

43. Information about Joyce Brown, op. cit.

44. Wickenhaver, J. (1991, June 25). Menace in the streets. *Manhattan Spirit*, pp. 2, 16.

45. Information on the Larry Hogue case is taken from Dugger, C. W. (1992, September 3). Threat only when on crack, homeless man foils system. *New York Times*, pp. A1, B4; Dugger, C. W. (1992, December 23). Judge orders homeless man hospitalized. *New York Times*, pp. B1–B2; Dugger, C. W. (1993, July 28). Son to house troubled man feared on West Side. *New York Times*, pp. B1, B4; Dugger, C. W. (1994, July 15). Larry Hogue is recaptured while at bank. *New York Times*, pp. B1–B2.

46. Fiegel, M. (1994, March 30). The Rip Van Winkle of psychiatry [Letter]. *Wall Street Journal*.

47. Sandler, S. (1992, November 17). The West Side has lost patience. *New York Times*, p. A15.

48. Will, G. F. (1987, November 19). A right to live on a sidewalk? *Washington Post*, p. A23.

49. Maier, G. J. (1989). The tyranny of irresponsible freedom [Editorial]. *Hospital and Community Psychiatry*, 40, 453.

50. Bonovitz, J. C., & Bonovitz, J. S. (1981). Diversion of the mentally ill into the criminal justice system: The police intervention perspective. *American Journal of Psychiatry*, 138, 973–976.

51. Blumenthal, R. (1989, November 16). Emotionally ill pose growing burden to police. *New York Times*, pp. A1, B2.

52. Jacobs, C. (1994). *Criminalization of Californians with mental illness* [Mimeo]. California Alliance for the Mentally Ill.

53. Husted, J. R., Charter, R. A., & Perrou, B. (1995). California law enforcement agencies and the mentally ill offender. *Bulletin of the American Academy of Psychiatry and the Law*, 23, 315–329.

54. Gillig, P. M., Dumaine, M., Widish, J., Hillard, J. R., & Grubb, P. (1990). What do police officers really want from the mental health system? *Hospital and Community Psychiatry*, 41, 663–665.

55. Tobar, H. (1991, August 25–26). When jail is a mental institution. *Los Angeles Times*.

56. Simpsons arraigned. (1993, May 20). *Burt County Plaindealer*.

57. Blumenthal, op. cit.

58. Woodruff, N. (1994, September 27). Whitefish woman holds police at bay with pistol. *Kalispell Daily Inter Lake*, p. A4.
59. Blumenthal, op. cit.
60. Ibid.
61. Kraft, B. P. (1993, July 10). Suspect pleads guilty in slaying of police officer. *Jackson Clarion-Ledger*, p. 1.
62. Hart, C. N. (1993, September/October). Tragedy raises many questions. *Mental Health Advocate*, p. 2. Alliance for the Mentally Ill of Minnesota.
63. Cop killer was hostile loner who liked to feed birds. (1994, October 3). *Kalispell Daily Inter Lake*, p. 3.
64. N.M. gunfire kills three. (1994, May 28). *Denver Post*, pp. 1B, 8B.
65. Holden, D. (1994, November 27). Relatives say Zmyewski was severely mentally ill. *Huntsville Times*, pp. A1, A8.
66. Quinn, C. (1995, March 1). Officer dies of gunshot wound. *Winston-Salem Journal*, pp. A1, A4.
67. Marcus, E. (1991, October 18). Police fired 17 shots at Md. man. *Washington Post*, pp. C1, C6.
68. Tabor, M. B. W. (1992, May 30). Mother denies police version of son's killing. *New York Times*, p. A23.
69. Ginn, S. (1994, October 17). Mother says son was trying to salvage his life. *Riverside Press-Enterprise*, pp. B1, B3.
70. Barrionuevo, A. (1995, May 20). Workers say slain autistic teen had shown no violent behavior. *Dallas Morning News*, p. 3.
71. Hansen, D. (1995, March 8). Police shoot, kill armed man. *Spokane Spokesman-Review*, pp. A1, A7.
72. Insane cuts. (1995, August 27). *St. Petersburg Times*, p. 9.
73. Hibdon, K., & McLean, B. (1995, December 19). Officer, attacker shot. *Ventura Star*, pp. A1, A8.
74. Weaver, N. (1994, October 4). Mental health cuts unlock doors to new treatments. *Sacramento Bee*, p. 8.
75. Kelley, W. (1992). Unmet needs. *Journal of the California Alliance for the Mentally Ill*, 3, 28–30.
76. Shermeister, C. (1985, April 4). A swift descent into consuming madness. *Sheboygan Press*, pp. 1, 8.
77. Blais, M. (1987, May 24). Trish. *Tropic: Miami Herald Sunday Magazine*, pp. 7–16.
78. Swados, E. (1991). *The four of us*. New York: Farrar, Straus & Giroux.
79. Dearth, N., Labenski, B. J., Mott, E. M., & Pellegrini, L. M. (1986). *Families helping families: Living with schizophrenia*. New York: Norton.
80. Suchetka, D., & Martin, B. (1989, February 27). N.C. family's final solution was murder. *Charlotte Observer*, pp. 1A, 8A.

Chapter 6: Looking Backward: Where We Have Been

1. Cruel and inhumane [Editorial]. (1994, September 11). *Cleveland Plain Dealer*, p. 12.
2. Deutsch, A. (1937). *The mentally ill in America*. New York: Columbia University Press, p. 123.
3. Maisel, A. Q. (1946, May 6). Bedlam 1946. *Life*, pp. 102–118.

4. Sareyan, A. (1993). *The turning point: How men of conscience brought about major change in the care of America's mentally ill.* Washington, DC: American Psychiatric Press, p. 67.
5. Maisel, op. cit.
6. Deutsch, A. (1948). *The shame of the states.* New York: Harcourt Brace.
7. Groman, M. (1947). *Oklahoma attacks its snake pits.* Norman: University of Oklahoma Press.
8. Sloat, B. (1994, September 8). Prison horrors for mentally ill, report reveals. *Cleveland Plain Dealer*; Sloat, B. (1994, September 9).
9. Sloat, op. cit.
10. Okin, R. L., Borus, J. F., Baer, L., & Jones, A. L. (1995). Long-term outcome of state hospital patients discharged into structural community residential settings. *Psychiatric Services, 46,* 73–78.
11. Okin, R. L., Dolnick, J. A., & Pearsall, D. T. (1983). Patients' perspectives on community alternatives to hospitalization: A follow-up study. *American Journal of Psychiatry, 140,* 1460–1464.
12. Sacks, O. (1991, February 13). Forsaking the mentally ill. *New York Times,* p. A23.
13. Panzetta, A. F. (1985). Whatever happened to Community Mental Health: Portents for corporate medicine. *Hospital and Community Psychiatry, 36,* 1174–1179.
14. Wing, J. K. (1960). Pilot experiment in the rehabilitation of long-hospitalized male schizophrenic patients. *British Journal of Preventive and Social Medicine, 14,* 173–180.
15. Braun, P., Kochansky, G., Shapiro, R., Greenberg, S., Gudeman, J. E., Johnson, S., & Shore, M. F. (1981). Overview: Deinstitutionalization of psychiatric patients, a critical review of outcome studies. *American Journal of Psychiatry, 138,* 736–749.
16. Attkisson, C., Cook, J., Karno, M., Lehman, A., McGlashan, T. H., Meltzer, H. Y., O'Connor, M., Richardson, D., Rosenblatt, A., Wells, K., & Williams, J. (1992). Clinical services research. *Schizophrenia Research, 18,* 605.
17. Lamb, H. R. (1988). Deinstitutionalization at the crossroads. *Hospital and Community Psychiatry, 39,* 941–945.
18. Okin, R. L. (1987). The case for deinstitutionalization. *Harvard Mental Health Letter, 4,* 5–7.
19. Talbott, J. A. (1979). Deinstitutionalization: Avoiding the disasters of the past. *Hospital and Community Psychiatry, 30,* 621–624.
20. Talbott, J. A. (1985). Our patients' future in a changing world. *American Journal of Psychiatry, 142,* 1003–1008.

CHAPTER 7: NEW INITIATIVES IN FUNDING

1. Califano, J. A. (1993, April 1). The last time we reinvented health care. *Washington Post,* p. A23.
2. Inglehart, J. K. (1993). The American health care system. *New England Journal of Medicine, 328,* 896–900; Inglehart, J. K. (1995). Medicaid and managed care. *New England Journal of Medicine, 332,* 1727–1731.
3. *Annual Statistical Supplement, Social Security Bulletin.* (1995). Washington, DC: Social Security Administration. Most of the data on SSI and SSDI were also taken from this annual publication.

4. Kiesler, C. A. (1980). Mental health policy as a field of inquiry for psychology. *American Psychologist, 35,* 1066–1080.

5. Taube, C. A., Goldman, H. H., & Salkever, D. (1990, Spring). Medicaid coverage for mental illness: Balancing access and costs. *Health Affairs,* 5–18.

6. *Public mental health systems, Medicaid re-structuring and managed behavioral healthcare* [Mimeo]. (1995). Alexandria, VA: National Association of State Mental Health Program Directors.

7. Morgan, D. (1993, April 13). Are cash-starved states "looting" Medicaid coffers? *Washington Post,* p. A17; and Morgan, D. (1993, February 7). Medicaid loopholes closing for strapped states. *Washington Post,* p. A23.

8. Lave, J. R., & Goldman, H. H. (1990, Spring). Medicare financing for mental health care. *Health Affairs,* 19–30.

9. Annual Statistical Supplement, op. cit.

10. MacDonald, H. (1995, Winter). Welfare's next Vietnam. *City Journal,* pp. 23–38.

11. Ibid.

12. Jencks, C. (1994). *The homeless.* Cambridge, MA: Harvard University Press, p. 38. See also MacDonald, op. cit.

13. Smolkin, S. (1995). *Characteristics of food stamp households Summer 1993.* Washington, DC: U.S. Department of Agriculture, p. 45.

14. Information on HUD programs was obtained from Ms. Sylvia Oliver, Informations Systems Division, U.S. Department of Housing and Urban Development, September 7, 1995, and from other federal officials knowledgeable about these programs but who did not wish to be named.

15. Memorandum from Director of Mental Health and Behavioral Sciences Service, Department of Veterans Affairs, to the National Alliance for the Mentally Ill, April 22, 1993.

16. Annual Statistical Supplement, op. cit.

17. Memorandum from Director of Mental Health and Behavioral Sciences Service, op. cit.

18. Torrey, E. F. (1988). *Nowhere to go.* New York: Harper & Row, pp. 221–228.

19. Lutterman, T., Hollen, V., & Hogan, M. (1993). *Funding sources and expenditures of state mental health agencies: Revenue/expenditure study results fiscal year 1990.* Alexandria, VA: National Association of State Mental Health Program Directors.

20. Brill, H., & Patton, R. E. (1962). Clinical-statistical analysis of population changes in New York State mental hospitals since introduction of psychotropic drugs. *American Journal of Psychiatry, 19,* 20–35.

21. Lerman, P. (1981). *Deinstitutionalization: A cross-problem analysis.* (DHHS Publication No. ADM 81–987). Washington, DC: U.S. Government Printing Office, pp. 68, 100.

22. Gronfein, W. (1985). Incentives and intentions in mental health policy: A comparison of the Medicaid and the community mental health programs. *Journal of Health and Social Behavior, 26,* 192–206.

23. *Health, United States, 1987.* (1988). (DHHS Publication No. PHS 88-1232). Washington, DC: U.S. Government Printing Office.

24. Morrissey, J. P. (1989). The changing role of the public mental hospital. In D. A. Rochefort (Ed.), *Handbook on mental health policy in the United States* (p. 273). Westport, CT: Greenwood Press.

25. Talbott, J. A. (1981). The national plan for the chronically mentally ill: A programmatic analysis. *Hospital and Community Psychiatry, 32,* 699–704.

26. Manderscheid, R. W., & Sonnenschein, M. A. (1994). *Mental health, United States, 1994.* Center for Mental Health Services (DHHS Publication No. SMA 94-3000). Washington, DC: U.S. Government Printing Office, p. 103.

27. Kiesler, C. A., & Simpkins, C. G. (1993). *The unnoticed majority in psychiatric inpatient care.* New York: Plenum, p. 196.

28. Ibid., p. 231.

29. White, C. L., Bateman, A., Fisher, W. H., & Geller, J. L. (1995). Factors associated with admission to public and private hospitals from a psychiatric emergency screening site. *Psychiatric Services, 46,* 467–472.

30. Eisenhuth, B. (1983). Profiles of the street people. *Hospital and Community Psychiatry, 34,* 818.

31. Besharov, D. J. (1995, June 11). The welfare balloon. *Washington Post,* p. C3.

32. The funding sources for mental health programs in Iowa were kindly provided by Mr. Larry Allen, Management Analyst, Iowa Department of Human Services, Des Moines, Iowa.

33. The discharged chronic mental patient. (1974, April 12). *Medical World News,* pp. 47–58.

34. Dorwart, R. A., & Hoover, C. M. (1994). A national study of transitional hospital services in mental health. *American Journal of Public Health, 84,* 1229–1234.

35. Gilbert, P. L., Harris, M. J., McAdams, L. A., & Jeste, D. V. (1995). Neuroleptic withdrawal in schizophrenic patients: A review of the literature. *Archives of General Psychiatry, 52,* 173–188.

36. Kissling, W. (1994). Compliance quality assurance and standards for relapse prevention in schizophrenia. *Acta Psychiatrica Scandinavica, 89*(Suppl. 382), 16–24.

37. Davidson, R. (1991, December 9). A mental health crisis in Illinois. *Chicago Tribune,* p. 20.

38. Herbert, B. (1993, September 5). Mental health failures. *Washington Post,* p. A15.

39. Karras, A., & Otis, D. B. (1987). A comparison of inpatients in an urban state hospital in 1975 and 1982. *Hospital and Community Psychiatry, 38,* 963–967.

40. Geller, J. L. (1992). A report on the "worst" state hospital recidivists in the U.S. *Hospital and Community Psychiatry, 43,* 904–908.

41. Torrey, op. cit., p. 15.

42. Torrey, E. F., Stieber, J., Ezekiel, J., Wolfe, S. M., Sharfstein, J., Noble, J. H., & Flynn, L. M. (1992). *Criminalizing the seriously mentally ill.* Washington, DC: National Alliance for the Mentally Ill and Public Citizen Health Research Group.

43. Sheehan, S. (1982). *Is there no place on earth for me?* Boston: Houghton Mifflin.

44. Moran, A. E., Freedman, R. I., & Sharfstein, S. S. (1984). The journey of Sylvia Frumkin: A case study for policymakers. *Hospital and Community Psychiatry, 35,* 887–893.

45. Herbert, op. cit.

46. Collet, M. (1981, December 15). The crime of mental health. *Valley Times* (Pleasanton, CA).

47. Rapid rise in children on SSI disability rolls follows new regulations. (1994). (GAO/HEHS-94-225). Washington, DC: U.S. General Accounting Office.

48. MacDonald, op. cit.

49. Ibid.

50. McManus, M. C., & Frieson, B. J. (1989, June 1). Relinquishing legal custody as a means of obtaining services for children who have serious mental or emotional disorders. Testimony for Subcommittee on Human Resources, Committee on Ways and Means, U.S. House of Representatives, June 1, 1989.

51. Cohen, R., Harris, R., Gottlieb, S., & Best, A. M. (1991). States' use of transfer of custody as a requirement for providing services to emotionally disturbed children. *Hospital and Community Psychiatry, 42,* 526–530.

52. Torrey, *Nowhere to go,* op. cit.

53. Torrey, E. F., Bigelow, D. A., & Sladen-Dew, N. (1993). Quality and cost of services for seriously mentally ill individuals in British Columbia and the United States. *Hospital and Community Psychiatry, 44,* 943–950; *Toward rebalancing Canada's mental health system.* (1991). Toronto: Canadian Mental Health Association.

54. *Block grants: Characteristics, experience, and lessons learned.* (1995). (GAO/HEHS-95-74). Washington, DC: U.S. General Accounting Office.

55. Pasamanick, B., Scarpitti, F. R., & Dinitz, S. (1967). *Schizophrenics in the community: An experimental study in the prevention of hospitalization.* New York: Appleton-Century-Crofts; Davis, A. E., Dinitz, S., & Pasamanick, B. (1974). *Schizophrenics in the new custodial community: Five years after the experiment.* Columbus: Ohio State University Press.

56. Polak, P. R., & Kirby, M. W. (1976). A model to replace psychiatric hospitals. *Journal of Nervous and Mental Disease, 162,* 13–22.

57. Burns, B. J., & Santos, A. B. (1995). Assertive community treatment: An update of randomized trials. *Psychiatric Services, 46,* 669–675. See also Torrey, E. F. (1986). Continuous treatment teams in the care of the chronic mentally ill. *Hospital and Community Psychiatry, 37,* 1243–1247.

58. Wolff, N., Helminiak, T. W., & Diamond, R. J. (1995). Estimated societal costs of assertive mental health care. *Psychiatric Services, 46,* 898–906.

59. Deci, P. A., Santos, A. B., Hiott, D. W., Schoenwald, S., & Dias, J. K. (1995). Dissemination of assertive community treatment programs. *Psychiatric Services, 46,* 676–678.

60. Teague, G. A., Drake, R. E., & Ackerson, T. H. (1995). Evaluating use of continuous treatment teams for persons with mental illness and substance abuse. *Psychiatric Services, 46,* 689–695.

61. Dincin, J., & Witheridge, T. F. (1982). Psychiatric rehabilitation as a deterrent to recidivism. *Hospital and Community Psychiatry, 33,* 645–650; Bond, G. R. (1984). An economic analysis of psychosocial rehabilitation. *Hospital and Community Psychiatry, 35,* 356–362; Dincin, J. (Ed.). (1995). A pragmatic approach to psychiatric rehabilitation: Lessons from Chicago's thresholds program. *New Directions for Mental Health Services, 68.* San Francisco: Jossey-Bass.

62. Interview with Kenneth Dudek, October 5, 1995.

63. Fairweather, G. (Ed.). (1980). The Fairweather Lodge: A twenty-five year retrospective. *New Directions for Mental Health Services, no. 7;* and Fairweather Lodge model. (1986). In B. A. Stroul (Ed.), *Models of community support services: Approaches to helping persons with long-term mental illness.* Rockville, MD: National Institute of Mental Health.

64. Fairweather, G. W., & Fergus, E. O. (1988). *The lodge society: A look at community tenure as a measure of cost savings.* East Lansing: Michigan State University.

65. Norwood, L., & Mason, M. (1982). *Evaluation of community support programs in Texas.* Austin: Texas Department of Mental Health and Mental Retardation.

66. Information is from Mary T. Sullivan, Bellevue, Washington, chairperson of the Public Relations Committee of the Association of Advanced Practice Psychiatric Nurses, June 27, 1995.

67. Information is from the American Academy of Physician Assistants, Alexandria, Virginia, July 28, 1995.

68. Sherman, P. S., & Porter, R. (1991). Mental health consumers as case management aides. *Hospital and Community Psychiatry, 42*, 494–498.

69. Solomon, P., & Draine, J. (1994). Family perceptions of consumers as case managers. *Community Mental Health Journal, 30*, 165–176.

70. Hilzenrath, D. S. (1994, July 25). The quandry over mental health care costs. *Washington Post*, p. C3; Hamilton, J. O., & Galen, M. (1994, August 8). A furor over mental health. *Time*, pp. 66–69.

71. Lurie, N., Moscovice, I. S., Finch, M., Christianson, J. B., & Popkin, M. K. (1992). Does capitation affect the health of the chronically mentally ill? *Journal of the American Medical Association, 267*, 3300–3304.

72. Cole, R. E., Reed, S. K., Babigian, H. M., Brown, S. W., & Fray, J. (1994). A mental health capitation program: I. Patient outcomes. *Hospital and Community Psychiatry, 45*, 1090–1096; Reed, S. K., Hennessy, K. D., Mitchell, O. S., & Babigian, H. M. (1994). A mental health capitation program: II. Cost-benefit analysis. *Hospital and Community Psychiatry, 45*, 1097–1103.

73. Reed, S. K., & Maharaj, K. (1994). Effects of capitation on health of the chronically ill. *Pharmaco Economics, 6*, 506–512.

74. Schlesinger, M. (1989). Striking a balance: Capitation, the mentally ill, and public policy. In D. Mechanic & L. H. Aiken (Eds.), *Paying for services: Promises and pitfalls of capitation.* New Directions for Mental Health Services, no. 43. San Francisco: Jossey-Bass.

75. Freudenheim, M. (1995, April 11). Penny-pinching H.M.O.s showed their generosity in executive paychecks. *New York Times*, p. D1; Jenks healthcare business report. (1994, September 24). CEO compensation was obtained from Disclosure Inc., Bethesda, MD.

76. Hymovitz, C., & Pollock, E. J. (1995, July 13). Cost-cutting firms monitor couch time as therapists fret. *Wall Street Journal*, pp. 1, 4.

77. Freudenheim, M. (1995, April 28). A bitter pill for H.M.O.s. *New York Times*, p. D1.

78. Blair, L. (1995, October 18). Stop giving incentives for denying psychiatric care. *Cedar Rapids Gazette*, p. 5.

79. Meyers, J. (1995, July/August). Thank you to everyone who attended the Medco outreach meeting. *Alliance of the Mentally Ill of Blackhawk County Newsletter*, p. 2.

80. Crisis in mental health [Editorial]. (1995, September 18). *Des Moines Register*, p. A4.

81. Moran, M. (1995, August 18). R.I. managed care company severely penalized by state. *Psychiatric News*, pp. 1, 18.

82. Bass, A. (1995, April 27). State warns HMOs on Medicaid. *Boston Globe*, p. 1.

83. Don, J. K. (1988, May/June). Mental health care: A "big picture" look from a company president's perspective. *Federation of American Health Systems Review*, pp. 25–27.

84. Hart, B. (1995, February 28). "Rent-a-docs" not much help to mentally ill. *Phoenix Gazette*.

85. Woolhandler, S., & Himmelstein, D. U. (1995). Extreme risk—the new corporate proposition for physicians. *New England Journal of Medicine, 333,* 1706–1708.

86. Wells, S. M. (1995). Exploring the promises and pitfalls of managed care. *Access, 7,* 1–4.

87. Kent, S., Fogarty, M., & Yellowlees, P. (1995). A review of studies of heavy users of psychiatric services. *Psychiatric Services, 46,* 1247–1253.

88. Isaac, R. J., & Armat, V. C. (1990). *Madness in the streets.* New York: Free Press, p. 95, quoting a July 24, 1989, interview with Dr. Saul Feldman.

89. Myerson, A. R. (1994, June 29). Hospital chain sets guilty plea. *New York Times,* p. D1.

90. Kerr, P. (1991, November 24). Mental hospital chains accused of much cheating on insurance. *New York Times,* p. A1; Sharkey, J. (1994). *Bedlam: Greed, profiteering, and fraud in a mental health system gone crazy.* New York: St. Martin's Press, pp. 75, 133, 136.

91. Schulte, F., & Bergal, J. (1995, November 26–29). Managed health care foundering in Florida; Taxes help pay for perks; Some HMO applicants lack health credentials; and Medicaid cost makes managed care the only option. Ft. Lauderdale *Sun-Sentinel.*

92. Schulte, F., & Bergal, J. (1995, November 26). Florida operators branch out. Ft. Lauderdale *Sun-Sentinel.*

93. Priest, D. (1993, January 15). Health care organizations back national database to rate their plans. *Washington Post,* p. A24.

94. Quint, M. (1995, February 24). Taking the pulse of H.M.O. care. *New York Times,* p. D1.

95. Noble, H. B. (1995, October 30). Study rates health plans in 5 areas around U.S. *New York Times,* p. 14.

96. Gill, T. M., & Feinstein, A. R. (1994). A critical appraisal of the quality of quality-of-life measurements. *Journal of the American Medical Association, 272,* 619–626.

97. Price, P., & Harding, K. (1995). Quality of life [Letter]. *Lancet, 346,* 445.

98. Lehman, A. F. (1996). Measures of quality of life among persons with severe and persistent mental disorders. *Social Psychiatry and Psychiatric Epidemiology, 31,* 78–88.

99. Wachal, M. (1994). The Oregon health plan: Managing by outcomes. In F. D. McGuirk, A. M. Sanchez, & D. D. Evans (Eds.), *Outcome issues in a managed care environment* (pp. 65–77, Appendix C). Boulder, CO: Western Interstate Commission for Higher Education.

100. Gerber, G. J., Coleman, G. E., Johnston, L., & Lafave, H. G. (1994). Quality of life of people with psychiatric disabilities 1 and 3 years after discharge from hospital. *Quality of Life Research, 3,* 379–383.

101. Awad, A. G. (1995). Quality of life issues in medicated schizophrenic patients. In C. Shiriqui & H. Nasrallah (Eds.), *Contemporary issues in the treatment of schizophrenia* (pp. 735–747). Washington, DC: American Psychiatric Press.

102. Lehman, op. cit.

103. Srebnik, D. (1995). Outcomes accountability project [Personal communication]. University of Washington, Department of Psychiatry.

104. Redelmeier, D. A., Molin, J. P., & Tibshirani, R. J. (1995). A randomised trial of compassionate care for the homeless in an emergency department. *Lancet, 345,* 1131–1134.

105. Murphy, M. C. (1995, December 18). Personal communication.

106. Rockwell, D. A., Pelletier, L. R., & Donnelly, W. (1993). The cost of accreditation: One hospital's experience. *Hospital and Community Psychiatry, 44,* 151–155.

107. *Outcome-based performance measures.* (1993). Towson, MD: Accreditation Council on Services for People with Disabilities.

108. Veit, S. W., & Stye, K. C. (1994). Performance outcome: Applications in mental health decision support. In F. D. McGuirk, A. M. Sanchez, & D. D. Evans (Eds.), *Outcome issues in a managed care environment* (pp. 53–56). Boulder, CO: Western Interstate Commission for Higher Education.

109. New managed care "report card" to measure patients' satisfaction. (1995, October 6). *Psychiatric News,* p. 8.

110. *Survey of the state: Alabama's mental illness services.* (1994). Alabama Alliance for the Mentally Ill.

111. *Care of persons with mental illness: A ranking of area programs in North Carolina.* (1992). North Carolina Alliance for the Mentally Ill.

112. *A survey of community mental health boards for FY 90-91.* (1993). Alliance for the Mentally Ill of Michigan.

113. Pearson, R. (1995, October 14). Mental health chief steps down. *Chicago Tribune,* p. 6.

114. Jencks, op. cit.

115. The President's Commission on Mental Health. (1978). *Report of the task panel on state mental health issues* (Vol. 4). Washington, DC: U.S. Government Printing Office, pp. 1991–2000.

CHAPTER 8: FROM LEGAL FOLLY TO COMMON SENSE: THE RIGHT TO GET WELL

1. The rights of the insane [Editorial]. (1883). *Alienist and Neurologist, 4,* 714. Cited by Geller, J. L. (1992). A historical perspective on the role of state hospitals viewed from the era of the "Revolving Door." *American Journal of Psychiatry, 149,* 1526–1533.

2. Siegel, L. M. (1981, March 3). Feeling the chill. *New York Times,* p. A19.

3. Howard, P. (1994). *The death of common sense.* New York: Random House, pp. 45, 49.

4. Treffert, D. A. (1985). The obviously ill patient in need of treatment: A fourth standard for civil commitment. *Hospital and Community Psychiatry, 36,* 259–264.

5. Isaac, R. J., & Armat, V. A. (1990). *Madness in the streets: How psychiatry and the law abandoned the mentally ill.* New York: Free Press, p. 26.

6. Ibid., p. 262.

7. The discharged chronic mental patient. (1974, April 12). *Medical World News.*

8. Ennis, B. J. (1972). *Prisoners of psychiatry.* New York: Harcourt Brace Jovanovich, p. 7.

9. Klein, J. (1983). The least restrictive alternative: More about less. *Psychiatric Quarterly, 55,* 106–114.

10. Munetz, M. R., & Geller, J. L. (1993). The least restrictive alternative in the postinstitutional era. *Hospital and Community Psychiatry, 44,* 967–973.

11. Ibid.

12. Terez, T. (1986, September). Commitment: The law vs. psychiatry. *Ways,* pp. 18–20.

13. Isaac & Armat, op. cit., p. 128.

14. Appelbaum, P. S. (1994). *Almost a revolution: Mental health law and the limits of change.* New York: Oxford University Press, p. 28.
15. Isaac & Armat, op. cit., p. 137.
16. Schaeffer, P. (1980, January). Court rules that mental patients have right to refuse treatment. *Clinical Psychiatry News,* p. 1.
17. Gould, R. E., & Levy, R. (1987, November 27). Psychiatrists as puppets of Koch's roundup policy. *New York Times,* p. A35.
18. *Involuntary psychiatric commitment a crack in the door of Constitutional freedoms* [Information letter]. (1994). Los Angeles: Citizens Committee on Human Rights, p. 16.
19. Ibid., pp. 4 & 12.
20. Breggin, P. R. (1974). The killing of mental patients. In *Madness Network News Reader* (pp. 149–154). San Francisco: Glide Publications. See also Gorman, C. (1994, October 10). Prozac's worst enemy. *Time,* pp. 64–65.
21. Isaac & Armat, op. cit., p. 126.
22. Ibid., p. 115.
23. Ibid., p. 116.
24. Sundrum, C. J. (1995). Patient advocacy in the United States. *International Journal of Mental Health, 23,* 3–26.
25. Isaac & Armat, op. cit., p. 241.
26. Siebert, A. (1995, August 4). "Successful schizophrenia." Presented at Alternatives '95 conference, St. Paul, MN.
27. Information on this case is taken from: Courts says killer can't be forced to be sane enough to die. (1992, October 21). *New York Times;* and Dennis, D. (1993, January/February). Medicate to execute. *The Angolite,* pp. 35–48.
28. Lamb, H. R., & Mills, M. J. (1986). Needed changes in law and procedure for the chronically mentally ill. *Hospital and Community Psychiatry, 37,* 475–480, quoting Roth.
29. Carmody, D. (1984, December 17). The tangled life and mind of Judy, whose home is the street. *New York Times,* pp. B1, B10.
30. Rimer, S. (1985, November 27). At 28, a prologue of promise, but a life in rags. *New York Times,* p. B4.
31. Evans, S. (1985, January 24). Senate panel hears appeal to ease rules in District. *Washington Post,* pp. C1, C6.
32. Torrey, E. F., Stieber, J., Ezekiel, J., Wolfe, S. M., Sharfstein, J., Noble, J. H., & Flynn, L. M. (1992). *Criminalizing the seriously mentally ill.* Washington, DC: National Alliance for the Mentally Ill and Public Citizen Health Research Group, p. 51.
33. Ibid., p. 51.
34. Tobar, H. (1991, August 25–26). When jail is a mental institution. *Los Angeles Times.*
35. McFarland, B. H., Faulkner, L. R., & Bloom, J. D. (1989). Chronic mental illness and the criminal justice system. *Hospital and Community Psychiatry, 40,* 718–723.
36. Lafave, H. G., Pickney, A. A., & Gerber, G. J. (1993). Criminal activity by psychiatric clients after hospital discharge. *Hospital and Community Psychiatry, 44,* 180–181.
37. Appelbaum, op. cit.
38. Ibid., p. 43.
39. Acker, C., & Fine, M. J. (1989, September 12). Desperate for help, sometimes parents lie. *Philadelphia Inquirer.*

40. Wyatt, R. J. (1991). Neuroleptics and the natural course of schizophrenia. *Schizophrenia Bulletin, 17,* 325–351.

41. McEvoy, J. P., Schooler, N. R., & Wilson, W. H. (1991). Predictors of therapeutic response to haloperidol in acute schizophrenia. *Psychopharamacology Bulletin, 27,* 97–101.

42. Lieberman, J., Koreen, A., Loebel, A., Geisler, S., Alvir, J., & Volkow, N. (1994). Evidence for sensitization in the early stage of schizophrenia [Abstract]. *Neuropsychopharmacology, 10,* 2015.

43. Waddington, J. L., Youssef, H. A., & Kinsella, A. (1995). Sequential cross-sectional and ten-year prospective study of severe negative symptoms in relation to duration of initially untreated psychosis in chronic schizophrenia. *Psychological Medicine, 25,* 849–857.

44. Post, R. M., Leverich, G. S., Altshuler, L., & Mikalauskas, K. (1992). Lithium-discontinuation-induced refractoriness: Preliminary observations. *American Journal of Psychiatry, 149,* 1727–1729.

45. Appelbaum, op. cit., p. 138, citing an unpublished report from the Massachusetts Department of Mental Health, July 7, 1988.

46. Zito, J. M., Craig, T. J., & Wanderling, J. (1991). New York under the Rivers decision: An epidemiologic study of drug treatment refusal. *American Journal of Psychiatry, 148,* 904–909.

47. Farnsworth, M. G. (1991). The impact of judicial review of patients' refusal to accept antipsychotic medications at the Minnesota Security Hospital. *Bulletin of the American Academy of Psychiatry and the Law, 19,* 33–42.

48. Weiden, P. J., & Olfson, M. (1995). Cost of relapse in schizophrenia. *Schizophrenia Bulletin, 21,* 419–429.

49. Kraepelin, E. (1971). *Dementia praecox and paraphrenia.* Huntington, NY: Robert E. Krieger, p. 26. (Original work published 1919)

50. Amador, X. F., Flaum, M., Andreason, N. C., Strauss, D. H., Yale, S. A., Clark, S. C., & Gorman, J. M. (1994). Awareness of illness in schizophrenia and schizoaffective and mood disorders. *Archives of General Psychiatry, 51,* 826–836.

51. David, A., Buchanan, A., Reed, A., & Almeida, O. (1992). The assessment of insight in psychosis. *British Journal of Psychiatry, 161,* 599–602; and personal communication from Dr. David, January 18, 1993.

52. Grisso, T., & Appelbaum, P. S. (1995). The MacArthur treatment competence study. *Law and Human Behavior, 19,* 149–174.

53. Woodley, H. G. (1991). *Certified.* In R. Porter (Ed.), *The Faber book of madness* (p. 4). London: Faber and Faber. (Original work published 1947)

54. Young, D. A., Davila, R., & Scher, H. (1993). Unawareness of illness and neuropsychological performance in chronic schizophrenia. *Schizophrenia Research, 10,* 117–124.

55. McEnvoy, J. P., Freter, S., Everett, G., Geller, J. L., Appelbaum, P. S., Apperson, L. J., & Roth, L. (1989). Insight and clinical outcome of schizophrenic patients. *Journal of Nervous and Mental Disease, 177,* 48–51; McEnvoy, J. P., Appelbaum, P. S., Apperson, L. J., Geller, J. L., & Freter, S. (1989). Why must some schizophrenic patients be involuntarily committed? The role of insight. *Comprehensive Psychiatry, 30,* 13–17.

56. Lysaker, P., Bell, M., Milstein, R., Bryson, G., & Beam-Goulet, J. (1994). Insight and psychosocial treatment in schizophrenia. *Psychiatry, 57,* 307–315.

57. Amador, X. F., Strauss, D. H., Yale, S. A., & Gorman, J. M. (1991). Awareness of illness in schizophrenia. *Schizophrenia Bulletin, 17,* 113–132.
58. Lin, I. F., Spiga, R., & Fortsch, W. (1979). Insight and adherence to medication in chronic schizophrenics. *Journal of Clinical Psychiatry, 40,* 430–432.
59. Telephone interviews with anonymous Project Reachout staff, August 1995.
60. Miller, R. D. (1992). Need-for-treatment criteria for involuntary civil commitment: Impact in practice. *American Journal of Psychiatry, 149,* 1380–1384.
61. Krauthammer, C. (1988, December 23). The homeless who don't want help. *Washington Post,* p. A19.
62. Durham, M. L. (1985). Implications of need-for-treatment laws: A study of Washington State's Involuntary Treatment Act. *Hospital and Community Psychiatry, 36,* 975–977.
63. Miller, op. cit.
64. Rubenstein, L. S. (1985). APA's model law: Hurting the people it seeks to help. *Hospital and Community Psychiatry, 36,* 968–972.
65. Holden, C. (1985). Broader commitment laws sought. *Science, 230,* 1253–1255.
66. Hardin, H. (1993, July 22). Uncivil liberties. *Vancouver Sun.*
67. Lamb & Mills, op. cit.
68. Backlar, P. (1995). The longing for order: Oregon's medical advance directive for mental health treatment. *Community Mental Health Journal, 31,* 103–108.
69. Bullfinch, T. (1959). *Mythology.* New York: Dell, p. 193.
70. Torrey, E. F., & Kaplan, R. J. (1995). A national survey of the use of outpatient commitment. *Psychiatric Services, 46,* 778–784.
71. Hiday, V. A., & Scheid-Cook, T. L. (1987). The North Carolina experience with outpatient commitment: A critical appraisal. *International Journal of Law and Psychiatry, 10,* 215–232.
72. Hiday, V. A., & Scheid-Cook, T. L. (1989). A follow-up of chronic patients committed to outpatient treatment. *Hospital and Community Psychiatry, 40,* 52–59.
73. Van Putten, R. A., Santiago, J. M., & Berren, M. R. (1988). Involuntary outpatient commitment in Arizona: A retrospective study. *Hospital and Community Psychiatry, 39,* 953–958.
74. Zanni, G., & deVeau, L. (1986). Inpatient stays before and after outpatient commitment. *Hospital and Community Psychiatry, 37,* 941–942.
75. Hiday & Scheid-Cook, op. cit.
76. O'Keefe, C., & Potenza, D. (1995). *Mandated treatment, it works!* Poster presented at the annual meeting of the Institute on Psychiatric Services, Boston.
77. Bloom, J. D., Williams, M. H., & Bigelow, D. A. (1992). The involvement of schizophrenic insanity acquittees in the mental health and criminal justice systems. *Psychiatric Clinics of North America, 15,* 591–604.
78. Van Putten et al., op. cit.
79. Pasamanick, B., Scarpitti, F. R., & Dinitz, S. (1967). *Schizophrenics in the community.* New York: Appleton-Century-Crofts, pp. 57–58.
80. Kapur, S., Ganguli, R., Ulrich, R., & Raghu, U. (1992). Use of random-sequence riboflavin as a marker of medication compliance in chronic schizophrenics. *Schizophrenia Research, 6,* 49–53.
81. Hobby, G. L., & Deuttschle, K. W. (1959). The use of riboflavin as an indicator of isoniazid ingestion in self-medicated patients. *American Review of Respiratory Diseases, 80,* 415–423.

82. Ellard, G. A., Jenner, P. J., & Downs, P. A. (1980). An evaluation of the potential use of isoniazid, acetylisoniazid, and isonicotinic acid for monitoring the self-administration of drugs. *British Journal of Clinical Pharmacology, 10,* 369–381.

83. Wright, E. C. (1993). Non-compliance—Or how many aunts has Matilda. *Lancet,* 342, 909–913.

84. Sherill, M. (1992, January 19). Out there. *Washington Post,* p. F6, citing a survey done by social scientists at Columbia University.

85. Hardin, op. cit.

86. Krauthammer, C. (1985, January 4). For the homeless: Asylum. *Washington Post.*

87. *Annual Statistical Supplement,* Social Security Bulletin. (1995, August). Washington, DC: Social Security Administration.

88. Shaner, A., Eckman, T. A., Roberts, L. J., Wilkins, J. N., Tucker, D. E., Tsuang, J. W., & Mintz, J. (1995). Disability income, cocaine use, and repeated hospitalization among schizophrenic cocaine abusers: A government-sponsored revolving door? *New England Journal of Medicine, 333,* 777–783.

89. Satel, S. (1995). When disability benefits make patients sicker [Editorial]. *New England Journal of Medicine, 333,* 794–796.

90. Barry, K. L., Fleming, M. F., Greenley, J., Widlak, P., Kropp, S., & McKee, D. (1995). Assessment of alcohol and other drug disorders in the seriously mentally ill. *Schizophrenia Bulletin, 21,* 313–321.

91. Satel, S. (1995, July 17). The wrong fix. *Wall Street Journal,* p. A16.

92. Ibid.

CHAPTER 9: FROM THE WOODY ALLEN SYNDROME TO BRAIN DISEASE

1. Kraepelin, E. *Concerning the influence of acute diseases on the causation of mental illness.* Unpublished doctoral dissertation, kindly provided by the late Professor Michael Shepherd, Institute of Psychiatry, London.

2. Sicherman, B. (1967). *The quest for mental health in America, 1880–1917.* Ann Arbor: University Microfilms, p. 155. This thesis was published by Arno Press, New York, in 1980.

3. See, for example, the debate about "moral insanity" and the role played by Gray in the trial of the man who killed President James A. Garfield, in Rosenberg, C. E. (1968). *The trial of the assassin Guiteau.* Chicago: University of Chicago Press.

4. Sicherman, op. cit., p. 365.

5. Ibid.

6. Ibid., pp. 333, 364.

7. Ibid., pp. 278, 367.

8. See Torrey, E. F. (1992). *Freudian fraud: The malignant effect of Freud's theory on American thought and culture.* New York: HarperCollins, p. 91ff.

9. Ibid., pp. 240–244.

10. McHugh, P. R. (1995). What's the story? *American Scholar, 64,* 191–203, quoting Dr. Elvin Semrad.

11. Rogow, A. A. (1970). *The psychiatrists.* New York: G. P. Putnam's Sons, p. 147, quoting Stevenson.

12. Chisholm, G. B. (1946). The reestablishment of peacetime society: The responsibility of psychiatry. *Psychiatry, 9*, 3–11.
13. Davis, K. (1938). Mental hygiene and class structure. *Psychiatry, 1*, 55–65.
14. Much of this material, including quoted testimony, is taken from Hearings before the Senate Subcommittee on Territories and Insular Affairs on S.2518 and S.2973, 84th Congress, February 20 and 21, 1956. Washington, DC: Government Printing Office, 1956.
15. Robinson, D. (1965, January 26). Conspiracy USA: The far right fights against mental health. *Look*, pp. 30–32.
16. Mental health mania [Editorial]. (1957, December 30). *Manchester Union Leader.*
17. Marmor, J., Bernard, V. W., & Ottenberg, P. (1960). Psychodynamics of group opposition to mental health programs. *American Journal of Orthopsychiatry, 30*, 330–345.
18. Hearings before the Senate Subcommittee (note 14) op. cit.
19. Schmuck, R., & Chesler, M. (1967). Superpatriot opposition to community mental health programs. *Community Mental Health Journal, 3*, 382–388.
20. Calvert, G., & Neiman, C. (1971). *A disrupted history.* New York: Random House, p. 37.
21. Marcuse, H. (1971, February). Letter to Angela Davis. *Ramparts*, p. 22.
22. Brown, N. O. (1959). *Life against death: The psychoanalytical meaning of history.* New York: Vintage Books, p. 322.
23. Roszak, T. (1969). *The making of the counter culture.* Garden City: Anchor Books, p. 84.
24. Goodman, P. (1960). *Growing up absurd.* New York: Vintage Books.
25. King, R. (1972). *The party of Eros.* Chapel Hill: University of North Carolina Press, p. 78.
26. Sale, K. (1973). *SDS.* New York: Random House, p. 205.
27. Mead, M. (1928). *Coming of age in Samoa.* New York: William Morrow.
28. Torrey, op. cit.
29. Menninger, K. (1969). *The crime of punishment.* New York: Viking Press (paperback ed.), p. 28.
30. Menninger, K. (1968). The crime of punishment. *Saturday Review of Literature*, September 7, pp. 21–25.
31. Kaminer, W. (1992). *I'm dysfunctional, you're dysfunctional.* Reading, MA: Addison-Wesley.
32. Sykes, C. J. (1992). *A nation of victims.* New York: St. Martin's Press.
33. Sykes, C. J. (1992, November 2). I hear America whining. *New York Times*, p. A19.
34. Yolles, S. F. (1966). The role of the psychologist in Comprehensive Community Mental Health Centers: The National Institute of Mental Health view. *American Psychologist, 21*, 37–41.
35. Duhl, L. J. (1968). The shame of the cities. *American Journal of Psychiatry, 124*, 1184–1189.
36. Dumont, M. (1968). *The absurd healer: Perspectives of a community psychiatrist.* New York: Science House, p. 26.
37. See Torrey, E. F. (1988). *Nowhere to go.* New York: Harper & Row, pp. 129–130, 134–136.
38. Eisenberg, L. (1981). In J. Joffe & G. Albee (Eds.), *Prevention through political action and social change* (pp. 8–9). Hanover, NH: University Press of New England.

39. Rogow, A. A., op. cit., p. 126.

40. Torrey, *Nowhere to go*, op. cit., pp. 103–106.

41. *President's Commission on Mental Health* (Vol. 1, p. 9). (1978). Washington, DC: U.S. Government Printing Office.

42. Carter, R. (1992, November 17). How we make mental health worse. *USA Today*, p. 13A.

43. Smith, C. J., & Hanham, R. Q. (1981). Deinstitutionalization of the mentally ill: A time path analysis of the American States, 1955–1975. *Social Science and Medicine*, 15D, 361–378.

44. Goldman, H. H., & Gattozzi, A. A. (1988). Balance of powers: Social Security and the mentally disabled, 1980–1985. *Milbank Quarterly*, 66, 531–551.

45. Jencks, C. (1994). *The homeless*. Cambridge, MA: Harvard University Press, p. 37.

46. Carlson, M. (1993, May 31). A cause of her own. *Time*, p. 60.

47. Gore, T. (1993, Winter). Children and mental illness. *Phi Kappa Phi Journal*, pp. 16–17.

48. Pear, R. (1993). Administration rethinking mental-health coverage. *New York Times*, p. C7.

49. Harsh realities get spotlight at APA's legislative institute. (1994, April 1). *Psychiatric News*, p. C1.

50. Diagnostic and Statistical Manual of Mental Disorders. (1952, 1968, 1980, 1987, & 1994). Washington: American Psychiatric Association.

51. Kirk, S. A., & Kutchins, H. (1994, June 21). Is bad writing a mental disorder? *New York Times*, p. C1.

52. Kessler, R. C., McGonagle, K. A., Zhao, S., Nelson, C. B., Hughes, M., Eshleman, S., Wittchen, H. U., & Kendler, K. S. (1994). Lifetime and 12-month prevalence of *DSM-III-R* psychiatric disorders in the United States. *Archives of General Psychiatry*, 51, 8–19.

53. Goleman, D. (1994, January 14). 1 in 2 found to suffer mental disorder. *New York Times*, p. A20.

54. Hearings on Mental Health, Subcommittee of the Committee on Interstate and Foreign Commerce, House of Representatives, July 10–11, 1963. Washington, DC: U.S. Government Printing Office, p. 23.

55. Torrey, *Nowhere to go*, pp. 144–150.

56. Olfson, M., & Pincus, H. A. (1994). Outpatient psychotherapy in the United States: I. Volume, costs, and user characteristics. *American Journal of Psychiatry*, 151, 1281–1288.

57. Mack, J. E. (1994). *Abduction: Human encounters with aliens* (Rev. ed.). New York: Ballantine Books.

58. Grinfeld, M. J. (1995, July). Harvard mulls fate of its alien-abduction expert. *Psychiatric Times*, p. 13.

59. For details, see Marks, P. (1993, April 4). At Allen custody trial, therapists seem almost like family. *New York Times*, p. A37; Span, P. (1993, April 10). The poop on Mia's pooch. *Washington Post*, p. C1; Span, P. (1993, May 4). Here comes the judgment! *Washington Post*, p. C1; Henneberger, M. (1994, October 9). Managed care changing practice of psychotherapy. *New York Times*, p. C1; Weber, B. (1992, August 20). Woody in New Yorkers' eyes: A tarnished idol? *New York Times*, p. B1.

60. Olfson & Pincus, op. cit.

61. Pollack, D. A., McFarland, B. H., George, R. A., & Angell, R. H. (1994). Prioritization of mental health services in Oregon. *Milbank Quarterly, 72,* 515–550.

62. Rich, S. (1995, July 21). Can health care be reduced to the terms of an equation? *Washington Post,* p. A19.

63. New Hampshire State Legislature. (1981). Chapter 492, 126–B:7, Allocation of funds.

64. Bray, D. (1990). *Psychiatric inpatient services within a comprehensive mental health system. The public mental health hospital in a community-based system of care* [Proceedings from a national conference]. Columbia, SC: South Carolina Department of Mental Health.

CHAPTER 10: LOOKING FORWARD: WHERE WE SHOULD BE GOING

1. Shadish, W. R., Lurigio, A. J., & Lewis, D. A. (1989). After deinstitutionalization. The present and future of mental health long-term care policy. *Journal of Social Issues, 3,* 1–15.

2. Wallace, M. (1993, January 2). Can no one help tragic young men like Ben? *Daily Mail,* p. 3.

3. Zito, J. (1994). Diminished responsibility. *Nursing Times, 90,* 42–43.

4. Reforming community care. (1994, February 25). *London Times,* p. 13.

5. Ramsay, S. (1994). Clues to homicide by the mentally ill. *Lancet, 344,* 607.

6. Dean, M. (1994). Delays in mental health reform. *Lancet, 334,* 1008.

7. Nemiah, J. C. (1988). Review of M. A. Jiminez, *Changing faces of madness. American Journal of Psychiatry, 145,* 1595–1596.

8. State official ordered to live at troubled home. (1995, August 11). *Washington Post,* p. A2.

Index

Abandonment *vs.* freedom, 162
Accidents, fatal, 20
Accountability, 112–113, 114
  and performance contracting, 131–140
Accreditation Council on Services for People with
  Disabilities, 135–136
ACLU, *see* American Civil Liberties Union (ACLU)
Ada County Jail, Idaho, 37
Adoption Assistance and Foster Care Act, 110
Aetna Insurance, 121, 123
Agnews State Psychiatric Hospital (California), 13,
  36, 62
AIDS/HIV, 21, 33, 195
Aid to Families with Dependent Children (AFDC),
  92
Aid to the Permanently and Totally Disabled
  (APTD), 96, 100
Alabama, 76, 137, 144, 207
Alameda County, California, 17
Alaska, 37, 96, 112, 158, 171, 172, 173, 203
Albuquerque, New Mexico, 76
Alcan Aluminum, and managed care, 120
Alcohol/drug abuse, 4, 10, 17, 22, 29, 38, 48, 49,
  50, 98, 120, 164, 165, 190, 197, 198, 199
Allen, Woody, 167, 186, 188, 234
Alliance House, 130
Alliance for the Mentally Ill (AMI), 77, 137, 152,
  190. *See also* National Alliance for the Mentally
  Ill (NAMI)
Alzheimer's disease, 5, 10, 149, 160, 181, 187
AMBHA, *see* American Managed Behavioral
  Healthcare Association (AMBHA)
American Association for Marriage and Family
  Therapy, 181
American Association on Mental Deficiency, 135
American Civil Liberties Union (ACLU), 143. *See
  also* Civil libertarians
American Counseling Association, 181
American Legion, 173
American Managed Behavioral Healthcare
  Association (AMBHA), 137
American Psychiatric Association, 44, 88, 145, 168,
  169, 170, 177, 182
  model law for involuntary commitment, 158
  questionnaire on Barry Goldwater, 177–178
  Task Force, 17
Ancora hospital (New Jersey), 63
Antabuse, 161, 200
Antidepressants, 6
Antipsychotics, 5, 99, 161

APTD, *see* Aid to the Permanently and Totally
  Disabled (APTD)
Arizona, 9, 39, 51, 121, 123, 125, 158, 160, 161,
  206
Arkansas, 10, 51, 110, 206
Arlington Developmental Center, Tennessee, 201
Arthur Bolton & Associates, *see* Bolton, Arthur
Asbury Park, New Jersey, 65
Atlanta, 39, 58
Atlantic City, New Jersey, 65
Auburn, Washington, 129
Austin State Hospital, Texas, 42
Australia, 116, 193
Autism, 6, 10

Balloon theory, 35
Baltimore, 6, 9, 17, 19, 20, 22, 59, 81, 131
Bazelon Center for Mental Health Law, 153, 158
Behavioral Healthcare, 126
Behavioral Health Network, 129
Bellevue Hospital, 69, 71
Benefits, income, 163–166, 198
Berkeley, 175
Big Sur, California, 175
Birch, John (Society), 173
Black Panthers, 142
Blair (1973 study), 213
Block grants, 98, 111, 113–114, 197
Blood levels, monitoring medication compliance,
  161
Blue Cross–Blue Shield, 129
Boise, Idaho, 37
Boston, 17, 18, 81
  Prison Discipline Society, 26
Brain abnormalities, 4–5, 155, 168. *See also* National
  Brain Research Institute
British Columbia Civil Liberties Association, 162.
  See also Civil libertarians
Bronx, 69
Brooklyn, 54, 68, 69, 76
Buffalo, 34
Burt County (Nebraska) Plaindealer, 74
Businesses using managed care companies, 120–121

California, 9, 10, 13, 17, 28, 32, 35, 36, 39, 41, 42,
  45, 62, 76, 92, 96, 99, 112, 130, 131, 143, 147,
  160, 171, 173, 175, 178, 180, 196, 206
Camberwell district, London, 46
Cambridge, Massachusetts, 54
Camden, New Jersey, 57, 65

Canada, 56, 113, 133, 134–135, 151, 193
Cancer research, 195
Capitation, 122
Care Data (New York research firm), 131
Carter, Jimmy, 56, 139, 179–180
    President's Commission on Mental Health,
        10–11, 179–180
Carter, Rosalynn, 179–180, 234
Carve-out/carve-in systems, 121
Case managers, mentally ill as, 119–120
Catholic Franciscans, 131
Census Bureau, 16
Center of Forensic Psychiatry, 54
Centers for Disease Control, 199
Central City Hospitality House, 21
Central Park, 68, 188
Central State Hospital, Louisiana, 148
CHAMPUS, 123, 127
Charter Medical Corporation, 121
Chartley House, 129
Chester County, South Carolina, 79
Chicago, 16, 29, 107, 177
Chickens-in-the-air metaphor, 109
Child guidance movement, 169
Child Mental Health Interest Group, 181
Children, custody issue, 110
Children, labeling as disabled, 109–111
Chlorpromazine, 8, 99
Church of Scientology, 146
Cincinnati, 74
Citizens Commission on Human Rights, 146
Civil libertarians, 70
    American Civil Liberties Union (ACLU), 143
    British Columbia Civil Liberties Association,
        162
    New York Civil Liberties Union, 67, 71, 153
    psychiatrists, 146
Civil rights era of the 1960s, 142
Clark University, 168
Cleveland Plain Dealer, 81, 84
Cleveland State Hospital, Ohio, 82
Clinton, Bill, 120, 131, 181, 183
Clozapine, 5, 129
Clubhouse model/programs, 6, 65, 117–118, 130,
    202
CMHCs, see Community Mental Health Centers
    (CMHCs)
Cocaine use, 164
Colorado, 29, 119, 121, 131, 158, 206
Columbia Law School, 150
Columbia University student uprisings, 174
Columbus State Hospital, Ohio, 41
ComCare, 125
Command hallucinations, and prediction of
    violence, 52
Commitment, involuntary, see Involuntary
    commitment/treatment
Commonsense model, 151
Communism, 171, 173
Community, and assessment of treatment outcomes,
    138–140
Community Mental Health Centers (CMHCs), 9,
    14, 37, 98, 112, 174, 176–177, 178, 184–185
Community Patrol, 65
Comorbidity Study, National, 183
Conditional release, 153, 159–160, 161, 197

Confidence, diminished in psychiatrists/mental
    health system, 56
Connecticut, 29, 92, 96, 142, 206
Conscientious objectors, World War II, 83
Conservatives, and mental health, 170–177
Conservatorships, 160
Consumer case managers, 119–120
Consumer survey/interview, 134
Continental Health Plans of Miami, 128
Continuity of care, 124–125
Continuum/spectrum concept of mental
    disorders/health, 167, 168, 170, 198
Contracting, performance, 139–140
Cost-benefit (social/economic), and medical care
    rationing, 189–190
Cost-shifting, to federal government, 91–99
    consequences of, 99–111
    fiscal contribution, federal vs. state/local (1963,
        1985, 1994) (Table 7.2), 98
    solution to (only logical), 111–114
Council, see National Advisory Mental Health
    Council
Council for Exceptional Children, 135
Counseling, supportive, 6
Creedmoor State Hospital (New York), 24
Custody issue, children's, 110

Dade County Jail, 34
Dallas Association of Mental Health, 172
Dallas County Jail, 42
Damage to brain, secondary to trauma, 10
Dane County, Wisconsin, 160
Dangerousness, 56, 144, 145, 157, 197
    exaggerated to obtain judicial order, 152
Daughters of American Revolution, 172, 173
Death rate, elevated, 19
Deaths in jail, 34
Deinstitutionalization, 8–11, 205–207
    balance sheet (assessing outcome of), 85–88
    benefits of, 85
    and cost-shifting to federal programs, 99–111,
        144
    effects of:
        on families, 77–79
        and homelessness, 21–24
        increase in mentally ill recipients of SSI, 96
        and jails and prisons, 35–42, 45
        in a large city (New York, New York), 66–73
        on public services/police, 73–77
        in a small town (Ocean Grove, New Jersey),
            62–66
    history, 81–90
    legal push of changed commitment laws, 144
    magnitude of, 8–11, 180, 205–207
Delaware, 10, 112, 172, 207
Delaware County AMI, 152
Delusions, type of (and prediction of violence), 52
Democratic Party, and mental health professions,
    178
Demonstration projects, 200
Denver County Jail, 25, 28
Des Moines, Iowa, 21, 124
Detreatmentization, 88
Devine, Texas, 62
Diabetes, 156, 162
"Dine and dash," 38

Disability Insurance Trust fund, *see* Social Security Disability Income (SSDI)
Disabled, 109–111, 135
Discrimination, 57
Disorders, mental (classification of), 182
District of Columbia, *see* Washington, DC
Diversion of resources, 183–186
Donahue show, 71
Dumping patients, 125–126
Dwelling Place, 15

East Cambridge Jail, Boston, 27
Eastern Lunatic Asylum (first psychiatric hospital in United States), 81
East Orange, New Jersey, 65
Economic cost-benefit, 189
EDPs (emotionally disturbed persons), 68
Eisenhower, Dwight, 178
Elavil, 6
Electroconvulsive therapy (ECT), 6
Elizabeth, New Jersey, 65
Emergency detentions, 37
Employment programs, 6
England, 19, 46, 50, 52, 86, 116
Epidemiologic Catchment Area (ECA) surveys, 48, 164, 183, 199
Epilepsy, 10, 156, 188
Erie County Holding Center, 34
Esalen Institute, California, 175

Fact magazine, 177–178
Fairfax, Virginia, 55
Fairness, and medical care rationing, 190
Fairview State Hospital, Pennsylvania, 104
Fairweather Lodge model, 6, 116, 118, 202
Families, effects of mental illness crisis on, 77–79
Family, and assessment of treatment outcomes, 138–140
Family Advocate, 138
Federal Civil Rights Law, 143
Federal government:
    cost-shifting to, 91–99
    federal programs, 91–99
    recommended role of, 199–201
Financial incentives, optimal system of, 197
Florida, 9, 34, 37, 39, 40, 76, 84, 112, 119, 127, 131, 145, 206. *See also* Miami
Follow-up, minimal, 107
Food stamp program, 93, 97, 100, 102, 144
Ford, Gerald, 179
For-profit companies, 127–131, 197
    good one (example), 128–129
Fort Lauderdale, Florida, 18, 127
Foster care drift, 110
Fountain House clubhouse model, 6, 65, 116, 117, 118, 130
Freezing to death, 19
Freud, Sigmund, 168–170, 173, 174, 175, 181, 186
Friends and Advocates of the Mentally Ill, 71
Fromm, Erich, 169
Funding initiatives, new, 91–140
Funding systems, complexity of (public psychiatric services) (Figure 7.2), 106

Gaithersburg, Maryland, 76
Garfield, James A., 232

General Accounting Office (GAO), 110
Georgia, 39, 58, 111, 179, 207
Ghettoization/psychiatric ghettos, 14, 61–79
Goldwater, Barry, 177, 178
Government, *see* Federal government
Grand Atlantic Hotel, 63, 65
Grand Rapids, Michigan, 55
Greater Boston Legal Services, 147
Great Falls, Montana, 75
Green Spring Health Services, 121, 123
Greystone Park hospital (New Jersey), 63
Guardianships, 160, 197

Halfway houses, community resistance to, 56
Hallucinations, type of, and prediction of violence, 52
Haloperidol, 161
Hamilton County, Ohio, 74
Hartford, Connecticut, 18
Harvard, 71, 150, 185
Hawaii, 3, 29, 147, 158, 203
HCFA, *see* Health Care Financing Administration (HCFA)
Health Care Financing Administration (HCFA), 132, 135, 200
Health insurance/managed care systems, 120–121
Health Reform Task Force, Mental Health Work Group, 181
Hell's Kitchen, 15
Helplessness *vs.* dangerousness, criteria for commitment, 157–158
Hemet, California, 76
Hernandez, Ismael, 128
Hinckley, John, 57
Hinds County (Mississippi) Detention Center, 33
Hitler, 169
HIV/AIDS, 21, 33, 195
HMOs, *see* Managed care
Homelessness, and mental illness, 13–24
    arrest/incarceration rates, 30–31
    causes of, 21–22
    and deinstitutionalization, 21–24
    families, effects on, 78
    illustration ("murder of a shopping bag lady"), 14–16
    magnitude of problem, 16–18, 85, 149–150
    quality of life, 18–21
Home Owners Association, 65
Homicides, 44, 49, 57–58, 68, 194
Hospitals, general (psychiatric treatment in), 103–104
Hospitals, psychiatric:
    history of, in United States, 81–82
    inpatients, number of (1950–1995), 9, 101
    moving mentally ill from jails to hospitals (1800s), 25–28
    moving mentally ill from hospitals to jails (1970s, 1980s), 28–31
    reform movement, 82–85
    worst in U.S. (public), 3
House of Representatives, 110
    Public Health Subcommittee, 84
    Un-American Activities Committee, 171
Housing, insufficient low-income, 22
Housing, subsidized, 97–98
Houston, Texas, 3

Howard Hughes Medical Institute, 195
HUD, 16, 19–20, 93, 97–98
Human Affairs International, 121, 123
Huntsville, Alabama, 76
Hygiene, see Mental hygiene movement
Hypertension, 156

Iannotta, Phyllis, 13, 14–16, 21, 85, 201–202, 209
IBM, and managed care, 120
Iceland, 49
Idaho, 29, 37, 206
Illinois, 58, 112, 137, 138, 206. See also Chicago
IMD (institution for the treatment of mental diseases) exclusion, 102
Indiana, 206
"Infection, psychic," 169
Insight, 154–156
Integrated Delivery Systems, 112
International Health Related Quality of Life Society, 133
Involuntary commitment/treatment:
    barriers/restrictions, 77, 142–148, 157. See also Law, mental health/illness
    and Canadian health care system, 113
    criteria for, states that have broadened, 158
    legal safeguards against abuse, 162
    and managed care, 125
    model law for involuntary commitment, 158
    need for, 156–163, 197
    need-for-treatment criteria, 157
    treatment of outpatients, 159–160
Iowa, 9, 103, 105, 121, 122, 123–124, 160, 206
Isoniazid, 161

Jackson, Mississippi, 58, 75
Jackson, Senator Henry, 172
Jails/prisons, and the mentally ill, 25–42, 150–151
    and deinstitutionalization, 35–42
    historical perspective:
        moving mentally ill from jails to hospitals (1800s), 25–28
        moving mentally ill from hospitals to jails (1970s, 1980s), 28–31
    jury sentencing (due to diminished confidence in psychiatric hospitals), 56
    magnitude of problem, 31, 85–86
    Menninger's recommendations, 176
    mercy bookings, 39–40
    and police departments (easier than commitment), 74–75
    quality of life, 31–35
        suicides, 33
        infectious diseases, 33
        deaths in (three cases described), 34
    violence in, 31, 32, 53–54
JCAHO, see Joint Commission on Accreditation of Healthcare Organizations (JCAHO)
Jefferson County Jail, Kentucky, 33
Jersey City, New Jersey, 65
John Birch Society, 173
Johns Hopkins University, 139
Johnson, Lyndon B., 92, 146, 177
Joint Commission on Accreditation of Healthcare Organizations (JCAHO), 132, 135, 136, 200
Juries, 56
Juvenile delinquency, 169

Kalispell Police Department, Montana, 75
Kallinger, Joseph ("the Shoemaker"), 57
Kansas, 39, 130–131, 147, 158, 160, 207
Kansas City, Missouri, 45, 53
Keansburg, New Jersey, 65
Keene, New Hampshire, 129
Keener Men's Shelter, New York City, 23–24
Kennedy, John F., 178, 180, 184
Kennedy International Airport, 16
Kentucky, 33, 37, 38, 58, 59, 147, 206
King County, Washington, 37, 42, 129
Kingston hospital, 147
Kings View Hospital, Reedley, California, 130

Lanterman-Petris-Short (LPS) Act (1969), 36, 41, 143–144
Law, mental health/illness, 197
    consequences of, 148–154
    and issues of insight, 154–156
    "lawyers' first victory," 143
    legal barriers to treatment, 141, 142–148
    legal solution to mental illness crisis, 162, 197–198
    most visible consequences of, 149–150
    need for involuntary treatment, 156–163
Least restrictive setting, 11
Legal issues, see Law, mental health/illness
Legal Services, 146–147, 148
Lehman Quality of Life Interview, 133
Lennon, John, 57
Lessard v. Schmidt, 144, 145, 147
Liability for damages, mental health law, 153
Liberal political thought, and mental hygiene movement, 168–169
Life magazine, 62, 84
Lithium, measuring blood levels of, 161
London's Institute for Psychiatry, 154
London Zoo, 193, 194
Long Beach, New York, 13, 61–62
Long Branch, New Jersey, 65
Long Island commuter train, 68
Los Angeles, 3, 17, 18, 22, 23, 30, 55, 58, 59, 112, 151, 173, 177
    police force, 39–40, 74
    County Jail, 31, 32, 33, 42, 53–54
Louisiana, 39, 148, 150, 206
Louisville Homecare Project, 115, 119
LPS, see Lanterman-Petris-Short (LPS) Act (1969)
Lubbock, Texas, 172
Luce, Henry R., 83, 84
Lyons, 74

MacArthur Foundation, 53
McCarthy, Mary, 169
McCoy, Joy, 152
Macdonald, Dwight, 169
McDonald, Bobby, 75, 76
Madison, Wisconsin, 6, 38, 39, 116
    stories of local tragic events involving mentally ill individuals (1988), 59
Magellan Health Services, 121, 123
Magnetic resonance imaging (MRI), 4
Maine, 59, 206
Main Street House, 63, 65
Malone, Senator George, 172

Managed care, 120–126
  CEOs' compensation, 123
  problems with, 122–129
    continuity of care, 124–125
    denying priority services, 126
    profit motive, 123–124
    skimming/dumping patients for profit,
      125–126
  studies assessing effectiveness for severe mental
    illness, 122
Manhattan State Hospital, 23
Manic-depressive illness, 181, 188
  discontinuing lithium, irreversible worsening of
    symptoms, 152
  and insight, 154
  research allotments, 195
  suicide rate, 8
  treatment of, 5–6
Maricopa County, Arizona, 123
Marlboro State Psychiatric Hospital (New Jersey),
  62–64
Marx, 169, 174, 175
Maryland, 76, 131, 206. See also Baltimore
  University of, 133
Marysville Prison, 35, 84
Massachusetts, 10, 23, 26, 40, 54, 58, 87, 96, 104,
  117, 119, 121, 123, 124, 145, 206
Mayors, Conference of, 18, 210
Mead, Margaret, 174, 175, 233
Medco, 121, 124, 123
Media:
  and discrimination, 60
  in New York, sympathy subsiding, 71
  and violence and mental illness, 56–60
Medicaid, 92–94
  block grant, see Block grants
  costs, 93, 118, 185, 186, 196
  cost-shifting, 91, 92–94, 102
  and deinstitutionalization, 8, 100, 101, 144
  disincentives, 164
  and managed care, 120, 121, 123, 124, 127
  rationing (Oregon), 189
  restrictions, 89, 103–104, 105, 116, 117, 115,
    119
Medical care rationing, 188–191
Medical schools, recommendation for, 199
Medicare, 8, 93, 94–95, 100, 127, 144, 164, 196
Medication(s), 5–8
  compliance:
    effective methods for improving, 160
    methods for monitoring, 161
    right to refuse, 148–149
      and death sentence, Louisiana, 148–149
Medication(s), failure to take:
  and prediction of violence, 50–51, 59, 79, 197
  and rationing, 190
  reasons for, 154–156
Medigrant, 113
Memphis, 200
Mendota State Hospital, Wisconsin, 39, 72
Menninger, Karl, 175–176
Mennonites, 130
Mental Health Consumer Survey/Interview, 134
Mental Health Law Project, Washington, DC,
  142–143, 153
Mental Health Study Act of 1955, 84

Mental Health Work Group, 181
Mental hygiene movement, 167–170
Mental illness crisis/mental health system:
  cost of care/treatment for (1995), 4
  cost-shifting to federal government, 91–99
  definition of severe mental illness, 4
  deinstitutionalization, see Deinstitutionalization
  divorcing from mental illness from mental health,
    186–188, 191, 198–199
  funding, new initiatives, 91–140
  historical perspective ("looking backward"),
    81–90
  and homelessness, 13–24
  and jails/prisons, 25–42
  percentage population having (1995), 4
  prioritizing services, 188–191
  reform, merging of mental illness with mental
    health and social, 167–170
  research over past decade, 4–5
  solutions ("looking forward"), 193–203
  and violence, 43–60
  why not even worse, 151–152
Merck, 121, 123
Mercy bookings, 39, 40
Merit Behavioral Care, 120, 123–124, 125
Methadone, 161
Miami, 3, 34, 62, 78, 128
Michigan, 30, 54, 55, 59, 116, 118, 137, 160, 207
Milwaukee Legal Services, 147
Minneapolis, 20, 75, 122
Minnesota, 59, 75, 122, 153, 206
Minute Women, USA, 171
Mississippi, 37, 58, 75, 92, 207
Missoula, 75
Missoula County Jail, Montana, 34
Missouri, 53, 103, 206
Monadnock Family Services, Keene, New
  Hampshire, 129, 130
Monoamine oxidase inhibitor (MAOI), 6
Montana, 33, 34, 37, 75, 76, 112, 206
Movies, and mental illness, and violence, 57
MRI, see Magnetic resonance imaging (MRI)
Multiple sclerosis, 5, 149, 187, 188
Multnomah Community Ability Scale, 133
Murder of shopping bag lady, 14–16
Muscular dystrophy research, 195
Mussolini, Benito, 170
"My Brother Might Kill Me," 47, 78

NAMI, see National Alliance for the Mentally Ill
  (NAMI)
Napa State Hospital, California, 41, 45
Nardil, 6
NARSAD, see National Alliance for Research on
  Schizophrenia and Depression (NARSAD)
National Academy of Sciences, 139
National Advisory Mental Health Council, 4, 5, 17,
  187
National Alliance for Research on Schizophrenia
  and Depression (NARSAD), 195
National Alliance for the Mentally Ill (NAMI), 29,
  30, 31–32, 47, 51, 57, 138–139. See also
  Alliance for the Mentally Ill (AMI)
National Association for Mental Health, 170
National Association of State Mental Health
  Program Directors, 94

National Brain Research Institute, 187, 198, 199
National Center for Health Statistics, 102
National Committee for Mental Hygiene, 168, 169, 170
National Committee for Quality Assessment, 131
National Institute on Child Health and Human Development, 187
National Institute of Mental Health (NIMH), 4, 14, 46, 48, 100, 115, 118, 147, 148, 176, 184, 187, 188, 195, 198
National Institute of Neurological Disorders and Stroke, 187, 198
National Institutes of Health, 188, 195, 199
National Mental Health Association, 181
National Neuropsychiatric Institute, 184
National Science Foundation, 188, 195
National Zoo, 20
NBC television employee, 69
Nebraska, 74, 121, 123, 160, 206
Neighborhood Service Centers, New York City, 177
Neighborhood Watch program, 65
Neurological impairment, and violence, 51
Nevada, 10, 29, 203, 207
Newark, New Jersey, 65
New Hampshire, 10, 39, 92, 113, 116, 129, 136, 161, 172, 190–191, 206
New Jersey, 27, 57, 145, 206
  Ocean Grove ("deinstitutionalization in a small town"), 62–66
New Mexico, 37, 38, 76, 195, 206
New Orleans, 39
Newton, Kansas, 130–131
New York/New York City, 13
  AIDS/HIV, 21
  deinstitutionalization/ghettoization, 61, 63, 66–73, 86, 99–100, 206
  hospitals, 23–24, 44, 81, 82, 107, 147, 153
  incidents/vignettes, 47, 51, 58, 78, 150, 202
  jails/prisons, 30, 33, 42
  Keener Shelter, 23–24
  managed care, 122
  measurement of public mental health programs, 137
  Medicaid/SSI use, 92, 110, 114
  mental hygiene movement, 169
  models/programs, 6, 65, 117, 131, 157, 177
  physician assistants, 119
  police, 73–74
  Protection and Advocacy program suit, 147
  and single responsibility funding, 112
  Woody Allen/Mayor Ed Koch, 186
New York Civil Liberties Union, 67, 71, 153
New York State Commission on Quality of Care for the Mentally Disabled, 137, 138
New York State Psychiatric Institute, 45
New York Technical College, 69
New Zealand, 193
Niebuhr, Reinhold, 83
Nixon, Richard, 173, 178, 179, 180
Nonprofit companies, 127–131, 197
Norpramin, 6
North Carolina, 76, 94, 119, 137, 158, 160, 207
North Dakota, 112, 160, 206
Northwestern University, 16

Northwest Mental Health Services, Seattle, 128–129
Nursing, psychiatric, 119
Nursing homes, 91, 102, 116

Obesity, 190
Obsessive-compulsive disorder, treatment of, 6
Ocean Grove, New Jersey ("deinstitutionalization in a small town"), 62–66
O'Connor v. Donaldson, 145
Ohio, 23, 34, 56, 59, 74, 84, 112, 128, 206
  milestone (beginning of deinstitutionalization era), 82–85
Oklahoma, 30, 206
Old-Age, Survivors, and Disability Insurance (OASDI) program, 96
Old Age Assistance (OAA), 95
Ontario, 113
Oppenheimer, J. Robert, 83
Oppositional defiant disorder, 182
Orange County, California, 17
Oregon, 38, 106, 121, 131, 133, 139, 147, 151, 160, 161, 171, 189, 190, 191, 206
Oregon Quality of Life Scale, 133
Outpatient psychiatric care, 116
  commitment, 160, 197
  involuntary treatment, 159–160

PacifiCare, 127–128
PACT, see Program for/in Assertive Community Treatment (PACT)
Palo Alto Veterans Administration Hospital, 118
P and A Act, see Protection and Advocacy for Individuals with Mental Illness Act (P and A Act)
Panic disorder, severe, treatment of, 6
Pap smears, 189
Paranoid delusions, and prediction of violence, 52
Parkinson's disease, 5, 181, 187, 188
Parnate, 6
Paternalism vs. personal autonomy, 86–87
Patient care indicators, 136
Payee, representative, 165
Pelican Bay Prison, 213
Pennsylvania, 38, 112, 119, 131, 155, 201, 206
Pepper, Claude, 84
Performance contracting, 139–140
Performance Partnership Grants, 139
Philadelphia, 17, 29, 40, 43–44, 57, 58, 73, 81, 152, 177
Phoenix, 62, 125
Physician assistants, 119
Physicians Healthcare Plans, 128
PIA-NME, see Psychiatric Institutes of America—National Medical Enterprise (PIA-NME)
Pilgrim State Hospital, New York, 13, 67, 82
Pittsburgh, 53, 155
Plano, Texas, 76
Police, 73–77, 150–151
Politicalization of mental health/illness, 170–174, 199
  presidential politics, 177–182
Port Authority Bus Terminal, 15
Portland, Oregon, 62, 171
Posttraumatic stress disorder, 186

Pound, Ezra, 173
Prairie View Mental Health Center, Newton, Kansas, 130–131
Prince Edward Island, 113
Prioritizing mental health/illness services, 188–191, 199
    criteria (proposed) for, 189–191
Priority services, denying, 126
Prisons, see Jails/prisons, and the mentally ill
Professionals, mental *health vs.* mental *illness*, 185
Profit motive, 123–124
Program for/in Assertive Community Treatment (PACT), 6, 65, 116–117, 202
Progressive transinstitutionalism, thesis of, 35
Project Reachout, 157
Protection and Advocacy agencies/programs, 148, 153
    recommendation to abolish, 198
Protection and Advocacy for Individuals with Mental Illness Act (P and A Act), 147
Providence, Rhode Island, 18
Provincial health care systems, Canada, 113
Proxies, health care, 160
Prozac, 6, 88
Psychiatric hospitals, see Hospitals, psychiatric
Psychiatric Institutes of America—National Medical Enterprise (PIA-NME), 127–131
Psycho, 57
Public Citizen Health Research Group, 29, 31–32, 37, 40, 51
Public services, effect of mental illness crisis on, 73–77
Pulliam, Emmett, 55–56

Quality of Life, 133
Quality of Life Scale, 134
Queens, 67, 69

Rape, and homeless women, 20–21
Rape, in jails, 32–33
Rationing, 188–191
Reagan, Ronald, 57, 114, 180, 181
Reciprocity, interstate, 159, 198
Red Bank, New Jersey, 65
Reformers, psychiatric (1880s), 26–27
Rehabilitation, 6
Reich, Wilhelm, 169, 175
Rennie v. Klein, 145
Reno, Nevada, 18
Rent-a-doc, 125
Representative payee, 198
Repulsion, 57
Research:
    over past decade, 4–5
    "ultimate solution," 194–196
        government role, 199
Resources, diversion of, 183–186
Retardation, mental, 8, 10, 96
Rheumatoid arthritis, 156
Rhode Island, 10, 85, 124, 147, 158, 160, 206
Riboflavin detection test, 161
Right to get well, 141–166
Right-to-refuse medication campaign, 145
Riverside county, California, 138
Rochester, New York, 51, 58, 122

Rockefeller Center, 69
Rockland State Hospital, New York, 82
Rogers v. Okin, 145, 147, 153
Roosevelt, Eleanor, 83
Roosevelt, Franklin, 178
Rosenberg, Gary, 58
Rubenstein, Leonard, 158, 231
Rudd, Mark, 174
Russia, 172
Rutgers University, 100, 101

Sacramento, 112
Sacramento County, California, 33
St. Elizabeth's Hospital (Washington, DC), 24, 46, 107, 143, 150
St. Francis Residence, New York City, 131
St. Patrick's Cathedral, Manhattan, 69
Salem, Oregon, 106
Salmon, Thomas, 169
Salt Lake City, Utah, 129–130
Salvi, John, 58
San Antonio State Hospital, 62
San Diego County Jail, 42
San Francisco, 9, 18, 20, 57, 58
San Jose, California, 13, 62
San Mateo County, 36, 130
Santa Clara County, 36
Schizoaffective disorder, treatment of, 5
Schizophrenia, 181, 188
    healthy, valid condition, 148
    and insight, 154, 155
    research on, 195
    suicide rate, 8
    treatment of, 5, 6
Scientologists, 146
Scottish Rite of Freemasonry, 195
SDS (Students for a Democratic Society), 174, 175
Seattle, 37, 42, 58, 158
Selective serotonin reuptake inhibitor (SSRI), 6
Self-determination, 11
Senate Subcommittee on Health and Education, 84
Sheboygan, Wisconsin, Mental Health Center, 77
Shephard-Pratt Hospital, Baltimore, 131
Shopping bag lady, murder of, 14–16
"Siberia USA," 170–174, 178
Sickness Impact Profile, 134
Simi Valley, California, 76
Simmons, Officer Rickey Joe, 75
Simpkins, Celeste, 103, 104
Sinclair, Upton, 168
Single responsibility funding, 111–114, 196–197
    advantages, potential, 114–120
    and greater innovation in human resources, 118–119
Sipple, David, 76
Skimming patients, 125–126
Smoking, 190
Social cost-benefit, 189
Social reform/liberal thought, and mental hygiene movement, 168–169
Social Security Disability Income (SSDI), 20, 93, 96–97, 144, 163–166, 180, 181, 196, 198
Somaticism in psychiatric thought, 168
South Carolina, 29, 39, 59, 79, 206
South Dakota, 112, 207

Southwest Denver Mental Health Services, 115
Soviet Union, 171
Spectrum concept of mental disorders:, 182–186
Spock, Benjamin, 174, 175
Spokane, Washington, 76
SSDI, see Social Security Disability Income (SSDI)
SSI, see Supplemental Security Income (SSI)
Standards/enforcement, 200
Stanley, Theodore and Vada (Foundation), 195
States:
    deinstitutionalization (magnitude of, for each),
        205–207
    departments of mental health (recommended
        abolished), 188, 198
    and single responsibility funding, 112
Staten Island ferry, 68
Staten Island's South Beach Psychiatric Center, 15
Steadman, Henry, 30, 45, 60, 212, 213, 216, 218
Stigma of mental illness, 56, 57
    Stigma Clearinghouse, National, 57
Stockholm, 48
Strokes, 10. See also National Institute of
    Neurological Disorders and Stroke
Students for a Democratic Society (SDS), 174, 175
Suicide, 8, 29, 33, 64, 194
Sullivan v. Zebley, 109
Supplemental Security Income (SSI), 92, 93, 95–96,
    100, 102, 109, 110, 144, 163–166, 180, 181,
    196, 198
Sweden, 48, 50

Tacoma, Washington, 13
Tampa, Florida, 76
Tardive dyskinesia, 200
Television characters, and mental illness
    stereotyping, 56
Tennessee, 39, 51, 84, 111, 121, 123, 200, 206
Texas, 38, 42, 51, 62, 76, 112, 118, 119, 158, 172,
    206
Thorazine, 8, 99
"Thorazine Alley," 63
Tourism/tourist towns, 39, 65
Transinstitutionalization, 13, 35, 88, 91, 102–103
Travis County Jail, Texas, 42
Treatment, see Involuntary commitment/treatment;
    Medication(s); Medication(s), failure to take
Treatment outcomes, measurement of, 131–140,
    197, 199
Trenton hospital (New Jersey), 63
Trespassing, 39
Trilling, Lionel, 169
Trotsky, Leon, 169, 175
Truman, Bess, 84
Truman, Harry, 178
Tuberculosis, 149, 156, 161, 168
Twins, identical, 4–5

UCLA Neuropsychiatric Hospital, 135
UCLA School of Medicine, 164
UFO abduction therapy, 183, 185–186
Ulysses contracts, 160
Uncoordinated provision of care, 105–109
United Behavioral Systems, 124

United Cerebral Palsy Association, 135
United Healthcare, 123, 124
U.S. Behavioral Healthcare, 121, 123, 126
United States government, see Federal government
Upper Darby Township, Philadelphia, 73
Urban Institute, 16
Urinary markers, monitoring medication
    compliance, 161–162
Utah, 121, 129–130, 160, 172, 206

Valley Mental Health, Salt Lake City, Utah,
    129–130
Valley Storefront, 130
Value Behavioral Health, 120, 123
Value Health Inc., 123
Vanderbilt University, 103
Van Gogh, Vincent, 1
Vermont, 10, 112, 160, 206
Veterans Administration (VA), 63, 93, 98–99,
    163–166, 195, 198
Victim culture, 176
Vietnam antiwar demonstrations, 175
Violence, 14, 43–60, 86, 149–150, 151, 197
    and mental illness, and the media, 56–60
    predictors of, 49–53
    relationship with mental illness, 44–49
    walking time bombs in the community, 53–56
Virginia, 55, 81, 117, 138, 206
Voluntary outreach services, 157
Volunteerism, 65
Volunteers of America, 24, 131

Washington, DC, 21, 24, 49, 58, 72, 78, 107, 143,
    153, 160, 203, 207
Washington state, 13, 30, 38, 42, 76, 119, 121, 123,
    129, 158, 160, 206
University of Washington, 134, 165
Western State Hospital (Washington), 13
West Virginia, 9, 10, 39, 92, 147, 206
Whitefish, Montana, 75
"White House cases," 46
"Wild Man of West 96th Street," 72
Willard Asylum, 82
Williamsburg, Virginia, 81
Winston-Salem, North Carolina, 76
Wisconsin, 10, 38, 39, 72, 96, 116, 144, 147, 151,
    160, 172, 206
Women, severely mentally ill and homeless, 20–21
Woody Allen Syndrome, 167, 186
Worcester, Massachusetts, 26, 53
World Federation for Mental Health, 170, 172
World Health Organization, 171–172
World Trade Center, 68
Wyatt v. Stickney, 144, 145
Wyman Way Co-op, 129
Wyoming, 29, 37, 112, 207

Yolo County, California, 17

Zebley v. Sullivan, 96
Zoloft, 6
Zoo incidents, 20, 193, 194